Crisscrossing Borders in Literature of the American West

CRISSCROSSING BORDERS IN LITERATURE OF THE AMERICAN WEST

Edited by Reginald Dyck
and Cheli Reutter

First published in 2009 by PALGRAVE MACMILLAN® in the United States – a division of St. Martin's Press LLC, 175 Fifth Avenue, New York, NY 10010.

Where this book is distributed in the UK, Europe and the rest of the world, this is by Palgrave Macmillan, a division of Macmillan Publishers Limited, registered in England, company number 785998, of Houndmills, Basingstoke, Hampshire RG21 6XS.

Palgrave Macmillan is the global academic imprint of the above companies and has companies and representatives throughout the world.

Palgrave® and Macmillan® are registered trademarks in the United States, the United Kingdom, Europe and other countries.

ISBN-13: 978-0-230-61343-0
ISBN-10: 0-230-61343-8

Library of Congress Cataloging-in-Publication Data

Crisscrossing borders in literature of the American West / edited by Reginald Dyck and Cheli Ruetter.
    p. cm.
  Includes bibliographical references.
  ISBN 0-230-61343-8 (alk. paper)
  1. American literature—West (U.S.)—History and criticism. 2. American literature—20th century—History and criticism. 3. West (U.S.)—Intellectual life. 4. West (U.S.)—In literature. 5. Transnationalism in literature. 6. Cultural pluralism in literature. 7. Working class in literature. I. Dyck, Reginald. II. Ruetter, Cheli.

PS271.C76 2009
810.9'35878—dc22   2008028393

A catalogue record of the book is available from the British Library.

Design by Macmillan Publishing Solutions

First edition: March 2009

10 9 8 7 6 5 4 3 2 1

Printed in the United States of America.

CONTENTS

Acknowledgments

First we would like to thank our contributors for their rigorous dedication to this project.

Cheli would like to acknowledge the Fulbright Commission, the Albert-Ludwigs-Universität Freiburg, and Wolfgang Hochbruck for their support in the development of this project. She would also like to thank Emory Elliott, Steve Axelrod, Susan Griffin, and Kwakiutl Dreher, and, of course, her mentor, Stanley Corkin. She gratefully acknowledges her family, and especially her children, Justin and Mindy, who have accompanied her in various adventures in pursuit of new views on the American West.

Reg would like to acknowledge the support of Capital University, Office of the Provost. His role in the project began during his sabbatical and continued with the help of a Gerhold Research Grant. In addition, Reg would like to acknowledge his father, Ruben Dyck, who, although he taught biology, encouraged us children in the humanities; his mentor, John McKenna, who helped induct him into the pleasures of the discipline; and his brother Stan Dyck, history professor, who through many conversations introduced him to new ways of thinking about the West. Reg would also like to extend a special thank you to Kaori Fujishiro.

Renny Christopher's "Louis Owens's Representations of Working-Class Consciousness" is reprinted from *Louis Owens: Literary Reflections on His Life and Work,* edited by Jacquilyln Kilpatrick (University of Oklahoma Press, 2004). Robert Crooks' essay "From the Far Side of the Urban Frontier: The Detective Fiction of Chester Himes and Walter Mosley" first appeared in a somewhat different form in *College Literature* 22.3 (October 1995): 68–90. Robert McKee Irwin's "Helen Hunt Jackson's *Ramona:* A Transnational Reading of the Old West" adapted from his "*Ramona* and Postnationalist American Studies: On 'Our America' and the Mexican Borderlands," in *American Quarterly* 55.4 (2003): 539–67 (© The Johns Hopkins University Press. Adapted with permission of The Johns Hopkins

University Press). Portions of Steven Rosendale's "The American West in Red and Green: The Forgotten Literary History of Social Justice Environmentalism" also appear in his *City Wilderness: US Radical Fiction and the Forgotten Literary History of Social Justice Environmentalism* (University of Iowa Press, forthcoming).

NEW MODELS FOR WESTERN LITERARY STUDIES

Reginald Dyck

> *The boundaries of the American West . . . doors pretending to be walls.*
>
> —*Richard White*

You can never step into the same West twice, spatially or temporally. And yet the West is there, conceptually and geographically, complexly bordered while not contained within lines. Both the borders and the identities they help delineate have continued to change in response to shifting material conditions. Thus, Richard White opens his history of the West with, "The boundaries of the American West are a series of doors pretending to be walls" (3). Bordered spaces, whether doors or walls, embody power struggles, systematic oppressions, and a multitude of conflicting desires.

Today a controversial national wall dividing Northwest Mexico from the Southwest United States attempts to control dialectical engagements, including migration and return, across this line constructed in sand. Long delays and new requirements at the border between Canada and the United States indicate that all is not peaceful at the Peace Arch either. These, however, are not the only national boundaries that mark the West and its literary studies. Some nations have drawn lines to support their imperial interests, and others to maintain communal identity and protect themselves against invaders.

The Kashaya Pomo nation, for example, has experienced continual devastating threats to its borders from a series of nations intent on empire. For centuries they lived within clear political boundaries on the coast and hills of what became central California. Their external relations remained stable until the advent of the Russian Empire in 1811. Later, the enslavement and displacement that came with Mexican political control again altered the Kashaya Pomo's political status. Threats to their right to self-determination only intensified with U.S. occupation and the dominance of capitalist forms of production. Stripped of land ownership, Pomo Indians were segregated onto rancherías. Some of these later gained federal status, but termination created another destructive change in their political position. When federal recognition was granted to the Federated Indians of Graton Ranchería, the Kashaya Pomo people became part of a new political arrangement. This is just one example of nations that have shaped and been shaped by the many borders that continue to intersect across the West.

National boundaries, however, are not the only ones that matter. Many borders are crossed and recrossed in this critical anthology. Cumulatively, the essays here engage the West as a complex process and place, with recognizable yet contested and fluctuating lines that immigrants and emigrants, readers and writers, and saints and sinners continue to crisscross. All these border crossers carry with them cultural, political, economic, and moral structures that require adaptation as they traverse the lines of the West.

To better apprehend this region of complex borders, Western literary studies should look across disciplinary boundaries for new paradigms. The shifting perspectives of other regional studies, the hemispheric approaches of comparative American studies, and the steps and missteps taken within American studies to employ a transnational perspective can all offer new models for reconfiguring Western literary studies. Each offers strategies for better understanding the past and engaging contemporary conditions of the West.

In the special 2006 issue of *American Literature*, "Global Contexts, Local Literatures: The New Southern Studies," Kathryn McKee and Annette Trefzer's preface presents an important model for a new regional sense of place. Rather than defining the South in contradistinction to the North (or the West to the East), we might see both the South and the West as enmeshed in hemispheric relations. From this standpoint, regional divisions appear much more porous than is suggested by traditional studies caught up with issues of a unified regional identity. Also, hemispheric relations become a two-way process of exchanging goods, ideas, people, and much more.

The South becomes much more than an exporter of Faulknerian fictions, and the West more than a purveyor of national myths.

Tara McPherson argues in a later essay that Southern studies must "move beyond . . . fetishizing sameness in Southern studies" (698). This means, for example, recognizing Arkansas-based Wal-Mart as a modern reflection of traditional Southern labor strategies that are now exported around the world. Southern studies should be useful, she argues, in explaining "the complex histories of this reality and, I hope, in helping us maneuver for change." This can be accomplished by extending Southern studies to include regional labor policies, commercial practices, demographic changes, as well as "vibrant models of resistance" that have been developed (696–97). As the essays in this anthology make clear, Western literary studies similarly face challenges in engaging a New West represented by Microsoft executives, Native uranium workers, or a black Los Angeles detective. The past is not left behind in this complexly diverse West but rather reconfigured, and so made more usable for creating productive new analytical models.

These models need to include the hemispheric exchanges of people who are now central to the economy and culture of the New South as well as the New West. Immigrants with low-wage jobs are essential to both economies. Leon Fink's *The Maya of Morgantown: Work and Community in the Nuevo New South* analyzes the establishment of a transplanted Guatemalan Maya community in North Carolina. Incorporating communities like this offers another new model for conceptualizing regions. In opposing long-established Southern employment relationships, these low-wage immigrant workers dialectically engaged Southern labor practices. Their story can prompt us to consider related issues in the West: the nature of immigration and resistance to it, the ways people accept and challenge dominant cultural and economic paradigms, the historical and contemporary experience of marginalized workers, and the struggles to change work relations. Essays in this volume's first section offer models for Western scholars taking up many of these issues.

McKee and Trefzer in their preface explain another way that new regional conditions can impact literary studies: "A globally inflected Southern studies can productively defamiliarize texts and problems" (685). The essays here accomplish this for Western literary studies as they revitalize Western texts such as *Ramona* by placing them in a hemispheric context. They also challenge us to reconfigure our regional literary boundaries to include writers such as Brianda Domecq of Mexico and Isabel Allende of Chile. Paul Giles notes that a hemispheric focus can shift historical attention from, for example, the Civil War to the U.S.-Mexican wars of the nineteenth century. Yet Giles is aware that these reconstructed stories work against "popular reactions against globalization" that support "nostalgic misrepresentations" that turn back to reassuring nationalistic stories (649). Desirée A. Martín's essay makes the shift in historical attention by focusing on a borderland heroine while also confronting the issue of popular nostalgic reactions.

The essays by scholars from Germany and from areas of expertise other than English also globalize Western literary studies in important ways, for example, by deconstructing and reconstructing Western icons from alternative ideological perspectives. In his essay "The New American Studies: A Lesson from the Borderlands," Robert McKee Irwin insists that scholars must learn the necessary languages for hemispheric work and then develop dialogues with scholars outside the U.S. academy (519). His present essay exemplifies this engagement. The global strategies of this anthology help resist the U.S. academic tendency toward "intellectual provincialism" (Fishkin 36).

Yet methodological dilemmas and dangers lurk in these new regional models, as in any analytical constructions. Caroline F. Levander and Robert S. Levine, introducing a 2006 special hemispheric studies issue of *American Literary History,* caution that the United States too often is still accepted as the default unit in transnational American studies (400). We must consider to what extent we are willing to decenter Western literary studies. This shift in focus, however, is not without its own dilemmas. A number of scholars have addressed the danger of cultural imperialism inherent in crossing national boundaries (see, for example, Irwin's "The New American Studies"). The essays in the last section of this volume, "Transnational Wests," offer ways for redressing the usual imbalance while recognizing, as Levander and Levine encourage, the asymmetry and interdependency of nation-state development throughout the hemisphere (400). A transnational pluralism that overlooks power differentials is not the answer needed, as Cheli Reutter's discussion of Allende makes clear.

Moreover, in its effort to combat intellectual provincialism, Western literary studies intent on crisscrossing borders must not forget what German scholar Winfried Fluck forcefully argues:

> The United States is a paradigmatic, agenda-setting modern society and no talk about the crisis of the nation-state can distract from the fact that there is enough nation-state left to affect all of us

decisively. . . . American power is thus still a major issue for the rest of the world.   (29)

Even if we resist making the United States "the default unit of intellectual engagement" (Levander and Levine 400), we must not ignore its position in the world. This means that transnational perspectives must recognize and analyze the multifaceted aspects of U.S. power while resisting hegemonic ideas of U.S. exceptionalism that recognize others as exotic markers of difference rather than as cultures and nations in their own right.

The role of the nation-state has other complex aspects for transnational Western literary studies. For non-Native scholars particularly, Native literature and culture must be afforded a similarly transnational analysis. As suggested by the above example of the Kashaya Pomo people, American Indians throughout the hemisphere often claim boundaries that establish tribal sovereignty. My essay recognizes Simon Ortiz's engagement with the complex issue of sovereignty as he considers land and water rights. Many tribally centered writers and scholars aim to strengthen rather than dismantle national borders by claiming an international rather than an intranational or multicultural relationship with the United States. Nevertheless, they recognize that Native national borders also continue to be crossed and recrossed in both threatening and productive ways.

The Western Hemisphere, a cartographic concept going back to the 1600s, predates the stirrings of nationalism in the Americas, and therefore many call for a hemispheric analytical framework to take precedence over a nationalistic one. Used dialectically, however, both offer Western literary studies the necessary political and cultural categories for analysis. Thus transnational or hemispheric studies extend the insights of postnational analysis without reasserting the dominance of the United States and the U.S. West. Perspectives from across the ocean can do the same. If so, is there still a place for literary studies of a region so often used emblematically for the nation? The essays in the final section offer a positive answer by reconceptualizing the West transnationally. The authors recognize that regions, nations, and hemispheres are not based on intrinsic relationships between geography and politics, but are shifting cultural constructions that have acute political implications.

After these conceptual transformations, is there still a "there there" (to borrow Gertrude Stein's phrase)? Martin Bone's essay "(Re)inventing the (Post)southern 'Sense of Place'" asks whether a sense of place can survive the postmodern challenge to referentiality, a bedrock of much past work in both Southern and Western literary studies. And in its materiality, has the West become mainly an interchangeable collection of ranchettes, gated communities, managed parks, strip malls, and slums created by capitalism's homogenizing efficiency? Bone suggests that we may be imprisoned by traditional ideas of place that do not reflect new realities.

Bone refers to Frederic Jameson's comment that place no longer exists in our world, or it does only in a much feebler sense. Because of our loss of "thereness," we need to recreate our sense of place, but in new ways. Jameson explains in *Postmodernism*:

> Disalienation . . . involves the practical reconquest of a sense of place and the construction or reconstruction of an articulated ensemble which can be retained in memory and which the individual subject can map and remap along with moments of mobile, alternative trajectories. (51)

The conflict between loggers and environmentalists, now part of the Western collection of legends, exemplifies the deep alienation produced as both groups' cognitive maps turn out to depict a narrowly static sense of place. These maps lack the dialectical outlook needed to help both groups grasp new conditions while not minimizing their real, material conflicts.

Western literary studies can help us create "articulated ensemble[s]" that engage a new sense of place for the West. The red/green approach of Rosendale's essay is just one of this anthology's dialectical investigations into the meaning of place. The contributors offer new micromaps or orienteering outings that reconceptualize a region that often seems alien from traditional perspectives. Shifting through time and space, their essays work to "disalienat[e]" us by providing satisfying standpoints from which to view an ever-changing West.

*   *   *

The idea of maps, with their conceptualizations of regional space, brings us back to the place of the borders the essays here crisscross. Maps not only mark dividing lines but also show ways of negotiating them. In the preface to her seminal book *Borderlands/La Frontera: The New Mestiza*, Gloria Anzaldúa extends the new mestiza consciousness beyond the Southwest to include border regions of cultures, races, as well as individuals' shared experiences. She then adds, "It's not a comfortable territory to live in, this place of contradictions" (18).

Touring the other side of borders, however, is not the same as living in borderlands. Settings that cross national lines have long been a staple of Western U.S. literature. Cormac McCarthy's *All the Pretty Horses*, a relatively recent example, makes clear the lack of mestiza consciousness in traditional Western border crossings. Mexico, the setting for most of the novel, is the protagonist's heart of darkness, an exotic place of escape when his normal, U.S. world unravels. Rather than the primitivism of Conrad's Congo, the Other side here is defined by brutal lawlessness and rigid social hierarchies. For the protagonist, crossing the Rio Grande means entering an alien world. Even if his home place has been lost, hope for recovery only exists on the northern side of the river. Going south is in the end only an excursion. Instead of touring the Other, the "Crisscrossing" of our title calls for mutuality. It is shorthand for the stance Anzaldúa makes in *Borderlands/La Frontera*, a manifesto that continues to challenge us.

> But it is not enough to stand on the opposite river bank shouting questions, challenging patriarchal, white conventions. A counterstance locks one into a duel of oppressor and oppressed. . . . At some point, on our way to a new consciousness, we will have to leave the opposite bank, the split between the two mortal combatants somehow healed so that we are on both shores at once. (100)

One important obstruction to this healing process is the "bourgeois fascination with 'authentic' and 'exotic' cultures" (Curiel 13). Scholars can resist exoticization and the trap of authenticity by acknowledging power differences and ideological implications when crossing cultural borderlands. We also need to recognize that within the United States and the West, class hierarchies may be the toughest borders to cross. Renny Christopher's essay makes this point as she addresses mixed-blood and mixed-class identities in Louis Owens's work.

To these two cautions we should add Pablo Vita's fundamental corollary: "Almost all recent border studies and theory fail to pursue the possibility that fragmentation of experience can lead to the reinforcement of borders instead of an invitation to cross them" (qtd. in Andrews and Walton 615n4). In attempting to reinforce some borders, dismantle others, and traverse many more, we as scholars must self-reflexively recognize and take responsibility for the implications of our efforts.

As these cautions make clear, creating new maps or models for Western literary studies is perilous work. Sonia Saldivar-Hull, introducing the second edition of *Borderlands/La Frontera*, observes that the book "continues to offer a radical (re)construction of space in the Americas" (13). The essays here contribute to this important reconstruction project from a specifically regional point of view.[1] The contributors' maps, while created from previous ones, offer alternative, partial representations of a region. They are guides for creating a new sense of place in our time.

*   *   *

As the essays here demonstrate, much has changed since the Western Literature Association published *Updating the Literary West* (1997). Now over a decade old, it registered an important shift in the field.[2] SueEllen Campbell's essay explains new developments in the field at that time:

> What's new is a widespread critical rethinking of traditional stories (histories, myths, texts, interpretive paradigms) of the American West, a rereading and retelling of these stories as complex, multivocal fragments of discourse thoroughly embedded in equally complex and intertwined social, cultural, political, economic, and ecological networks. (6)

For this critical rethinking, Campbell recognizes the influence of American studies scholars like Richard Slotkin and Annette Kolodny, the New West History, environmental studies that include ecofeminism and deep ecology, the natural sciences, and geography. In the volume's next essay, "Feminism, Women Writers and the New Western Regionalism," Krista Comer describes a new emphasis on female sexuality, working class culture, environmental health, imperial conquest rather than heroic pioneer effort, and racial identity and the history of race relations. These developments created not just an updated field but a fundamentally refigured one.

The same year as the publication of *Updating,* Forrest G. Robinson edited a special issue of *Arizona Quarterly* on the New West History, a key influence at the time on Western literary studies. The fact that Robinson himself and most of the contributors are literary scholars suggested a close (though conflicted) connection between these fields.[3] In their introduction, Jerome Frisk and Robinson note that New West historians "re-tell regional history from the point of view of the oppressed, colonized and conquered; they wish to speak out for the interests of women, minorities, and the environment."

They also add urbanism to their list of new developments (11). This list generally matches the observations by Campbell and Comer. Frisk and Robinson astutely recognize the limitations of the New West history, which also find parallels in the essays of *Updating* as both historians and literary scholars participated in the social, cultural, and multicultural turns: "The New West Historians are not generally concerned with exposing the hidden economic and political interests that motivated actions, movements, and discourses" (6).

These limitations identify some of the new developments in Western literary studies as scholars have further expanded as well as transformed the methodologies and scope of the field. For example, the second section of this anthology, focusing on the working-class West, is indebted to the New West historians' bottom-up approach. Yet these essays do confront the ideological investments and power dynamics of Western development. The claims of the New West historians are more assumed than argued in this anthology, even as a number of essays recognize the continuing ideological significance of Turner's frontier thesis. Although rugged individualism and frontier divides have taken on new forms in contemporary society, their resonance in certain contexts remains strong.

Building on these past developments, *Crisscrossing Borders in Literature of the American West* offers new models for defining and analyzing the literature of the West. It represents a fast-changing field of crossings and recrossings with new possibilities and scholarly responsibilities. The three sections reflect important standpoints for considering Western literature; in each, the essays provide fruitful new models for engaging a reconfigured region.

*   *   *

The essays in the opening section, "A Postnational West," challenge the traditional borders that have often delineated both national and Western narratives. Postnational analysis certainly does not assume that the concept of nation will soon become obsolete (Curiel 1). Rather, it challenges the adequacy of a singular, unified national story that privileges some by excluding others. This project is particularly important since the U.S. national identity has so often been grounded in Western stories and icons set in the West that gain their explanatory power through strategic exclusions. Postnational analyses that engage previously excluded peoples and stories are not completely new since other approaches, Ethnic and Women's studies, for example, have questioned unified national stories for some time. Yet its self-reflexive questioning of borders is particularly relevant to contemporary Western literary studies. The undoing of previous exclusions, however, requires caution so as "not [to] equate and thereby confuse linguistic, cultural, ethnic, and national categories" (Rowe 24).

The four essays in this opening section engage in new ways the foundational story of westward expansion, the pioneer story. The first two consider new occupational or racial stories that transform frontier space. The second pair reframes or defamiliarizes traditional stories in challenging new ways.

Jeffery A. Sartain finds that middlebrow histories of the computer industry, from Tracy Kidder's *Soul of a New Machine* to Tom Wolfe's "Two Young Men Who Went West," consistently reuse the eighteenth- and nineteenth-century language of westward expansion to describe new technological developments. These narratives construct the computer industry as a new masculine proving ground by adapting the idea of the rugged individualist to techno creators and entrepreneurs. Yet the traditional Western story has considerable variation, from individual odyssey to building a community, and Sartain finds similar variations in the accounts of Silicon Valley, Silicon Alamo, and the men who led the charge.

Robert Crooks reconsiders Frederick Jackson Turner's concept of the frontier as the dividing line between civilization and savagery to establish a new analytical framework for the African American detective fiction of Chester Himes and Walter Mosley. He traces the use of frontier ideology as a justification for Indian wars and land expropriations to the present urban racial divide. The power dynamics in these two contexts are similar even if the forms of oppression and segregation differ. Recognizing detective fiction as descending from James Fenimore Cooper's frontier novels, this essay also shows how in this new context the basic western formula can generate, at least to some degree, strategies for resisting dominant economic and racial power structures embodied in the continuing frontier ideology of individualism. With a focus similar to the New West historians, this essay looks at the urban racial frontier from the Other side. Crooks compares the different possibilities for resistance that Himes and Mosley present. He finds in the West Coast novels of Mosley more tensions and ambiguities than resolutions to the problem of the urban color line.

As with the first two essays in this section, Rüdiger Heinze's "American Outsiders at the Center: Mormons and the West" questions Turnerian constructions of the West. His essay, and Homestead's, which follows, challenges common assumptions about historical or literary status. Heinze analyzes the integral yet liminal place Mormons hold in the story of the West and the nation. Although in many ways prototypical pioneers, they also challenged the Western individualistic ideology and took the vaguely religious underpinnings of Manifest Destiny much too seriously for an increasingly secular nation suspicious of a theocracy in its midst. For other Americans, consequently, Mormons continue to be "not-quite-other and too close to home." Heinze explores this "central outsider" paradox using two markedly different texts, the feature-length movie *Legacy*—currently the official Church of Jesus Christ of Latter-day Saints version of their pioneer past—and Tony Kushner's play *Angels in America*. Yet, for all their different ways of perceiving Mormons, both works acknowledge the paradoxical status this group has within Western and national narratives.

One might argue that the "central outsider" social position has a parallel in the literary hierarchy. Caught between the popular and the literary, middlebrow works sit on an uneasy border. Both Sartain's essay on computer industry histories and Crooks's on detective fiction raise postnational questions about middlebrow fiction as they question the nationalist assumptions in the texts they consider. The Cather scholar Melissa Homestead offers a different critique through her analysis of middlebrow writing strategies, marketing and circulation, and readership. Focusing on Willa Cather's *My Ántonia* and Bess Streeter Aldrich's *A Lantern in Her Hand*, Homestead acknowledges the power the pioneer story in both novels has for a national audience. At the same time she questions the literary hierarchy that values high art produced apparently without concern for the market while debasing middlebrow works that find a wide readership through sentimental engagement. Homestead undermines this hierarchy by strategically linking Cather to Aldrich, arguing that both authors embraced literary markets and middlebrow readerships. In addition, Homestead's essay challenges the usual exclusive focus on writers rather than readers. In a region (and nation) marked by the ideology of individualism, valorization of the author continues nearly unabated. Homestead's focus on readers and markets offers an important corrective.

In spite of its centrality to Western experience, class as an analytical category continues to receive only sporadic critical attention. Rowe argues,

> Far more likely to divide recent immigrants from US "national culture," as it is sometimes called, are social disparities in educational and

> economic opportunities. Class hierarchies, in other words, are far more
> divisive . . . than language or culture.   (24)

Immigrants are not alone in confronting class barriers. The essays in the second section, "Intersecting Stories: The Working-Class West," focus on this key aspect of the postnational critique.

In traditional constructions of the West, work has usually been associated with fur trapping, cowboying, and gun-slinging, occupations that are hardly even considered work. Similarly, Turner claimed that with the West functioning as a national safety valve, the steam would clean away the dangerous class consciousness associated with, say, Carnegie's steel mills or Pullman's manufacturing complex. As the three essays make clear, however, the West is not a class-free zone. Yet working-class concerns do not stand alone: this section's essays link class analysis with other important approaches. This is a key quality in their modeling new Western literary studies. For example, each essay acknowledges the important relationship between economic and environmental exploitation as it impacts the working class. In the first two, class analysis intersects with Native issues of identity, discrimination, and the destruction of the land. The third emphasizes the environmental justice critique in proletarian novels.

My own essay, "Indigenous Ways of Knowing Capitalism in Simon Ortiz's *Fight Back*," explains Ortiz's critique of capitalism as antithetical to Native values and survival. More than any other Native North American writer, Ortiz has confronted the structural causes of poverty and looked closely at work culture. This essay analyzes the way *Fight Back* depicts continuing racial and economic exploitation while at the same time celebrating the continuance of the Acoma people.

Renny Christopher, a leading scholar in working-class studies, focuses on identity by situating Louis Owens as both a mixedblood and mixed-class writer. Unlike much work on multiculturalism, "Louis Owens's Representations of Working-Class Consciousness" negotiates the common conceptual gap between individual subjectivity and the power relationships embedded in class structures. Owens's writing refuses to celebrate the possibilities of upward mobility. Instead, Christopher argues that it favors working-class values of community, interdependence, and connectedness, which are all allied with indigenous values. *Wolfsong* in particular focuses on work, with its protagonist caught between economic necessity and environmental destruction. The workplace in Owens's writing is a key location where Native identity and class status cross.

In a wide-ranging analysis of proletarian novels, "The American West in Red and Green" asserts that these 1930s works confront the prevailing social order by depicting the environmental destruction caused by capitalist production. Steven Rosendale, an author and editor who has challenged the boundaries of ecocriticism, first considers the way Eastern proletarian novels use idealized pastoral and pioneer tropes as a critique of and alternative to the barrenness of urban environments. However, Western proletarian novels, Rosendale demonstrates, challenge the pioneer legacy as they explore the relations between environmental and human exploitation. These novels, particularly Arnold B. Armstrong's neglected *Parched Earth*, presciently present a critique that predates by decades the work of the New West historians and ecocritics alike. In recognizing the environmental dimension of U.S. proletarian literature, this essay develops a new perspective both for environmental justice ecocritism and for the history of social activist literature.

The essays in the final section, "Transnational Wests," recognize that this region of study is not just of, by, or for the United States, but rather has historically been contested and traversed territory. Thus the "America" of our title references more than just the United States; it includes "*Nuestra América*," or "Our America," Cuban independence activist José Martí's term that includes Latin America in resistance to U.S. hegemony. Irwin's essay in this volume details the ways in which transnational analysis extends the postnational critique of the United States or the Western unified story of its origins and present condition.

To illustrate the continued hegemonic power of this story, Shelley Fisher Fishkin, in her 2004 American Studies Association presidential address, tells of her work on a literary guidebook for the National Parks Service and Oxford University Press trade publication division. Along with including sites such as the New Bedford Whaling District and Whitman's house, Fishkin wanted to include Angel Island, Wounded Knee, and the cabbage fields where Anzaldúa worked as a child. These sites did not fit the national story the publishers had in mind, and Fishkin finally withdrew the manuscript (17–18). One easily images that the publisher would have been even less inclined to include transnational Chilean and Californian sites from an Allende novel or a description of the border crossings of Teresa Urrea, the Saint of Cabora.

Later in her address, Fishkin usefully explains transnationalism as a field and method. "We'll pay increasing attention to the historical roots of multidirectional flows of people, ideas and goods and the social, political, linguistic, cultural, and economic crossroads generated in the process," she argues (22). Particularly relevant for Western literary studies in a transnational mode is her assertion that we must not only focus on immigrants but recognize "the endless process of comings and goings that create familial, cultural, linguistic and economic ties across national borders" (24). Yet, in considering the relationships between local and global or hemispheric spaces, we need to not overlook the continuing power and diverse meanings of nationalism. Robert Warrior, reminding us that Native peoples have political status as nations, also cautions that transnational economic relations are grounded in the structures of capitalism, a material reality that must be considered (808).[4]

The first three essays in "Transnational Wests" take a hemispheric approach, the first two by focusing on the boundary between Northwest Mexico and Southwest United States and the third reaching from Chile to California to the U.S. Midwest. The fourth crosses the Atlantic to explore the ideological critique embedded in German recreations of U.S. westerns. While recognizing asymmetries of power, transnational studies provide new opportunities for cross-border comparisons.

Robert McKee Irwin, a Mexicanist and leading scholar in hemispheric studies, challenges Western literary studies to take seriously the culture of the Mexican side of a shared boundary. His strategy is to first consider the Cuban poet and independence activist José Martí's use of the canonical Western novel *Ramona*. As Irwin challenges Martí's interpretation of Latin American racial harmony, he situates the novel within the context of the Northwest Mexican borderlands. Irwin uses *Ramona* as a case study that challenges the field to broaden its outlook so that it includes, in nonimperialist ways, intercultural relations in the Americas.

Martín embraces this challenge as she examines representations of Teresa Urrea, the popular border-crossing "Saint of Cabora." Martín's essay, "Possessing *La Santa de Cabora*," explores intercultural relations by following the historical character and her fictional representations as she crosses racial, class, religious, and national lines. Alienated from both Mexican and U.S. national identities because she is an Indian, a migrant, and a saint who is a woman challenging traditional sacred and human roles, Teresa Urrea exposes both the policing function of boundaries and the ways transnational identities can contest the universal national identities those boundaries work to sustain. Using the Mexican novelist Brianda Domecq's *La insólita historia de la Santa de Cabora* (*The Astonishing Story of the Saint of*

Cabora) (1990) as well as other contemporary sources, Martín calls us to embrace the contradictions of shifting border identities, as the borderland between Mexico and the United States continues to develop its own transnational culture.

Reutter's essay "Manifold Destinies" raises questions about the national and hemispheric implications of manifest destiny as it focuses on two works and authors not usually associated with Western literature. Both Isabel Allende's *Daughter of Fortune* and Toni Morrison's *Paradise* are set in the West but transgress its traditional borders, in part by having women of color as protagonists. However, Reutter finds Allende's novel to be only superficially transnational in spite of the multinational settings. Although its pluralism crosses national, racial, and gender borders, *Daughter of Fortune* sustains the traditional tropes and ideologies of the traditional Western and national constructions by, for example, endowing Chilean women characters with the role and stature traditionally held by the cowboys of western fiction. On the other hand, *Paradise* does challenge traditional stories by presenting an African American community struggling with its settler past and its own form of Manifest Destiny. Desperate to enforce community cohesion through their self-serving version of the past, the patriarchal leaders destroy their own revered story in attacking others who in many ways embody the town's desire to find a home in a foreign land. As with the women they attack, these men want to maintain their distinctive community. Ironically, they want to access a nationalist paradigm borrowed from the culture at large. Yet, by attacking a perceived threat from the outside, they undermine rather than preserve their own distinctiveness. Unlike Allende, Morrison does challenge traditional stories that without self-reflection present a utopian vision of a unified society.

The final essay, Hubertus Zander's "The Lonesome German Cowboy," analyzes changing German cultural constructions of Western myths and icons as representations of German national desires. Central to them is a skepticism about U.S. foreign policy. In parodying Karl May's widely read western novels, Michael "Bully" Herbig's 2001 movie, *Der Schuh des Manitu* (*Manitou's Shoe*), negotiates contemporary German skepticism about the new post–Cold War role that the United States has taken in world politics. May's novels themselves reflect earlier German dissent from the ideologies embedded in U.S. westerns. May challenged American exceptionalism with German Romanticism, and in doing so offered the more civilized *Edelmensch* (westman) as an alternative to the American cowboy. The 1960s film versions offer a different critique based on changing relations between Germany, the United States, and the Eastern Bloc. In these movies, the westman Old Shatterhand and his Apache blood brother Winnetou share a cooperative relationship rather than the antagonistic one between cowboys and Indians in U.S. Cold War westerns. This cooperative relationship suggested German hopes for a peaceful future threatened by U.S. imperialism. Herbig's *Manitou's Shoe* spoofs these 1960s movies and their hope for a new cooperative world. In this contemporary version of the western, Herbig acknowledges German skepticism about U.S. efforts to fulfill its Manifest Destiny by attempting to bring democracy to the rest of the world.

U.S. national stories that are rooted in the West, Manifest Destiny for example, continue to shape its relations with the hemisphere and the world as well as mark its own sense of identity. Too often this means that scholars from dominant groups and positions see with only single consciousness while forcing a double consciousness on others. Yet is it possible to have double consciousness without a veil? By implication, is it possible to have a Western literary studies that recognizes the many forms of difference that create borders within and around the region while neither reifying those borders nor discounting their power? In using W. E. B. Du Bois's terminology, I want to emphasize the high stakes in drawing lines. Du Bois, however, did not advocate erasing the color line any more than Anzaldúa advocated erasing borders. Our use of the term "crisscrossing" is intended to suggest that the essays here likewise do not erase borders but rather explore new perspectives and offer new models for understanding both the strength and the permeability of borders. Space without borders cannot become place, yet borders without crossings become walls rather than doors.

NOTES

1. Other works have recently contributed to reconstructing Western literary studies. Krista Comer's *Landscapes of the New West: Gender and Geography in Contemporary Women's Writing* (1999) is specifically feminist and postmodern in its cultural studies approach. *True West: Authenticity and the American West* (2004) focuses specifically, as editors William R. Handley and Nathaniel Lewis note, on "the conceit of western authenticity" (1). The essays in *Postwestern Cultures: Literature, Theory, Space* (2007), edited by Susan Kollin, analyze a wide range of cultural artifacts from the U.S. West. Claudia Sadowski-Smith's *Border Fictions: Globalization, Empire and Writing at the Boundaries of the United States* (2008) offers an overview beyond a specific region.

2. Nina Baym contextualizes *Updating the Literary West* by explaining the limitations of its earlier incarnation, *Literary History of the American West*. This volume, she argues, was outdated on its arrival in 1987, with its Turnerian focus on the frontier as key to national character. Baym suggests the same outdatedness for the field itself at that time (814–16). Max Westbook's preface to *Updating* offers a positive view of the previous volume, and by implication the field as well, by emphasizing continuities rather than radical shifts.

3. Robinson's 2004 review essay, "We Should Talk: Western History and Western Literature in Dialogue," explains that while literary scholars want to break down disciplinary barriers, historians are resistant in part because this move "directly challenges their disciplinary foundations" (132–33). At heart is the problem of representation, the relationship between the "imagined" and the "real" West. Krista Comer in "Literature, Gender Studies, and the New West History" offers a more thorough analysis of the relationship between these disciplines from a feminist perspective.

4. Warrior includes the following quote from Wai Chee Dimock:

> Transnationality . . . points not to the emergence of a new collective unit . . . but to the persistence of an old logic, the logic of capitalism. Market born and market driven, it is infinite in its geographical extension but all too finite in its aspirations. It offers no alternative politics, poses no threat to the sovereignty of the state. (808)

Dimock's view of transnationalism, focusing on economic structures, offers few possibilities for resistance. See my references in this essay to Anzaldúa for a more positive, cultural perspective. The challenge is to include both perspectives in our analysis.

Works Cited

Andrews, Jennifer, and Priscilla L. Walton. "Rethinking Canadian and American Nationality: Indigeneity and the 49th Parallel in Thomas King." *American Literary Quarterly* 18.3 (2006): 600–17.

Anzaldúa, Gloria. *Borderlands/La Frontera: The New Mestiza*. 1987. San Francisco, CA: Aunt Lutie, 1999.

Baym, Nina. "Old West, New West, Postwest, Real West." *American Literary History* 18.4 (2006): 814–28.

Bone, Martyn. *The Postsouthern Sense of Place in Contemporary Fiction*. Baton Rouge: Louisiana State University Press, 2005.

Campbell, SueEllen. "'Connecting the Countrey': What's New in Western Lit Crit?" 3–16. Western Literature Association.

Comer, Krista. "Feminism, Women Writers and New Western Regionalism: Revisiting Critical Paradigms," 17–34. Western Literature Association.

————. "Literature, Gender Studies, and the New Western History." *The New Western History: An Assessment.* Special issue of *Arizona Quarterly* 53.2 (Summer 1997): 99–134.

Curial, Barbara Brinson, David Kazanjian, Katherine Kinney, Steven Mailloux, Jay Michling, John Carlos Rowe, George Sánchez, Shelley Streeby, and Henry Yu. "Introduction." In *Post-Nationalist American Studies,* edited by. John Carlos Rowe. Berkley: University of California Press, 2000.

Fishkin, Shelley Fisher. "Crossroads of Cultures: The Transnational Turn in American Studies—Presidential Address to the American Studies Association, November 12, 2004." *American Quarterly* 57.1 (2004): 17–57.

Fisk, Jerome, and Forrest G. Robinson. "Introduction." *The New Western History: An Assessment.* Special issue of *Arizona Quarterly* 53.2 (Summer 1997): 1–15.

Fluck, Winfried. "Inside and Outside: What Kind of Knowledge Do We Need? A Response to the Presidential Address." *American Quarterly* 59.1 (2007): 23–32.

Giles, Paul. "Commentary: Hemispheric Partiality." *American Literary History* 18.3 (2006): 648–55.

Irwin, Robert. "The New American Studies: A Lesson from the Borderlands." *Comparative American Studies* 3.4 (2005): 514–25.

Jameson, Frederic. *Postmodernism: Or, The Cultural Logic of Late Capitalism.* Durham, NC: Duke University Press, 1991.

Levander, Caroline, and Robert S Levine. "Introduction: Hemispheric American Literary History." *American Literary History* 18.3 (2006): 397–405.

McKee, Kathryn, and Annette Trefzer. "Preface: Global Contexts, Local Literatures: The New Southern Studies." *American Literature* 78.4 (2006): 677–90.

McPherson, Tara. "On Wal-Mart and Southern Studies." *American Literature* 78.4 (2006): 677–90.

Robinson, Forrest G. "We Should Talk: Western History and Western Literature in Dialogue." *American Literary History* 16.1 (2004): 132–43.

Saldivar-Hull, Sonia. "Introduction." *Borderlands/La Frontera: The New Mestiza.* By Gloria Anzaldúa. 1987. San Francisco, CA: Aunt Lutie, 1999.

Warrior, Robert. "Native American Critical Responses to Transnational Discourse." *PMLA* 122.3 (2007): 807–8.

Westbook, Max. Preface. *Updating the Literary West,* xii–xv. Western Literature Association.

Western Literature Association. *Updating the Literary West.* Fort Worth, TX: Christian University Press, 1997.

White, Richard. *"It's Your Misfortune and None of My Own": A History of the American West.* Norman: University of Oklahoma Press, 1991.

PART I

A POSTNATIONAL WEST: NEW CHALLENGES TO OLD STORIES

CHAPTER 1

ELECTRONIC PIONEERS AND SILICON GUNSLINGERS: CONSTRUCTING HISTORIES OF THE U.S. COMPUTER INDUSTRY

Jeffrey A. Sartain

Modern electronic solid-state computing began in 1947 with the invention of the transistor, the small chip of silicon with miniscule gold wires embedded that makes all forms of modern computing possible.[1] The initial events that led to the modern computing culture took place simultaneously with a variety of critically important historical events in America, including McCarthyism, the beginning of the cold war, a postwar push for feminine domesticity, civil rights movements of all types, and a variety of cultural movements, including but not limited to the Beat aesthetic, the counterculture of the 1960s, the proliferation of television, the space race, New Journalism, rock and roll, and pop art.[2]

Since its inception, narratives about the computer industry have blended the frontier myth with stories of technological invention and commercial entrepreneurship. As Richard Slotkin explains in *Gunfighter Nation,* the contemporary deployment of the frontier myth represents how a "revised ideology acquires its own mythology, typically blending old formulas with new ideas or concerns" (6). Indeed, the computer industry's consistent rhetoric of determination, exploration, and innovation depends on formulaic elements borrowed from westerns and the frontier myth for cultural resonance. Much like the western genre in literature and film, the computer industry's deployment of the frontier myth and its attendant tropes can be read for ideological underpinnings and assumptions. Specifically, the computer industry's reliance on the frontier myth reifies a notion of masculine identity predicated on individualism and conquest. Computing narratives tend to feature an incarnation of Frederick Jackson Turner's quintessentially American "frontier man," who embodies the virtues of individualism, industry, creativity, ruggedness, and self-reliance (Turner 9). The frontier man has become the de facto model for describing the computer industry's entrepreneurs, inventors, engineers, and scientists in print.

As Susan Faludi notes in *Stiffed,* the idea of the frontier has long been a guarantee of American masculine identity (26–27). She argues that the foreclosure of the geographic frontier forces the cultural consciousness to come up with substitutes to give masculine identity in American culture a proving ground (30–40). By conflating the western and the computing industry, the traditional patriarchal culture secures some solid ground against the encroachments of contemporary identity politics. Much like mid-century film westerns, the computer industry's usage of the frontier myth continues "to assure the white male citizen that America was his" (Coyne 46).

Popular histories of the computer industry, like those written by Tracy Kidder, Stephen Levy, David Kushner, and Tom Wolfe, yield productive results when examined narratologically because these authors seek to ascribe a story arc to events in the recent past.[3] The various popular histories of computing that have appeared over the last three decades are remarkable for their consistent use formulaic of elements from the western.[4] As Michael Coyne observes, "There is considerable irony in a prosperous, technologically sophisticated society forging an idealized self-image from a Spartan past" (3). A more complete understanding of these narratives' fictive elements reveals the ideologies they reify, which are often startling because of their reliance on centuries-old biases and oppressions. Inasmuch as westerns can be analyzed to reveal the values of the particular cultural moment that produced them, so too can narratives that borrow formulaic elements from the western. As Stanley Corkin argues, "The benefit of such analysis lies in its power to show how popular productions convey social and cultural values, particularly at a time of change and duress" (5). Careful analysis of generic western conventions in relation to computer industry writing will help reveal the ideological assumptions underpinning a major facet of contemporary culture.

The classic western structure utilized by most popular histories of the computer industry posits the frontier to be explored/conquered as an Edenic wilderness of danger and possibility. To tame this "savage" frontier, rugged individualists are needed to extol the virtues of "civilization" in the wilderness. The role of explorer or conqueror or cowboy, as well as its constituent values, is reserved for masculine identity. Those who would impede the explorer are prefigured as feminine and feminized, further reinforcing the patriarchy and chauvinism of the culture pushing into the frontier. The traditional western, as well as computing narratives that borrow its formulaic elements and plot structures, are structured as mythic quests in which a hero must overcome great odds. Therefore, it is quite rewarding to look to the nature of the western hero for clues about the epistemological assumptions reified by the text. The bulk of western heroes contain within their characters some sort of unresolved, paradoxical conflict. The tension caused by this conflict is often at the root of the hero's journey in westerns, and gets carried forth in the litany of binary oppositions featured in westerns: good versus evil, the frontier versus civilization, law versus order, individualism versus community, masculine versus feminine, and many other binary oppositions (Wallmann 30–34).

The complexities of westerns that treat such binaries in dialectic tension most interest critics because the western's meaning and continued relevance directly stem from its epistemological ambivalence, signaled by the genre's often-paradoxical and complicated treatment of oppositional themes. While this is the dominant mode for most classic westerns, other westerns posit very simplistic relationships between characters that are usually painted in the broadest strokes possible. These westerns are often intended for a juvenile audience, such as the *Lone Ranger* serials in which a simplistic "good guys versus bad guys" logic rules. As Patricia Nelson Limerick warns in *The Legacy of Conquest*, "To celebrate the Western past with an open invitation is a considerable risk: the brutal massacres come back along with the cheerful barn raisings, the shysters come back with the saints, contracts broken come back with contracts fulfilled" (330). For Limerick, the tropes, symbols, and language of the western never appear unproblematically because they are always encoded in the larger history of violence, conquest, and oppression of the U.S. continental westward expansion.[5]

Coyne offers the distinction between "community" and "odyssey" westerns, which is perhaps even more useful than the simple-complex rubric for teasing out some of the extended connotations of the computer industry's frontier imagery. As Coyne outlines in *Crowded Prairie*:

> With very few exceptions . . . Westerns are likely to revolve around either a community, essentially a social construct, or an odyssey, which is primarily a literary device. Westerns with a community setting, despite their smaller geographical scale, were better suited to celebrate or criticize contemporary US politics, values and national identity, while odyssey Westerns—though frequently ranging wide over the frontier terrain—tended to favour [sic] narratives of personal obsession.   (6)

Coyne's community or odyssey binary isn't an exclusive schematic, though, as many westerns "might effortlessly contain elements of each" (7). By extending Coyne's argument to the contemporary computing narratives under examination, we can delineate the more socially concerned "community" narratives from the individually centered "odyssey" narratives.

In many ways, narratives describing the high-tech arena and computer industry have become a sanctuary for many traditional masculine values, reaffirming American culture's longstanding faith in the idea of the rugged individualist as pioneer and explorer, in this case revised and morphed into the image of the nerd and the hacker. Computing narratives like *Soul of a New Machine*, *Hackers*, *Masters of Doom*, and "Two Young Men Who Went West," which repurpose the terms of westward expansion to describe new technological developments, offer rich and rewarding insights into the contemporary ideologies reified within their pages. Through a more concrete understanding of the computer industry's juxtaposition of high-tech innovation with frontier rhetoric and imagery, we can more completely understand the oppressions that inhere in this particular reinscription of the discourse of westward expansionism.

*   *   *

Electronic Pioneers: *Soul of a New Machine* and *Hackers*

Tracy Kidder begins his Pulitzer-winning account of Data General Corporation's struggles to bring a new minicomputer to market, *Soul of a New Machine* (1980), with a scene involving one of Data General's top design engineers, Tom West, on a yachting vacation. In the opening scene, as the party runs into inclement weather, West's fortitude and stamina stand out among the seasick passengers and crew. Working for three days and nights tirelessly, West sails against the elements with a skill and dedication that causes the ship's captain to remark, "That fellow West is a good man in a storm" (7). Tellingly, Kidder opens his technological narrative with a story of a rugged individual, Tom West, successfully testing his personal mettle against the elements, remarking that West resembled "the ghost of an old-fashioned virtuous seaman" (4). In Kidder's narrative, the yachting vacation's inclement weather metaphorically stands in for the social, intellectual, and economic problems West later faces at Data General. Presciently describing West's skills and perseverance on the yacht, Kidder goes on to highlight how these virtues influence West's work life. West headed the Eagle minicomputer project at Data General, where he astutely hid his modifications to the computer's design and engineering specifications from management's prying eyes. West's insubordination was handsomely rewarded, though, when his unauthorized design for the Eagle minicomputer bailed the company out of an overcommitted project that was lagging further and further behind its projected timeline.

Whether on vacation or at work, West navigates perilous territory, first the ocean and then the so-called electronic frontier, and through his individual perseverance and fortitude, he achieves a greater good. As described by Data General manager Ken Holberger in *Soul of a New Machine,* West's actions "reminded him of the typical conclusion of one sort of Western. A town hires a gunslinger to clean it up, but when he's taken care of their problem, he's still a gunslinger and sooner or later the respectable citizens are going to run him out of town" (280). This particular plot formula from the western signals the text's ambivalence toward the violence and rugged individualism of the frontier. The gunslinger embodies a violence and savagery necessary to settle the frontier, but such values cannot comfortably coexist with the civilization they help engender. Such is the case in Kidder's text as well. West is rewarded for his iconoclasm and individualism while these very traits preclude his seamless integration into the larger community of Data General's corporate bureaucracy. Fundamentally, *Soul of a New Machine* contains elements of both the "community" and the "odyssey" westerns described by Coyne: "The community Western extols social adjustment, the odyssey Western is charitably disposed toward a strain of self-styled alienation" (7). On the side of community, the prosperity and survival of Data General—a social, economic, and technical community—is the end goal of the individuals described in *Soul of a New Machine*. Simultaneously, *Soul of a New Machine* describes West as the quintessential figure of individualist alienation, one of those protagonists who reify masculinist American ideologies into tangible archetypes.

Levy's work portrays the tension between the opposing values of individualism and community that tug at West and, in doing so, embodies the western's characteristic dialectic tension between the individual and the community. The traits Kidder uses to describe West are also picked up again in Evan Ratliff's twenty-year retrospective on *Soul of a New Machine,* "O, Engineers!" where Ratliff describes the aging West as a man "who could easily pass for a salty old sea captain." Ratliff goes on to describe *Soul of a New Machine* as "the high tech story by which all others are judged" because of its "glimpse into the mysterious motivations, the quiet revelations, and the spectacular devotions of engineers." Ratliff's article indicates the sweeping degree to which *Soul of a New Machine* helped crystallize the usage of western genre conventions to describe Silicon Valley.

Only four years later, Levy uses many of the same generic conventions from the western in his bestseller, *Hackers: Heroes of the Computer Revolution* (1984). Levy's work chronicles an industry shift from the complex epistemological tensions described in *Soul of a New Machine* to the individualism that pervades more recent computer industry writing.[6] *Hackers* tells the story of "computer programmers and designers who regard computing as the most important thing in the world" (7). The individuals Levy describes pursue computing as an ideal form, and many times they must accomplish their goals outside of sanctioned corporate, industrial, commercial, and academic institutions. Levy paints a picture of computer hackers who seek knowledge through exploration of forbidden systems (steam tunnels, computer networks, etc.), and it's through their unsanctioned explorations that they are able to solve problems in previously bureaucratized systems. Levy's hackers work on an intellectual frontier invested with all the resonances called forth by John G. Cawelti's description of the western's symbolic landscape—"a field of action that centers up on the point of encounter between civilization and wilderness, East and West, settled society and lawless openness" (*Adventure* 193). In Levy's narrative, the computer is the gateway to an Edenic wilderness of unexplored intellectual territory, simultaneously threatening and imbued with limitless possibility.

Levy and the programmers he profiles adopt the pejorative term "hackers" because, for them, the term signifies an individual's willingness to transgress boundaries and make whatever personal or institutional sacrifices are necessary to accomplish a task at hand.

Levy distills the attitudes embodied by the hackers he profiles into six principles he calls "The Hacker Ethic":

1. Access to computers—and anything that might teach you something about the way the world works—should be unlimited and total. Always yield to the Hands-On Imperative.
2. All information should be free.
3. Mistrust authority—promote decentralization.
4. Hackers should be judged by their hacking, not bogus criteria such as degrees, age, race, or position.
5. You can create art and beauty on a computer.
6. Computers can change your life for the better.   (Levy 39–49)

Levy spends the bulk of the book describing how the principles of the Hacker Ethic play out in the lives of notable early computer industry figures like Apple Computer founders Steve Jobs and Steve Wozniak, Microsoft founder Bill Gates, and a host of other early individuals who helped shape modern computing culture. All of the hackers Levy describes embody, at one point in their careers, the complex ideological tension between individuals and communities inscribed in the Hacker Ethic.

In the Epilogue to *Hackers*, Levy profiles "the last of the true hackers" (415), Richard Stallman, then a systems programmer at MIT's Artificial Intelligence lab.[7] As more and more bureaucracy appeared in the previously unrestricted forum of the Artificial Intelligence lab, Stallman grated against the shift from the Hacker Ethic's community emphasis to the individualism rising from commercialization and corporatization of computing. Stallman witnessed more and more hackers going "to work for businesses, implicitly accepting the compromises that such work entailed" (418), and thereby abandoning the complex dynamic between individuals and community suggested in the Hacker Ethic. Much like West in *Soul of a New Machine*, *Hackers* portrays Stallman as the embodiment of the complex tensions between opposing values of community and individuality, liberty and control. By the end of *Hackers*, though, Stallman is a tragic figure whose time has passed because of the industry's rampant commercialism and the new generation of hackers' myopic self-interest. The hackers seeking to corporatize and monetize their skills "delivered the fatal blow to what was left of the idealistic community [Stallman] loved" (419). The efforts of young hackers to cash in on computing pushed the once open and egalitarian computing culture down the slippery slope of capitalism, and Levy suggests that this was the beginning of the end for the ideal of altruistic, communitarian, and egalitarian values embodied by Stallman and the other early hackers.

Soul of a New Machine and *Hackers* recount the early days of the computer industry and its nascent subculture within many of the established conventions of the western. Kidder's and Levy's texts share the inherent dialectic tension of westerns, described by Cawelti, where "the forces of civilization and wilderness are in balance, the epic moment at which the old life and the new confront each other and individual actions may tip the balance in one way or another, thus shaping the future history of the whole settlement" (*Adventure* 193). As chronicled by Levy, the balance eventually tipped in favor of individuals' struggles for wealth and success in the new industry, and the importance of community diminished in favor of more individualized odyssey stories.

* * *

Silicon Gunslingers: *Masters of Doom* and "Two Young Men Who Went West"

Frontier imagery and its attendant ideologies of individualism, progress, and conquest are nearly universal in popular histories of the computer industry. Recent computing narratives tend to take these values and naturalize them without their attendant oppositions, though, focusing on drastically simplified versions of these values, eschewing the dialectic tension and ambiguity that characterize the complex ideological positions of more community-minded westerns. As a cultural landmark, Levy's *Hackers* chronicles the transition linking the complexity and tension appearing in *Soul of a New Machine* with the more simplistic narratives that dominate in recent years. For example, in David Kushner's *Masters of Doom: How Two Guys Created an Empire and Transformed Pop Culture* (2004), the tension between the opposing values that characterizes Kidder's and Levy's narratives is utterly absent. In *Masters of Doom,* the simplistic version of the western gunslinger has clearly won out, as Kushner takes great pains to describe the virtuoso genius of John Carmack and John Romero, the founders of Id Software and creators of the legendary videogame, *Doom* (1993). Kushner's use of gunslinger imagery is unsurprising because Carmack and Romero created the first-person shooter (FPS) videogame interface, where "the whole idea was to make the player feel as if he were *inside* the game," actively engaging in the violence of the shoot-'em-up science-fiction adventures characteristic of the

FPS genre (Kushner 80). Kushner extends the frontier imagery to describe Id Software's headquarters in Austin, Texas, as the "Silicon Alamo" because of the fierce creative and economic rivalries between the area's numerous videogame publishers and the personal rivalries between Carmack and Romero (243–61).

Kushner's use of gunslinger imagery is much less complex than Kidder's, and demands attention to the oversights inherent in contemporary deployments of Western imagery. Kushner's text overtly engages the symbols and language from the western genre, including one of the most famous sites in Western history, fiction, and myth—the Alamo. The story Kushner tells of this new Silicon Alamo largely follows Coyne's odyssey structure, relating a tale of individual achievement and conquest where the achievements of the characters do not create any sort of lasting community. Kushner explicitly describes the personal and professional challenges Carmack and Romero face as their company becomes the most powerful videogame publisher in the world in just a few short years. Kushner also regales readers with the excesses of the "Two Johns" as they celebrate their success by buying cars, houses, companies, and indulging in esoteric hobbies like space rocketry. At no point in *Masters of Doom* does Kushner ever nod to the dialectic tension of the community western, which gives some social and altruistic meaning to the violence and lawlessness of the gunslinger on the frontier. Rather, *Masters of Doom* is a story of individual achievement and skill that never leads to the kind of community-building and consolation characteristic of the community western. Instead, Kushner gives readers a very simplistic odyssey western, an unadulterated and unapologetic celebration of "personal obsession" (Coyne 6)—a spectacular, if only figurative, orgy of violence, conflict, and conquest that reifies a particular type of simplistic western hero.

Like Kushner's *Masters of Doom,* Tom Wolfe's "Two Young Men Who Went West" follows Coyne's odyssey structure, describing the individual achievements of Intel founder Bob Noyce. Wolfe frames his biographical account of Noyce with a history of Grinnell, Iowa, Noyce's hometown, founded by a dissenting Protestant and Congregationalist minister, Josiah Grinnell. Wolfe presents his version of the beginnings of the modern computer industry as a reiteration of the story of nineteenth century westward expansionism, driven by Protestant values of individualism, perseverance, work, and egalitarianism.[8] Throughout the piece, Wolfe explicitly argues that Noyce's successes in science and business were a direct result of the Protestant values internalized by Noyce at a young age. As Wolfe puts it, "Noyce had wandered away from the church itself. He smoked. He smoked a lot. He took a drink when he felt like it. He had gotten a divorce. Nevertheless, when Noyce went west, he brought Grinnnell with him . . . unaccountably sewn into the lining of his coat" (62). For Wolfe, describing the roots of modern computing culture, western tropes are not used unconsciously or lightly, but signal a larger ethos at work that ascribes these values to a fading form of masculinity, and may be seen as part of a larger effort to shore up the same masculinity against the supposed degradations of the latter part of the twentieth century.

Wolfe's use of western elements in "Two Young Men Who Went West" parallels Jane Tompkins's argument, that "[the western] is about men's fear of losing their mastery, and hence their identity, both of which the Western tirelessly reinvents" (45). In the mid-twentieth century, the implicit threats to masculine dominance presented by working women, minorities, civil rights, and the egalitarian impulses of the 1960s countercultures threatened to evacuate the privilege and dominance of a certain type of masculinity. As Manuel Martinez argues, threats to dominant patriarchal culture were embodied in the suburban postwar home front:

> The tension between domesticity and the projected desire to strike out for the frontier can be seen as a central antagonism between an individualism defined by personal, unrestricted movement and the forces of an immobilizing and effeminizing domesticity and bourgeois vacuity in the workplace and home. (77)

The frontier, figured as the opposite of the emasculating home front, becomes a liminal space where traditional forms of masculinity can be aggressively reasserted. As part of the culture after World War II, Faludi argues, the reappearance of the values of traditional masculinity signals the ways in which postwar masculinity was attempting to assert its dominance after the upheavals resulting from wartime efforts.

Indeed, in "Two Young Men Who Went West," we can see that the pictures Wolfe paints of women are limited to very traditional stereotypes. Women are exclusively portrayed as sex objects, mothers, caretakers, or manual laborers. Exploited on all fronts as facilitators for the men in their lives, even the professional women who are the men's engineering colleagues and counterparts are only mentioned in passages describing them as "terasexy" (43) because they can participate in the repressive masculine discourse of the electronics industry. Women who can't adopt this discourse don't possess the prerequisites to continue to be "interesting" in Wolfe's schematic, and therefore are subjected to marginalization, divorce, grueling wage slave labor, or being ignored altogether. In Wolfe's text, women seem to exist solely to help men in their lives—a turn that simultaneously objectifies and subjugates women into a subservient, subordinate role. By using the language of the frontier to describe women in such chauvinistic terms, Wolfe implicitly links the electronics industry with the western's repressive attitudes toward gender. "Two Young Men Who Went West" simultaneously transcribes and reinscribes these repressive gender attitudes in contemporary culture.

Although Wolfe's treatment of gender and gender roles is disturbingly simple, his treatment of the individual or community dialectic is much more nuanced and complex. The oppositional tension is most apparent in the text's cryptic ending, where Wolfe describes the untimely, accidental death of Eagle Computer's CEO, Dennis Barnhart, on the day his new company began trading stock publicly. At the end of the business day, Barnhart found his personal stock to be worth $9 million. As Wolfe describes it in the final lines of "Two Young Men Who Went West":

> [Barnhart] and a pal took his Ferrari out for a little romp, hung their hides out over the edge, lost control on a curve in Los Gatos, and went through a guardrail, and Barnhart was killed. Naturally, that night people in the business could talk of very little else. One of the best known CEOS in the Valley said, "It's the dark side of the Force." He said it without a trace of irony, and his friends nodded in contemplation. They had no term for it, but they knew exactly what Force he meant.   (65)

In "Two Young Men Who Went West," the ending serves as a sort of cautionary tale about the necessity to temper the individualist drives of the industry with community-oriented impulses. As Wolfe describes Bob Noyce, the key values that return again and again are those he inherited from his Grinnell upbringing, the social and egalitarian values he used to model Intel's internal structure, which eschewed corporate hierarchies and seniority-based rewards. In the years since Intel's founding, the ethic of work and merit-based system of rewards that Noyce instilled at Intel have become the computer industry's standard operating model. Making a marked contrast with the story's preoccupation with Noyce's individualist odyssey, Wolfe seems to be offering the tragic Barnhart anecdote as a warning to those who only value the material rewards of the computer industry—consumer commodities and cash. At the end of "Two Young Men Who Went West,"

Wolfe offers readers a nod toward community values that temper the ethos of the rugged individualist. The success of Wolfe's narrative strategy, though, forestalling the emphasis on community until his closing lines, ultimately seems to reflect the diminished importance of community values in computer industry discourse in recent years.

* * *

OUTRIDERS ON THE ELECTRONIC FRONTIER

Beyond the sheer weight of technological innovation and the persistent drive for scientific progress, the western narrative appears to have been an important force in the quick cultural acceptance and assimilation of computers and computing culture. Histories tracing the beginning of the computer industry appear regularly in popular writing, signaling that the niche interest group of self-described nerds, geeks, and hackers has conquered the mainstream, and is now worthy to grace the covers of *Time, Newsweek,* and *Fortune.*[9] Rather than adopting the perspective of more complex westerns, recent computing narratives such as *Masters of Doom* and "Two Young Men Who Went West" maintain many tropes from the western, but they never address the ambiguities inherent in the genre. Instead, they center on the rewards of the western narrative of conquest without raising the bar for the responsibilities inherent in the rewards.

These are not the complex western narratives that seek places to form new communities in the frontier spaces. Rather, these are narratives so caught in the simplistic, individualistic versions of the western narrative that they almost completely eschew the frontiersman as community builder. Instead of building communities, Kushner's and Wolfe's characters participate in a capitalistic version of the frontier odyssey, populated only by rugged individuals. The critical reconciliation of the rugged individual with the community is one of the fundamental dialectics in the western genre, and it's almost entirely absent in recently published popular nonfiction about the computing industry.[10] For early computer industry chroniclers like Kidder and Levy, the attendant values of masculinity valorized in the western are sites of ideological contestation and dialectic tension. In contrast, more recent computing narratives like *Masters of Doom* and "Two Young Men Who Went West" create a myopic narrative of power and Manifest Destiny, reifying these quintessential American myths at both the thematic and stylistic levels. In all of these texts, the values exemplified by the protagonists are linked intrinsically with contemporary questions of gender and gender roles in high-tech industries. In Wolfe and Kushner, the tension and complexity resolve into a myopic and simplistic version of masculinity, a counterpart to the most juvenile western literature and film.

Popular writing about the computer industry is thoroughly enmeshed with the frontier myth, trafficking in imagery from the western genre in literature and film. Coyne believes that the western genre must be continually interrogated because, historically, the genre posited "American identity as mainly white and male, largely accepted racial supremacy as a given, romanticized aggressive masculinity and, ultimately, eulogized resistance to regulated society as the truest mark of manhood" (Coyne 15). In recent computing narratives, the electronic frontier is never settled; therefore, it's perpetually reserved as a playground for the types of impoverished masculinity that values individualism without community, exploration without consolidation, and the frontier without the domestic. By revealing the ideologies at work in these narratives, we can more astutely critique their oppressive usages in contemporary culture and highlight productive counter-discourses. As William Stahl observes, "Technology is enmeshed in ideologies and myths, ranging from fads and fashions up to the deepest symbols around which people structure their identities and order their societies" (16). Through deliberate, reflexive narratological examination, a concerned modern citizen can more completely understand the divisive and oppressive ramifications the computer industry's rhetoric has for an increasingly globalized world, where values of individualism and dominance must be balanced with their corresponding counterparts of community and collaboration.

NOTES

1. Three volumes stand out as solid comprehensive references for the history of computing. Paul E. Ceruzzi's *History of Modern Computing*, 2nd ed. (MIT Press, 2003); Martin Campbell-Kelly and William Aspray's *Computer: A History of the Information Machine*, 2nd ed. (Westview, 2004); and Georges Ifrah's *Universal History of Computing* (Wiley, 2001).

2. John Markoff's *What the Dormouse Said: How the 60s Counterculture Shaped the Personal Computing Industry* is a detailed examination of the specific historical and personal overlaps between the 1960s countercultural movements and the early computer industry.

3. Because this study analyzes discourse around the issues of contemporary computing and communications, many of the potentially rewarding texts for study are ephemeral. Therefore, to serve as representative

examples of the discourse, I've selected a few popular, successful, and important works that have helped to outline many of the fundamental practices of the discourse around computing.

4. For John G. Cawelti's extended discussion of the terminology and methodology of formula versus genre or mythography, see *Six-Gun Mystique* (64–61) and *Adventure, Mystery, and Romance* (5–36).

5. Beyond Limerick, my reading of revisionist Western history, often termed "New Western History," is particularly influenced by Richard White's *"It's Your Misfortune and None of My Own": A History of the American West* (1991) and William Cronon, George Miles, and Jay Gitlin's anthology, *Under an Open Sky: Rethinking America's Western Past* (1992).

6. Levy has continued to be an important narrator of the "computer revolution," frequently contributing to computer culture magazines like *Wired*, and writing many other books focused on computing culture.

7. Richard Stallman continues to be one of the most vocal activists for the communitarian aspects of computer culture through his work with open-source, free software. His work has significantly influenced the development and proliferation of open-source software systems, which have emerged as viable alternatives to corporate, proprietary software.

8. Max Weber, writing at the beginning of the twentieth century, discusses how this country's Protestant-cum-secular work ethic was instrumental in the success of capitalism in America in *The Protestant Ethic and the Spirit of Capitalism* (1930). Weber is an important intellectual figure for Wolfe, and Weber's work is instrumental in understanding the thematic arcs Wolfe ascribes to his subjects throughout his writing.

9. Bill Gates appeared on the June 5, 1995, cover of *Time Magazine* with the headline "Master of the Universe." Gates has appeared on *Time*'s cover eight times in all since his first appearance on the April 16, 1984, cover of *Time*, including a stint as *Time*'s Person of the Year in 2005 (December 26, 2005). For a complete gallery of Steve Jobs's magazine covers, visit http://www.kuodesign.com/pineapple/coverme/index.html. This archive has images of Jobs from the last twenty-five years of popular magazines, including his first appearance on *Fortune*'s cover (February 7, 1983), when he became the youngest individual to ever be featured on the cover.

10. Jeffrey Wallmann directly examines the individual or community dialectic in the Western *The Western: Parables of the American Dream* (1999) in his chapter entitled "Trailblazin" (36–56). Wallmann argues that since the western's inception, one of its fundamental paradoxes has been that "the hunters and trappers known as Mountain Men opened the wilderness to the very civilization they supposedly sought to escape" (37).

WORKS CITED

Cawelti, John G. *Adventure, Mystery, and Romance: Formula Stories as Art and Popular Culture.* Chicago: University of Chicago Press, 1976.

——. *The Six-Gun Mystique.* 2nd ed. Bowling Green: Bowling Green State University Popular Press, 1984.

Corkin, Stanley. *Cowboys as Cold Warriors: The Western and U.S. History.* Philadelphia: Temple University Press, 2004.

Coyne, Michael. *The Crowded Prairie: American National Identity in the Hollywood Western.* London: I. B. Tauris, 1997.

Faludi, Susan. *Stiffed: The Betrayal of the American Man.* 1999. New York: Harper, 2000.

Kidder, Tracy. *Soul of a New Machine.* 1981. New York: Avon, 1990.

Kushner, David. *Masters of Doom: How Two Guys Created an Empire and Transformed Pop Culture.* New York: Random, 2003.

Levy, Steven. *Hackers: Heroes of the Computer Revolution.* 1984. New York: Penguin, 1994.

Limerick, Patricia Nelson. *The Legacy of Conquest: The Unbroken Past of the American West.* New York: Norton, 1987.

Martinez, Manuel L. *Countering the Counterculture: Rereading Postwar American Dissent from Jack Kerouac to Tomás Rivera.* Madison University of Wisconsin Press, 2003.

Ratliff, Evan. "O, Engineers!" *Wired,* December 2000. http://www.wired.com/wired/archive/8.12/soul_pr.html

Slotkin, Richard. *Gunfighter Nation: The Myth of the Frontier in Twentieth-Century America.* Norman: University of Oklahoma Press, 1998.

Stahl, William A. *God and the Chip: Religion and the Culture of Technology.* Waterloo, Ontario: Wilfrid Laurier University Press, 1999.

Tompkins, Jane. *West of Everything: The Inner Life of Westerns.* New York: Oxford University Press, 1992.

Turner, Frederick Jackson. "The Significance of the Frontier in American History." *The Frontier in American History,* 1–38. 1920. New York: Krieger, 1975.

Wallmann, Jeffrey. *The Western: Parables of the American Dream.* Lubbock: Texas Tech University Press, 1999.

Wolfe, Tom. "Two Young Men Who Went West." *Hooking Up,* 17–65. New York: Farrar, Straus, and Giroux, 2000.

CHAPTER 2

From the Far Side of the Urban Frontier: The Detective Fiction of Chester Himes and Walter Mosley

Robert Crooks

> *They draw a line and say for you to stay on your side of the line. They don't care if there's no bread over on your side. They don't care if you die. And . . . when you try to come from behind your line they kill you.*
>
> —*(Wright 407)*

* * *

Western Frontier and Urban Frontier

In his 1893 essay "The Significance of the Frontier in American History," Frederick Jackson Turner recognized that with its closing, "the frontier" as signifier of geographical space was cut adrift.[1] Other conceptual and spatial divides along ethnic and racial lines had emerged almost simultaneously with the Western frontier, however, and were available to absorb and transform its conceptual significance. The most obvious was that between European and African Americans embodied in the codes, economy, and practices of slavery and subsequent segregation. Such lines of segregation became particularly sharp in urban settings. It is this urban manifestation of frontier ideology, and particularly the textual space opened up by crime fiction for an articulation of that frontier from its "other" side, that will concern me here.

Turner suggests, in an inchoate way, the need for and function of the particular ideological formation that drew a line between "white" civilization and "Indian" savagery, a term for which "black" criminal chaos could easily be substituted. In an attempt to account for the assumed ideological unity of the (European American) United States, Turner maps these differences onto a progressive cultural history stretching from the savage prehistory of Indian lands in a linear development to the industrial metropolitan centers of the East. Ignoring the lack of fit between this mapping and the uneven developments of various frontiers, Turner identifies the Indians as the unifying factor that transformed the various frontiers into a unity by posing a "common danger" of absolute otherness (15).

A continuous stream of diatribes against "Indianization" and the motif of the "good Indian," prominent in frontier narratives from James Fenimore Cooper through Zane Grey to the Daniel Boone television series, has helped in a variety of ways to reconcile a racially defined oppression with ideologies of egalitarianism and tolerance by posing frontiersmen and Indians as individuals free to choose European American civilization over Indian savagery.

From the European American perspective, then, the frontier wars were not wars of conquest, for the assertion of authority by the U.S. government to make legal claim to land occupied by Native Americans was tantamount to redefining Native Americans themselves as foreign intruders to be eradicated. Through this redefinition, the "Indian Question" was discursively linked to the "Slavery Question." Though the complete extermination of Native Americans and the mass transportation of black Americans "back" to Africa had many proponents, the compromise solution was collective oppression and exploitation facilitated by racial segregation, the containment of Native Americans and Native American culture on reservations, and the similar containment of African Americans through various forms of segregation.

This partitioning refocused the frontier ideology, which continued to map cultural and racial divisions, but in geographical terms now denoted relatively fixed lines of defense for the purity and order of European American culture. Such lines became particularly charged in cities like New York, Chicago, and Los Angeles, where population densities and the size of minoritized communities threaten individualist ideologies, since the collective experience of exploitation lends itself to collective resistance or rebellion. Thus the meaning of the other side of the frontier, in its urban manifestation, has been partly transformed: in mainstream European American ideologies, it now constitutes pockets of racial intrusion, hence corruption and social disease are to be policed and contained.

The association of black urban communities in particular with the criminal side of the urban frontier has historically been over-determined. Many of the African Americans migrating to the cities were forced to seek housing and then to remain in the poorest areas of the cities by discriminatory practices in housing, as well as in the workplace and schools (see, for instance, Glasgow, chapters 4 and 5). Furthermore, as Homer Hawkins and Richard Thomas point out,

> Most northern white policemen not only believed in the inferiority of blacks but also held the most popular belief that blacks were more criminally inclined by nature than whites. . . . For decades, white officials in northern cities allowed vice and crime to go unpoliced in black neighborhoods. This non-protection policy had the effect of controlling the development of black community by undermining the stability of black family and community life. (75–76)

Police indifference to black-on-black crime has been frequently noted in all regions of the United States[2] and persists to such an extent that Rita Williams exaggerates little, if at all, when she says that "African Americans know they can murder each other with impunity and absolutely no one will care" (115).

Inadequate policing of intracommunity crime, the saturation of black communities with liquor and gun stores, and gentrification supplement strategies of containment with those of eradication and displacement (on gentrification, see Smith 108–14). If the war of extermination and deterritorialization goes largely unrecognized, it is because the urban frontier works more through hegemony than through openly repressive force. All Americans can watch the physical and economic "self-destruction" of black communities on the nightly news, and conservative African American intellectuals can be co-opted into chastising blacks for failing to take responsibility for "their own" problems and the disintegration of their communities.[3] Meanwhile, the urban frontier serves the same purpose for capitalism, as did the Western frontier and the European colonial frontiers in general: the production of relatively cheap resources, including labor.

Though specific techniques of oppression and exploitation have changed, then, the frontier ideology remains largely intact, but displaced. Individualism, in particular, remains crucial in disguising a site of ideological struggle as a line of defense against crime and chaos or as the boundary of advancing modernization or "urban renewal" or "revitalization," and for disarming collective resistance. Hegemony works through negotiation, though, and resistance does exist, in however fragmented forms. In the remainder of this essay, I will consider one mode of resistance from the far side of the frontier, the emergence of African American detective fiction, a popular form that has the capacity both to represent and to enact resistance in social and literary terms.

*   *   *

CRIME FICTION AND THE RACIAL FRONTIER

Cultural historians such as Richard Slotkin and Alexander Saxton have argued persuasively that the hard-boiled American detective is a direct descendant of nineteenth-century frontier heroes like Natty Bumppo, liminal figures who crisscross the frontier, loyal to European American society but isolated from it through their intimate involvement with Native American others.[4] Indeed, Saxton sees the rapid emergence of the dime-novel detective in the late 1880s partly as a consequence of the closing of the frontier and a corresponding "credibility gap . . . between the occupational activities of [real contemporary miners and cowboys] and the tasks that western heroes were expected to perform" (336).

The importance of that genealogy is indisputable, I think, particularly for considering the ideological and cultural work of hard-boiled crime fiction. Hard-boiled crime fiction, possibly more than any popular formula, has been overwhelmingly dominated by the individualism that is crucial to frontier ideology. Though particular discourses do, of course, construct particular subject positions, their most important ideological work lies not in the construction of individual subjects, but rather in matrices of subject relations within a conceptual space. For that reason, we need to look beyond particular characters in adventure fiction to the dynamic spaces, and the intersubjective matrices, constructed by those fictions.

Given the overdetermined association of African Americans and crime in everyday life and the representations of that association as a natural result of essential racial characteristics, one might expect black crime and racial conflict to play a more central role in hard-boiled detective fiction. Although this is not the case, there are occasionally references to a racial frontier that marks the ultimate frontier, the absolute boundary of the "order" of the familiar, as in this passage from Mickey Spillane's *One Lonely Night*: "Here was the edge of Harlem, that strange no-man's-land where the white mixed with the black" (134).

This frontier dividing Harlem from the rest of Manhattan is represented from its far side in Chester Himes's novel of the same period, *A Rage in Harlem* (also known as *For Love of Imabelle*), as Jackson, the central character, on the verge of escape after a harrowing flight from the police, suddenly realizes that he has left Harlem and is "down in the white world with no place to go . . . no place to hide himself" (137). He turns back to face certain capture rather than go on. Himes does more than simply affirm the existence of the border, however: he explores its meaning as an ideological concept marking the exercise of white hegemony. In doing so he offers a conception of crime never more than tentatively articulated in European American detective novels by acknowledging an "underworld" that is "catering to the essential needs of the people" (49), perhaps not in ideal fashion but in a manner necessitated by the character of the socioeconomic system. A good deal of criminal activity in this fiction is a result of the U.S. economy's partitioning through segregation. Crime itself, then, is a potentially resistant practice.

Viewing crime as part, rather than as the breakdown, of a cultural system, Himes and, more recently, Walter Mosley construct a complex picture of crime and detection as a negotiation of cultural needs and values, operating within the black American subculture as a critique of white racial ideologies. Referring repeatedly and explicitly to the complex politics of race and class in the United States, they seek to disentangle justice and morality from white hegemony, fighting exploitation and violence within black communities while also attacking a social system that engenders crime. In short, they resist the assimilation of the far side of the frontier as "chaos" and "evil," favoring a conception of the frontier as a site of ideological struggle for rights and privileges between two American microcultures.[5]

The general grounds for such struggle are perhaps best summed up by Himes, commenting on "The Dilemma of the Negro Novelist in the U.S.A.": "Of course, Negroes hate white people, far more actively than white people hate Negroes. . . . Can you abuse, enslave, persecute, segregate and generally oppress a people, and have them love you for it? Are white people expected not to hate their oppressors?" (398–99).

Whatever differences there might be on specific details, Himes and Mosley agree in affirming the need for African American opposition to oppression and in rejecting the privilege of white supremacist ideology to diagnose and prescribe remedies for the situation of African Americans.

Self-policing of a community, even an oppressed one, is not necessarily complicitous with the oppressive order, of course, or at least not completely so. As I indicated earlier, crime within an oppressed community may be a form of resistance, but it is also a part of the larger, macrocultural economic and social structure. In the United States, that means crime is exploitative, for it acts out the imperatives of capitalist competition in a particularly unfettered manner. Therefore, as Manning Marable has pointed out, in relatively poor African American communities, like those of the Himes and Mosley novels, "the general philosophy of the typical ghetto hustler is not collective, but profoundly individualistic. . . . The goal of illegal work is to 'make it for oneself,' not for others. The means for making it comes at the expense of elderly Blacks, young black women with children, youths and lower-income families who live at the bottom of the working class hierarchy" (Marable 64). It is because of their need to resist the manifestations of individualist competition as criminal entrepreneurship that Himes's police detectives and Mosley's private investigator work in their own communities.

Aside from that common ground, however, the novels of the two series differ considerably, and these differences intersect in complicated ways with the construction of the urban or racial frontier in the two series. These constructions in turn reflect the contradictions produced by the ideological struggle between differing American microcultures. A dominant ideology tends to be self-sustaining, thanks to its greater access to means of reproduction like educational systems and mass communication media. Nevertheless, dominance and its reproduction can never be complete, never attend adequately to every extracultural force operating through travel, migration and immigration, international economic transactions, and so forth, or to every gap that develops in the intracultural social formation through uneven development. On the other hand, the pervasiveness of dominant ideologies tends to fragment and disperse the force of other microcultural modes of ideological resistance. Resistance is therefore always under pressure, faced with an incessant need to escape from or relocate itself within a space defined by the dominant microculture.

Michel de Certeau's *Practice of Everyday Life* still offers perhaps the most exhaustive attempt to theorize this locating of resistance, by positing two logical possibilities. Strategic resistance finds its space outside the domain of the dominant by attaching itself to an alternative, fully constituted ideology that exists elsewhere. Tactical resistance, on the other hand, works within the space of the dominant, exploiting the contradictions within that space as opportunities arise, but unable to hold on to what is gained in the tactical moment (34–39). The novels of Mosley and Himes can be usefully read as narratives representing, respectively, strategic and tactical resistance. To read the novels this way, however, also raises questions about the dichotomy de Certeau constructs, suggesting a more complicated relation between strategies and tactics.

Resistance in representational practices, of course, cannot operate in a straightforward manner. Fictional narratives in particular raise the question of the use of representation for resistance, since the diegetic world constructed by a narrative has an ambiguous, if necessary, relation to the world of everyday practice. Furthermore, the representation of resistance need not itself be a resistant practice (mainstream media coverage of the Los Angeles uprising in 1992 offers the most blatant recent demonstration). Therefore, in what follows, I will separate questions of representing resistance from the manner of representation, in this case, narration.

*   *   *

Representing Resistance

Representation and enactment of resistance to white hegemony is central to the detective fiction of both Himes and Mosley. In discussing these issues, I will consider the two writers in reverse chronological order for two reasons. In terms of representation, Himes's police detectives occupy a more complex and ambiguous ideological space. In terms of enactment, Himes's formal experimentation, especially in *Blind Man with a Pistol*, possesses a more radical potential than anything in Mosley's writing to date, though the latter also suggests directions for resistance unexplored by his precursor.

Unlike detective characters ranging from Mike Hammer or Kinsey Millhone, who despite many differences all bend the law only to better uphold it, Mosley's Easy Rawlins readily and unrepentantly acknowledges having been on the "wrong" side of the law himself. His detective work is described as being for the community and outside the white system of law, often performed on a barter basis and for people who "had serious trouble but couldn't go to the police"

(*Red Death* 5) because they themselves are already of material necessity living on the fringes of, if not outside, the law: "In my time
I had done work for the numbers runners, church-goers, business-
men, and even the police. Somewhere along the line I had slipped
into the role of a confidential agent who represented people when
the law broke down" (*White Butterfly* 17). This strategic position of
"confidential agent" is justified partly on the grounds that an African
American could not both work for the police and remain part of the
community. Speaking of Quinten Naylor, a black cop who figures in
the second and third novels, Rawlins says that he "got his promotion
because the cops thought that he had his thumb on the pulse of the
black community. But all he really had was me. . . . Even though
Quinten Naylor was black he didn't have sympathy among the rough
crowd in the Watts community" (*White Butterfly* 18–19).[6]

Within the narratives as a whole, the division between a communal African American order and white law proves tenuous. Mosley's
first three novels turn on problematic intersections of the white and
black communities of Los Angeles, focusing on figures who traverse
the unstable interstice between Daphne Monet/Ruby Hanks, an
African-European-American ("passing" for a "white" woman) who
likes the Central Avenue jazz dubs and black lovers; Chaim Wenzler,
a Jewish member of the American Communist Party who works
in and for the black community; and Robin Garnett, a rich young
white woman who has rebelled against her family and upbringing by
becoming a stripper and prostitute in Watts under the name of Cyndi
Starr. And in each case, Easy Rawlins is pressed into detective work
by forces from the white world as well: racketeer DeWitt Albright,
who plays on Easy's need for quick mortgage money after losing a job
(*Devil in a Blue Dress*); the IRS and FBI, who threaten to prosecute
him for tax evasion (*Red Death*); and the L. A. police, who threaten
to pin a series of murders on his friend Mouse (*White Butterfly*).
More important than these connections with the white community,
however, is Easy Rawlins's discovery that there is no simple way to
work for order and justice in his African American community when
what counts as "order" and "justice" is defined, at least in part, by
a dominant white supremacist ideology. Rawlins does not share the
common illusion of the privileged, that such terms can be defined
outside of ideology. He observes frequently that all people act
according to what they perceive to be their own best interests. That
leaves open, however, the question of whether a community that is
systematically disempowered by a dominant ideology can produce a
coherent strategic resistance.

Mosley's second novel, *A Red Death*, addresses the question most directly. At the beginning of the story Rawlins is summoned by an IRS investigator for tax evasion. Technically the charge is valid, because Easy failed to report as income the $10,000 that he acquired illegally, though in his own view he did so legitimately in *Devil in a Blue Dress*. FBI Agent Craxton then offers to help Rawlins cut a deal with the IRS, provided that he helps them get damaging information about Chaim Wenzler, a Polish Jew who survived the Holocaust and is a member of the Communist Party in the United States. Craxton appeals to Easy's patriotism, positing an alliance between them through an explicit statement of urban frontier logic: "The Bureau is a last line of defense. There are all sorts of enemies we have these days. . . . But the real enemies, the ones we have to watch out for, are people right here at home. People who aren't Americans on the inside" (50). Easy doesn't trust Craxton, insists that he will do the job only because he has no choice, and tells us that his own feelings about communism are "complex" because of the alliance between the Soviet Union and the United States during the war and Paul Robeson's professionally disastrous connections with Russia (47). However, he doesn't actually challenge Craxton's construction of the frontier between real Americans and un-Americans. Instead, he dismisses the idea of communist activity in the African American community and insists that he will help the FBI get Wenzler but won't work against his "own people" (53).

The rest of the narrative shows that any attempt to define such an internal frontier that aligns black and white interests against a common un-American enemy leads to unresolvable contradictions. Wenzler himself proves to be a sympathetic figure who works in the black community because of the links he sees between his own experience as a Jew in Poland and that of African Americans (91).[7] His main activities involve charitable work that Rawlins supports and aids. Furthermore, Wenzler's connections within the black community make any attempt to isolate him as an object of investigation impossible. Partly as a result of Rawlins's work, two black women and a black minister get murdered in addition to Wenzler, and Rawlins finds himself having to investigate the Garveyite African Migration group.

In short, Easy finds no reason to aid the FBI's investigation except to further his own economic interests, and he feels increasingly guilty about that. What is most interesting about the novel in ideological terms, however, is the response he works out to that guilt. One might expect that, seeing the impossibility of sharing the collective interests of the white-dominated U.S. government, Rawlins would decide between the two models for African American opposition offered by Wenzler's Communist Party and the African Migration group. Both, after all, draw upon oppositional ideological formations, one along class lines, the other along racial and cultural ones. Mosley uses an appeal to individualism to validate Easy's rejection of both collective positions. In each case Easy appeals to Jackson Blue, who might be described as the paradigmatic organic intellectual of Mosley's mid-twentieth century Watts. Jackson expresses his own rejection of the Migration agenda in terms of the cultural gap between Africa and African Americans: "We been away too long, man" (184). Shortly thereafter Easy himself echoes Jackson's rejection of the Migration movement, but with a crucial difference: "I got me a home already. It might be in enemy lands, but it's mine still and all" (190). Unlike Jackson's argument on grounds of collective, microcultural differences, Easy appeals to the imperative of individual property interests.

Jackson rejects communism on similar grounds of an unbridgeable difference of collective interests. While admitting that the communist economic agenda coincides with the interests of African Americans, he reduces the question of the Communist Party in America to the blacklist, and says that whites will eventually get off the list, but the situation of blacks will remain the same (197–98). Again Easy's rejection of collective action soon follows, based again on individual interests rather than microcultural ones: "It wasn't political ideas I didn't care about or understand that made me mad. It was the idea that I wasn't, and hadn't been, my own man. . . . Like most men, I wanted a war I could go down shooting in. Not this useless confusion of blood and innocence" (203).

The position reflected here aligns Easy with the individualist ideology that has crucially underpinned conservative frontier American politics, which helps explain why he is unable to reject the FBI's new frontier account of real and unreal Americans even though he distrusts Craxton. The positing of "American" as a collective cultural and ideological identity stands in direct contradiction with the notion that what makes one American is precisely radical "individuality." That contradiction has enabled the frontier ideology, in both its western and urban manifestations, to link an egalitarian political rhetoric with systematic aggression against Native Americans on the one hand, and the systematic underdevelopment of Black America meticulously documented by Marable on the other. Given the demand of political expediency, frontier ideology sometimes serves the establishment of national boundaries or internal partitions on the basis of an essentialist racial ideology that hierarchizes individuals by group identifications.

At other times, however, and in other geographical or cultural terms, the idea that all people are free individuals is used to argue that they fall on either side of the frontier lines through their own bad choices or personal failings. The logic of individualism coupled with that of nationalism and patriotism thus permits systematic and collective cultural aggression and oppression to be passed off as a policing action against one bad Indian like Cochise or Crazy Horse or Geronimo, or as the legitimate surveillance of a dangerous black leader like Martin Luther King or Malcolm X—or a communist like Wenzler. That Easy Rawlins falls into line with the ideology that claims that he can be his own man seems to confirm the accusation made by his friend Mouse: "You learn stuff and you be thinkin' like white men be thinkin'. You be thinkin' that what's right fo' them is right fo' you" (*Devil in a Blue Dress* 205). Thus, it is on very shaky ground indeed that Easy chides the black police officer Quinten Naylor: "You one' a them. You dress like them and you talk like them too" (*Red Death* 154).

The trajectory of Easy's particular negotiation of the contradictions of American culture can be traced, I think, to a lesson he learns from DeWitt Albright in the first novel of the series: "You take my money and you belong to me. . . . We all owe out something, Easy. When you owe out then you're in debt and when you're in debt then you can't be your own man. That's capitalism" (*Devil in a Blue Dress* 101). There is no necessary linkage between capitalism and white supremacist ideology, but just as racism can serve the interests of capitalism by ideologically fragmenting classes, so too can a capitalistic individualism undermine collective resistance to racism. Various sympathies notwithstanding, Easy's actions are structured by the drive to accumulate wealth, which drives wedges between him and the South Central community. At the end of *White Butterfly*, Easy announces his move to a section of West Los Angeles that "[m]iddle-class black families had started colonizing" (271). Significantly absent from the text is the recognition of the way this geographical sectoring of classes in the capitalist metropolis splits the interests of African Americans as a minoritized community—a phenomenon well understood by Bob Jones in Himes's *If He Hollers Let Him Go*: "When you asked a Negro where he lived, and he said on the West Side, that was supposed to mean he was better than the Negroes who lived on the South Side; it was like the white folks giving a Beverly Hills address" (48). Instead, Easy's casual use of the "colonizing" metaphor suggests the subordination of collective interests to the exigencies of white capitalism, which undermines strategic resistance organized around either class or community.

As police detectives, on the other hand, Chester Himes's Grave Digger Jones and Coffin Ed Johnson align themselves explicitly with the existing power structure, while nevertheless enacting a tactical resistance within that system. Although they ostensibly solve crimes, the solutions often turn out to be plausible but false. These solutions satisfy the white legal establishment, but also work to rid Harlem of committed criminals while sparing others, often "squares," who have gotten involved in crime through a desperate need for money, and offering them incentives to avoid further crime. Usually these fortunate survivors, like Jackson and Imabelle in *A Rage in Harlem* or Sissie and Sonny in *The Real Cool Killers*, marry at the end of the novels. In addition, Jones and Johnson's position within the law enforcement structure allows them to critique it directly, which they do most frequently by pointing out the roots of black crime in economic exploitation by whites.

Nevertheless, they take their orders and carry them out. As insiders, Grave Digger and Coffin Ed cannot mount any consistent resistance to white oppression. Rather, in the way that de Certeau cogently recognizes, they seize opportunities where they arise, never working directly against the interests of the police department, but twisting situations and police procedures in such a way as to subvert them and turn them to the benefit of the Harlem community.

Such tactical resistance proves as difficult to define and sustain as the strategic resistance attempted by Easy Rawlins, however, and that difficulty seems implicitly addressed by a trajectory that can be traced through the Grave Digger/Coffin Ed series. The pattern involves the way in which crime and policing, the relation between the two, and that between the two and the Harlem community, are conceived.

As I pointed out earlier, a passage in the first novel of the series radically defines crime not as a deviation from, but rather as an integral part of the U.S. economy, catering to "essential needs" of people that are not satisfied through "legitimate" business, or at least not satisfied uniformly, given the various kinds of inequalities that are also integral to the U.S. economy and culture. And far from standing in simple opposition to one another, the police and the organized crime system are also bound by economic relations. Himes's detectives are said to take "their tribute, like all real cops" (*Rage* 49), and as Coffin Ed succinctly puts it, "Crime is what pays us" (*Cotton* 100). Nonetheless, the novels insist on an order, a standard of tolerable or legitimate action, and that requires drawing a line, constructing a frontier. The passage on crime and the police in *A Rage in Harlem* reveals some of the contradictions that ordering raises, even within Himes's radical redefinitions:

> [Grave Digger and Coffin Ed] took their tribute, like all real cops, from the established underworld catering to the essential needs of the people—gamekeepers, madams, streetwalkers, numbers writers, numbers bankers. But they were rough on purse snatchers, muggers, burglars, con men, and all strangers working any racket. And they didn't like rough stuff from anybody else but themselves. (49)

Aside from the complicated question of what constitutes "essential needs" or legitimate access to "rough stuff," the inclusion of "strangers" in the list of those who cross the line of legitimacy is a particularly troubling one given the line drawn by whites that establishes all blacks as strangers outside Harlem. Jones and Johnson, by working for the white police, make themselves strangers both in and outside Harlem. The novels themselves acknowledge this tenuous position. Early in *The Heat's On*, Coffin Ed notices residents of a white-occupied apartment building watching them, and remarks, "They think we're burglars," to which Grave Digger replies, "Hell, what else are they going to think about two spooks like us prowling about in a white neighborhood in the middle of the night?" (16). In *Blind Man with a Pistol* a black woman appeals to the two for help when white policemen try to arrest her unjustly, and Grave Digger is forced to respond: "Don't look at me . . . I'm the law too" (59).

Theoretically, the problem is one that de Certeau's *Practice of Everyday Life* manages consistently to evade or finesse: since even dominant cultures are driven by ambiguities and contradictions emerging in the gap between ideologies and practices, how exactly is tactical resistance to be distinguished from complicity, or to put in terms that Himes might more likely use, how is justice to be distinguished from injustice?

Himes's novels themselves seem aware of this problem and try to address it by gradually shifting the position of Jones and Johnson from one of tactical resistance to one of strategic resistance. The claim that the two take their tribute from the underworld like all the rest of the cops is reversed in later novels, and in *Blind Man with a Pistol* they are described as martyrs for the cause of honesty:

> Now after twelve years as first-grade precinct detectives they hadn't been promoted. Their raises in salaries hadn't kept up with the rise of the cost of living. They hadn't finished paying off their houses. Their private cars had been bought on credit. And yet they hadn't taken a dime in bribes. (97)

It is from this position of unshakable honesty that Coffin Ed can ask in *The Heat's On*, "Is everybody crooked on this mother-raping earth?" (146) The immediate point of such passages seems to be the moral superiority of the two over the rest of the police force, yet the passages also work to legitimate Jones and Johnson's access to acceptable violence in Harlem on the same moral grounds. Thus Himes emphasizes the distance Grave Digger and Coffin Ed place between themselves and the Harlem community, a distance he otherwise tries to mitigate through occasional encounters between the detectives and acquaintances from their childhood. In effect, then, the resistant position of the detectives is established in terms of the individualist ideology that Mosley resorts to, because the legitimacy of Jones and Johnson's liberties with the law rests entirely on their individual moral quality, and has nothing to do with the inadequacy of the law itself. Collective resistance to a system of law and order based on collective oppression is therefore undermined altogether and the black detective located on what has been the good white side of the frontier all along. The project of collective opposition to a white supremacist culture succumbs to the fantasy of being one's own man.

Yet neither Himes nor Mosley embraces individualism unambiguously. *Blind Man with a Pistol* maps the end of multiple trajectories of the Harlem detective series, and where the career of Jones and Johnson leads to an ideological cul-de-sac, the narrative turns instead back to the Harlem community itself for a model of effective resistance. Indeed, the story is one of continual frustration for Grave Digger and Coffin Ed. They are forbidden by their superiors to use their prized pistols, forbidden to solve the murders that occur, and instead ordered to determine who is responsible for a series of riots in Harlem. The detectives offer one culprit themselves—Lincoln, who "hadn't ought to have freed us if he didn't want to make provisions to feed us" (135)—and they receive another answer from Michael X, a Black Muslim leader: "Ask your boss, if you really want to know . . . he knows" (174). Other culprits are produced by the narrative as a whole: an earnest but stupid integrationist organizer named Marcus Mackenzie; the leader of a Black Jesus movement named Prophet Ham, whose motives seem dubious; Dr. Moore, a racketeer who uses a Black Power movement as a front; and finally, a blind man with a pistol.

This multiplication of suspects, and the failure of the detectives to narrow the list to one guilty party, as the detective formula demands, suggests that the individualist question posed is the wrong one altogether. Instead, the novel suggests that riots are caused by a conjuncture of various personal interests with a general atmosphere of frustration, resentment, and hatred. The parable of the blind man with a pistol that forms the narrative's conclusion, displacing the conventional tying up of loose ends in the district attorney's office, is important in this regard. Superficially, the tale suggests that riots are caused by blind anger lashing out randomly. There is a crucial, though implicit, connection between this episode and the rest of the novel, however. Though the blind man starts shooting his pistol because of a complex misunderstanding and hits all the wrong targets, the one certain condition of possibility for the event is his fear and hatred of white people that is produced by the dominant racial ideology of the United States. It is the same ideology that creates the crowds necessary to turn an individual cause or scam into a riot, that allows Michael X to say with confidence, "Ask your boss . . . he knows" who's starting the riots, and impels Grave Digger to respond, "You keep on talking like that you won't live long" (175).

The turn away from individualist ideology, which permits right and wrong to be sorted out in terms of intrinsically good and bad guys, is manifested in other ways as well. For the first time in the series, Grave Digger and Coffin Ed have serious and repeated disagreements, not about facts or procedures in a specific case, but about their own role in general. Here's a representative passage, from a scene in which the detectives question a witness, a white woman named Anny:

> "You changed your race?" Coffin Ed interrupted.
> "Leave her be," Grave Digger cautioned.
> But she wasn't to be daunted. "Yes, but not to your race, to the human race."
> "That'll hold him."
> "Naw, it won't. I got no reverence for these white women going 'round joining the human race. It ain't that easy for us colored folks."
> "Later, man, later," Grave Digger said. "Let's stick to our business."
> "That is our business." (68)

In this reconsideration of their business, the detectives and the narrative itself suggest that the answer to the linked problems of racism and crime may not lie with them at all, but rather in collective resistance within the black community. In the earlier *Cotton Comes to Harlem*, a back-to-Africa movement is dismissed as a scam through which hustlers con the squares of Harlem, much in the same way that the Brotherhood, Black Jesus, and Black Power movements are dismissed in *Blind Man with a Pistol*. The Black Muslims also figure briefly in *Cotton Comes to Harlem* (114–16) and are not subject to the same satirical treatment, but neither are they dealt with in more than a passing way. However, Grave Digger and Coffin Ed's ultimate engagement with the Black Muslims in *Blind Man with a Pistol*, an alternative ending that immediately precedes the concluding parable, is marked by startling departures from character on the part of the detectives. For the first time in the series, their engagement with another character is free of both irony and paternalistic condescension. Having chafed at orders not to use their pistols throughout the novel, here they volunteer to surrender them as a gesture of their goodwill toward Michael X. And when Michael X does agree to talk to them, they listen with astonishing seriousness and humility to the man described unequivocally as "the master of the situation" (174).

I take the gesture of offering to hand over their pistols to be particularly significant because of the way it alters the position of the detectives constructed in *A Rage in Harlem* through the words "they didn't like rough stuff from anybody else but themselves" (49). This early position reproduces a dominant definition of legitimate access to violence. The gesture of laying down arms, while not reversing that definition, at least marks a refusal on the part of Jones and Johnson to uphold it actively.

The novel doesn't explicitly endorse the Black Muslims or lay out in any detail an effective oppositional strategy. Indeed, as I noted above, Grave Digger's last words to Michael X are a grim prediction of an imminent and violent death. In addition, sexual integration is tentatively held up earlier in the novel as the ultimate solution to racial inequality (64–65). I will not pretend to resolve the question of whether the proper form of black American resistance is tactical or strategic, terms that in this case coincide roughly with integrationist/ assimilationist and Black Nationalist agendas. The merits and weaknesses of each of these projects have been widely debated, and the problems are perhaps best summed up by Michele Wallace (citing Harold Cruse's *The Crisis of the Negro Intellectual*) in "Doing the Right Thing":

> Black political philosophy has always seesawed between an integra-tionist/assimilationist agenda and a cultural nationalist agenda. . . . Integrationism always ends up being an embarrassment to its black supporters because of the almost inevitable racism and bad faith of its white supporters; they are willing to "integrate" with a small portion of upper-class blacks only if the masses of poor blacks are willing to remain invisible and powerless. Cultural nationalism, on the other hand, has conventionally taken refuge in a fantasy of economic and political autonomy that far too often compounds its sins by falling into

precisely the trap of bigotry and racism (against gays, women, Jews, "honkies," and others) it was designed to escape.   (110)

Aside from the problems, though, integrationism and separatism need to be seen not in simple opposition to one another, but rather in triangulation with the ideology they resist, that of old or new frontier capitalist individualism. Thus far, Mosley's series, at the level of representation, has examined that triangulation and opted for individualism, viewing the collective possibilities of integration or separatism as they inevitably look from the individualist position: as individual choices amounting to something like voluntary club membership. Himes's series, on the other hand, finally leaves the triangulation as exactly that, an unresolved tension pulling the community of Harlem in different directions.

Mosley gestures toward a critique of individualism in a different way, by elaborating Easy's place within a community. His relationships with other characters like Jackson Blue, Mouse, and EttaMae are not merely glyphs that naturalize the authority of the central figure, as in most detective series, but rather change in significant connection to events of the narratives—Easy makes friends, loses them, feels the conflicts among his own various interests, and tries acutely enough not to set himself on a moral pedestal. As a result, those other characters attain a complex subjectivity that allows us to measure Easy's own limitations, making room for ironies at the level of textual narration if not at that of the first person narrator.

Himes's critique of individualism depends also on redefining crime again in *Blind Man with a Pistol*. Michael X implies that Harlem's crime is not a self-sustaining economy, as was suggested in *A Rage in Harlem*, and that the ultimate profit goes to the white community outside. In those terms, the irreducibly collective form of "crime," rioting, that preoccupies the novel also invalidates the individualist premises of American justice and law enforcement systems. Walter Mosley's series seems headed toward similar ends, since the historical trajectory of his series so far suggests that Easy Rawlins will eventually confront the Watts riots of 1965, just as *Blind Man with a Pistol* obviously alludes to the Harlem riots of 1964. The difference between the two series in their relation to the individualism central to frontier ideology extends beyond representations of crime and detection or policing, however. The Harlem series and Mosley's three novels employ quite different strategies of narrational enunciation that have implications as well for their relation to the urban frontier.

*   *   *

ENACTING RESISTANCE: HIMES, MOSLEY, AND NARRATION

Like most mass market fiction, detective novels generally have been formally fairly conventional. Although the detective story trades heavily on enigmas, withheld information, misdirection, and confusion, readers can generally depend on the detective to finally put all the scattered pieces in place to construct a single, accurate account of events. Walter Mosley's novels are no exception, assuming perhaps the most common form for hard-boiled detective novels since Raymond Chandler began the Philip Marlowe series: a first person narrative told by the detective. Though any narrative form can be manipulated to various ideological ends, this form lends itself to an individualist stance, especially in a formula where the central question might be articulated as "who has the one true version of the story?" The ideological frontiers that the detective novel generally constructs, between good and evil or justice and injustice, tend to get drawn around the figure of the narrating detective trying to negotiate a path of honesty in a corrupt world. Easy Rawlins agonizes over his own shortcomings and ethical blind spots—letting himself be manipulated into betraying his friends and community in *A Red Death*, forcing his wife to have sex against her will in *White Butterfly*, and so forth. He still seems to emerge, in his own accounts, as the most scrupulous and decent of the erring humans mired in the blindness of their cultural situations. In this respect Rawlins is hardly distinguishable from Philip Marlowe, Mike Hammer, or Kinsey Millhone, though as I suggested above, his meticulous placing within a community works against the monological form of the detective's narration.

Chester Himes offers no such vision of community micropolitics, but on the other hand, he established himself as a formal innovator from the beginning. In what seems an ingenious tactical response to the problem of writing novels set on the far side of the urban frontier, he rejected centering the novel in the perspective of the detectives, instead combining the narrational forms of the hard-boiled detective novel with that of criminal adventure narratives like James M. Cain's *Double Indemnity* or, to stretch definitions a bit, his own *If He Hollers Let Him Go* and *Lonely Crusade*. All the novels begin with so-called crimes and criminals, and the detectives often aren't introduced until several chapters into the narrative. Subsequently the point of view tends to shift back and forth, with some additional shifting on both sides of the law or crime divide. The limitations of each perspective are emphasized through a sprinkling of observations like "[Coffin Ed] hadn't discovered any lead to Uncle Saint, so he didn't know there were already three others dead from the caper" (*The Heat's On* 127). No single character ever acquires complete knowledge of events. The conventional aim of the detective novel, to restore or uphold an order we are asked to accept as legitimate, and the conventional aim of the criminal adventure thriller, to test the order but finally to succumb or be reconciled to it, are displaced by a negotiation that never leaves an established order entirely dominant or unquestioned.

This mixing of genres tends to subvert the adamant insistence of crime fiction on the accessibility of "truth" to an individual perspective and its containment within a single coherent narrative. Such resistance to a dominant fictional mode is still limited, nonetheless, by established conventions of reading. Setting the detective story against the criminal adventure story does not simply consign meaning and truth to a site of contestation. Rather, both narrative points of view are subordinated to that of the overarching narration that assures readers of getting a true account, even if it is denied to any diegetic subject. *Blind Man with a Pistol* carries narrational innovation further, however, in a way that undermines the assurance of a single, stable meaning.

It is impossible to tell how many riots occur, or when they occur in relation to other events of *Blind Man with a Pistol*. There are repetitions of names and features of characters without a clear indication in some cases of whether the same character is reappearing or whether another happens to have the same feature. There are italicized interludes whose relation to the rest of the story seems to vary considerably. For the most part, events seem organized according to a dear temporal order only within specific episodes.

This narrative disorder threatens the possibility of conventional narrative closure (aside from the fact that no closure is offered even nominally within some of the particular subplot sequences). If we nevertheless finish the novel and try to make sense of it, we are forced to seek some other principle of unity than a temporal sequence of events connected through a limited set of characters. What offers itself instead, I think, is a thematic coherence linking various episodes. And the point of that alternative mode of coherence, I think, is that the problems of racism and oppression cannot be thought through in the personal, individualistic terms that conventional narrative offers, but rather in terms of collective practices that invisibly link disparate individual stories. In other words, a novel like *Blind Man with a Pistol* reproduces ideological linkages as rhetorical ones, and therefore renders at least potentially visible in fiction what is generally concealed in the practices of everyday life in the United States.

This is only textual play, perhaps. But the frontier remains powerful as the text of American destiny. The disruption of narrative exemplified in Himes's *Blind Man with a Pistol* may offer one effective strategy for disrupting the urban frontier narrative by laying bare its ideological underpinnings and internal contradictions. Mosley's digressions into the micropolitics of community and between communities pull at the seams of the detective narrative in another way, undermining the traditional generic reassurance that the good guys and bad guys can be sorted out, and disrupted order reestablished. Pursuing this trajectory, investigating the genre as much as the crimes, may lead toward multiple stories that produce irreducibly multiple culprits. A radical rewriting of the urban frontier might thus help restore the fragmentation that Turner in 1893 was at pains to conceal.

NOTES

1. I am grateful to Bob Winston, Mike Frank, and Kalpana Seshadri-Crooks, as well as four anonymous readers for *College Literature*, for valuable critical comments on earlier versions of this essay. I should also note a general indebtedness to the work of Marxist and postmodern geographers such as Nell Smith, Derek Gregory, David Harvey, and Edward Soja, whose works inform my theoretical framework.

2. See, for example, Marable 113. The phenomenon has been so widespread as to be obvious even to a demonstrably racist novelist like Raymond Chandler (*Farewell* 11).

3. Judith Butler, in an essay on the first Rodney King trial, acutely analyzes a particular instance of white racist interpretive strategies that transform violence against African Americans as self-inflicted (20).

4. See Saxton 331–38 and Slotkin, "The Hard-Boiled Detective Story." Bethany Ogdon critiques the focus on the descent of hard-boiled fiction from frontier adventure narratives on the grounds that it tends to obscure specificities of the later genre (72–73). Ogdon's objections are aimed at a critical methodology focusing on motifs or archetypes, rather than questions of genealogy, however. Her own provocative reading of relations between hard-boiled fiction and fascist ideology is compatible with the present essay, if one acknowledges homologous relations between fascist and frontier ideologies.

5. While dealing here with issues of race and, to a lesser extent, of class, I have paid little attention to those of gender. That would require a much longer essay. I would, however, point out that Himes's novels seem to me blatantly misogynist and Mosley's at least highly problematic in the way they construct gender roles and relations. Interestingly, Mosley's Easy Rawlins becomes increasingly self-conscious about

gender relations in *White Butterfly*, and it is the novel's attention to conflicts between Easy's relation to his wife and the conventional masculinist trajectory of his detective work that offers the strongest challenge in Mosley's work to the identity of the detective fiction genre, which I will discuss in the final section of this essay.

6. Ellis Cashmore, in "Black Cops Inc.," points out that such assumptions of natural microcultural affinities were commonly made in the early assigning of African American police officers.

7. Easy Rawlins himself makes the same connection in *Devil in a Blue Dress:* "Many Jews . . . understood the American Negro; in Europe the Jew had been a Negro for more than a thousand years" (138).

WORKS CITED

Butler, Judith. "Endangered/Endangering: Schematic Racism and White Paranoia." *Reading Rodney King/Reading Urban Uprising*, edited by Robert Gooding, 15–22. London: Routledge, 1993.

Cain, James M. *Double Indemnity*. 1936. New York: Vintage, 1989.

Cashmore, Ellis. "Black Cops Inc.," 87–108. Cashmore and McLaughlin, 1991.

Cashmore, Ellis, and Eugene McLaughlin. *Out of Order? Policing Black People*. New York: Routledge, 1991.

Certeau, Michel de. *The Practice of Everyday Life*. Translated by Steven Rendall. Berkeley: University of California Press, 1984.

Chandler, Raymond. *Farewell, My Lovely*. 1940. New York: Vintage, 1988.

Glasgow, Douglas G. *The Black Underclass: Poverty, Unemployment and Entrapment of Ghetto Youth*. New York: Random, 1980.

Hawkins, Homer, and Richard Thomas. "White Policing of Black Populations: A History of Race and Social Control in America," 65–86. Cashmore and McLaughlin, 1991.

Himes, Chester. *Blind Man with a Pistol*. 1969. New York: Vintage, 1989.

———. *Cotton Comes to Harlem*. 1965. New York: Vintage, 1988.

———. "Dilemma of the Negro Novelist in the U. S. A." *New Black Voices: An Anthology of Contemporary Afro-American Literature*, edited By Abraham Chapman, 394–401. New York: Mentor, 1972.

———. *The Heat's On*. 1966. New York: Vintage, 1988.

———. *If He Hollers Let Him Go*. 1945. New York: Thunder's Mouth, 1986.

———. *Lonely Crusade*. 1947. New York: Thunder's Mouth, 1986.

———. *A Rage in Harlem*. 1957. New York: Vintage, 1989.

———. *The Real Cool Killers*. 1959. New York: Vintage, 1988.

Marable, Manning. *How Capitalism Underdeveloped Black America*. Boston: South End, 1983.

Mosley, Walter. *Devil in a Blue Dress*. New York: Pocket, 1990.

———. *A Red Death*. New York: Pocket, 1991.

———. *White Butterfly*. New York: Norton, 1992.

Ogdon, Bethany. "Hard-Boiled Ideology." *Critical Quarterly* 34.1 (1991): 71–87.

Saxton, Alexander. *The Rise and Fall of the White Republic: Class Politics and Mass Culture in Nineteenth-Century America.* London: Verso, 1990.

Slotkin, Richard. "The Hard-Boiled Detective Story: From the Open Range to the Mean Streets." *The Sleuth and the Scholar: Origins, Evolution, and Current Trends in Detective Fiction,* edited by Barbara A. Rader and Howard G. Zettler, 91–100. New York: Greenwood, 1988.

Smith, Neil. Contribution to discussion on "Housing: Gentrification, Dislocation and Fighting Back." *If You Lived Here: The City in Art, Theory, and Social Action* (a project by Martha Rosler), edited by Brian Wallis, 93–123. Dia Art Foundation discussions in Contemporary Culture 6. Seattle: Bay, 1991.

Spillane, Mickey. *One Lonely Night.* 40th anniversary edition. New York: Signet, 1951.

Turner, Frederick Jackson. "The Significance of the Frontier in American History." *The Frontier in American History,* 1–38. New York: Henry Holt, 1920.

Wallace, Michele. "Doing the Right Thing." *Invisibility Blues: From Pop to Theory,* 107–10. London: Verso, 1990.

Williams, Rita. "To Live and Die in L. A." *Transition* 59 (1993): 110–19.

Wright, Richard. *Native Son.* New York, Harper, 1993.

CHAPTER 3

AMERICAN OUTSIDERS AT THE
CENTER: MORMONS AND THE WEST

Rüdiger Heinze

In 1960, John F. Kennedy addressed the Greater Houston Ministerial Association on the issue of his Catholic faith. In the course of the speech, he maintained that "it is apparently necessary for me to state once again—not what kind of church I believe in, for that should be important only to me—but what kind of America I believe in" and that "contrary to common newspaper usage, I am not the Catholic candidate for president. I am the Democratic Party's candidate for President who happens also to be a Catholic" (Kennedy).

It is not without historical irony that some forty years later, during his unsuccessful presidential campaign, Mitt Romney, who "happens also to be" a Mormon,[1] recurrently harked back to this speech when questioned about his faith. In adopting Kennedy's rhetorically defensive, rather than merely explanatory gesture, Romney both repeated the curious dialectic and trope of the "central outsider" so prominent in America's religious past and demonstrated the ambivalent status that the Mormon religion still occupies in the contemporary United States. By referring to Kennedy, Romney pointed to a central historical and political figure and a central theme in American history, religious tolerance; but despite the fact that the official standing of the Mormon Church on core political issues such as abortion or gay marriage complies with the views of the Christian conservative base of the Republican Party, Romney saw the need to vindicate his faith.

This centrality versus marginality of the Latter-day Saints (LDS) Church has been debated for some time now. In his tellingly titled book *Religious Outsiders and the Making of Americans* (1986), the historian Laurence Moore holds that to become American means "to invent oneself out of a sense of opposition" (45); accordingly, "by declaring themselves outsiders, they [the original Mormons] were moving to the center" (46) and thus not only within the pale of Jacksonian ideology but also within the tradition of the American nation as founded and crucially shaped by religious dissenters. This dialectic has been challenged by another prominent commentator on Mormonism, Harold Bloom, on the grounds that contemporary Mormonism has moved from antinomianism to orthodoxy and has thus become mainstream and aligned on many issues with the Southern Baptists, Pentecostals, and other religious conservatives/fundamentalists (Bloom 88). But public and critical debates over Romney or a number of court cases over the constitutional right to free practice of religion, and thus polygamy, suggest that neither is the United States ready for a Mormon president, nor have its citizens fully come to terms with their quintessential—that is, most genuinely and originally American—religious group (Bloom 80–83), although the early times of violent conflict have passed.

The dialectical trope of the Mormons as central outsiders, then, appears to be still adequate. Neither are they central enough to be unquestioningly accepted into the Protestant mainstream, nor are they marginal enough to be ignored, relegated to insignificance, or demonized as pure Other. For this reason, this essay will adopt Terry Givens's hypothesis that "we are more disturbed at transgressive behavior displayed by our close counterparts than by utterly foreign entities" and his suggestion that instead of "marginal" we should use the term "liminal" "to characterize those constructions which operate in the *absence* of great distances . . . the place where the imagination, in its efforts to create complete alterity, meets empirical limitations, the constraints of observed and felt commonalities" (385–86, emphasis in the original). Historically, other groups have been more conspicuously recognizable and identifiable as different and other, which has facilitated their conceptual marginalization, expressed in nativism toward Chinese immigrants or colonialism towards Native Americans, for example. However, the Mormons "could not be easily categorized or identified in terms of foreign origins, racial markers, peculiarities of dialect or dress. Neither nativism nor imperialism was a feasible response to a group unsusceptible to such quick differentiation and exclusion from the body politic" (Givens 387). In short, the Mormons were and still are not-quite-other and too close to home.

If because of this liminality the Mormons continue to constitute a difficult and contested legacy for mythologies of the basic American "national stories," they do so specifically and most prominently regarding the American West. The Mormons were clearly pioneers and considered themselves so: one of their crucial doctrines is the divine revelation in 1847 to Brigham Young that they should organize companies westward "to go as pioneers" (Doctrine & Covenants 136). The creation of a "New Jerusalem" or Zion in the West was and is one of their chief—millenarian—agendas, so that for the Mormons, Manifest Destiny is indeed a sacred doctrine.[2] But their beliefs also contradict other crucial aspects of the myth of the West: among other things, their religious motivation stood in stark contrast to the economic definition at the heart of Manifest Destiny.[3] Their presence in the West represented a contradiction to Frederick Jackson Turner's claims, and their whole way of life was largely incommensurable with frontier life elsewhere. Their persecution and the subsequent western trek still constitutes a central aspect of their identity. Combined with their doctrinal view of the West as the geographical and teleological transubstantiation of the biblical Millennium and the New Jerusalem, the American West for the Mormons merges historical past, present, and future into a complex framework of meaning-making that at times adapts, at times converges with, and often departs from mainstream mythologies of the American West.

For this reason, I argue that Mormons' (self-)perception and myth-making indeed offers a new perspective on the American West. As an integral yet simultaneously liminal part of the myths of the American West and the correlative national stories, the story of the Mormons and their trail disrupts and possibly revises the more homogeneous, traditional versions of those stories.

This essay will discuss the particular, ambiguous, and liminal role of the Mormons in the mythologies of the West and the struggle for control over their perception. It will do so by analyzing and historicizing two key contemporary examples in the struggle: the feature-length movie *Legacy*—the current official Church of Jesus Christ of Latter-day Saints version of their pioneer past, shown at the Joseph Smith Memorial Building in the Salt Lake City Mormon Temple District—and Tony Kushner's play *Angels in America*. I hope to show that while the strategies of both texts are different, in one regard they are quite similar: they demonstrate the continuing liminal and paradoxical status of the LDS within narratives of the American West and the nation. Consequently, as I will further argue, they are particularly revealing for their specific ideological work in the context of the 1990s.

*   *   *

Almost from their very inception, the Mormons occupied a liminal social, political, and economic position in their immediate surroundings and, as they grew, within the United States in general. With their persecution and the subsequent move west, the clash between Mormons as prototypical American pioneers and simultaneously as continually harassed outsiders became an ambivalent and prominent part of the national story.

Originally the LDS were only one of many new or renewed religious movements during a period of Restoration between 1800 and 1830, frequently called the Second Great Awakening. They shared with many others the belief in the apostasy of the early Christian church after the death of the last disciples and in the restoration of true practice and gospel in their times to prepare for the advent of the Millennium (Abanes 83ff). More generally, they relied upon a heritage of ideas familiar to a wider American public, most prominently William Bradford's aspirations for the New World paradise, John Winthrop's City upon a Hill, Cotton Mather's preachings, and also the tradition of religious dissent inspired by Anne Hutchinson and Roger Williams (Arrington and Haupt, *Mormon* 3f).

Unlike most other groups that developed at the time, and despite the similarities of the Mormons to these groups, the Mormons were severely persecuted right from the beginning, and it is this persecution and the resulting move west that have deeply influenced historical and present Mormon identity (Norton 101) and brought about their liminal position in American history and society. Within the span of seventeen years the Mormons moved from western New York State (1830–31) over Ohio (1831–38), Missouri (1831–39), and Illinois (1839–48) to the Utah desert in the winter of 1846–47, and then still outside U.S. territory. Among the reasons for their persecution were their belief in additional scripture and continuous revelation, which in the eyes of legislators and the wider public made the Mormons unpredictable because it meant that at any time God might reveal an order adversarial to the law; their abolitionism; their increasing political influence—they voted en bloc; their by necessity communitarian and often exclusive economic practice; and, most notoriously, although only established in 1843, polygamy (which they "exchanged" for statehood in 1896), an apparent threat to monogamous marriage and thus to the cornerstone of Christian civilization (Handley 3; Arrington and Haupt, *Mormon* 44ff). After continuing incidents of mob violence and political conflicts such as the extermination order by the Missouri governor Lilburn Boggs in 1838 (officially rescinded only in 1976), Young, by then the leader (and thus prophet) of the largest remaining strain of the LDS movement, ordered the Mormon move to Utah to establish their own state of Deseret.

In settling the West and moving the frontier ever more westward, the Mormon pioneers participated in the fulfillment of Manifest Destiny. Indeed, some (not exclusively Mormon) historians have argued that the Latter-day Saints "were one of the principal forces in the settlement of the West" (Stegner 7).[4] In terms of religious beliefs, the Mormons again worked with well-known ideas and concepts (many of them prevalent, though naturalized, in secular narratives of the West). They employed the paradoxical typology of the desert found in the Bible that was important for the Puritans, pitting death against paradise, defeat against victory, and human struggle against eschatology (Austin 39–41).

However, as mentioned above, the Mormons are not easily incorporated into the mythological narratives of the West, primarily because of their polygamy and belief in continuous revelation. Unlike the prototypical pioneers, many of the Mormons were not experienced in farming and other like trades; also, they moved in large polyglot but unusually cohesive companies of extended families (Abanes 123ff). They shared provisions and resources and dealt with most adversities in cooperative efforts financed by tithes, practicing communal property ownership and economic practice closed to non-Mormons (Jackson 7ff). On the whole, they propagated communitarian and cooperative rather than individualist and competitive ideals. Instead of the rugged and self-reliant nomadic individual who pitted strong will against the wild, the Mormon Church propagated an orderly and disciplined family life in settlements that soon grew into grid cities with temples and a relatively well-developed infrastructure (see Abanes; Arrington and Haupt; *Mormon;* Jackson). In addition, they were an unexpected success in cultivating the Utah desert—contrary to pioneers' experience in other challenging places (Dakota, Montana) and to much Western experience being about failure, even if it is downplayed. As Eric A. Eliason summarizes:

> In the history of the American West, Utah's theocratic government and strongly communitarian attempts to build a just social order— often through central planning, community ownership of business

enterprises, and cooperative labor and financing—can be viewed as a particularly striking counterexample to Frederick Jackson Turner's hypothesis that the frontier experience brought into being American individualism, capitalism, and democracy. (12)

Thus, despite their self-perception as pioneers and as central outsiders within a tradition of religious dissent, the entire Mormon enterprise was regarded suspiciously by a wider American public. As R. Philip Loy points out, it might have seemed to many non-Mormons that Young was actually building a "church-controlled political empire" (60). Perhaps the best-known expression of the ambivalence toward the Mormon "kingdom" in the West are Mark Twain's descriptions in *Roughing It* of his visit to the "fairy-land, land of enchantment . . . and mystery" (88) and Zane Grey's *Riders of the Purple Sage*. Especially the latter emphasizes the Mormon's liminal position, as Handley explains:

> The Western formula's function—and a key to its popularity—is not simply to demonize an Other but also to resolve American contradictions about religious, sexual, and racial identity by casting the American hero [Lassiter] and Mormon villains in distinct but eerily similar roles in which they enact a family drama. (2)

Similar structures also permeate an enormous quantity of diatribes in all genres and media against the "vicious" and "relentless" Mormon proselytizers and polygamists.

At the same time, hardship and isolation (though not complete, see Arrington and Haupt, "Community") enforced not only cooperative concepts but also a "we vs. they" Manichean image of the world (Poll 166). Although the times of such openly hostile reception have passed, contemporary Mormon (self-)perception of their historical past does have to struggle with this tradition of the Mormons as liminal outsiders and its remnants in contemporary U.S. culture.

*   *   *

Two key examples of the contemporary ideological struggle over the perception of Mormons and their connection to the American West are *Legacy* (1990) and *Angels in America* (1992). Their comparison is particularly rewarding not only because they deal with the Mormons from apparently diametrically opposed perspectives and within different genres and styles, but also because they deal with conceptions of the American nation and its future in the context of the 1990s and meaning-freighted debates about the end of history and the new millennium. It is no coincidence that the Mormon production is called *Legacy* and not *Heritage,* while the subtitle of Kushner's play reads "A Gay Fantasia on National Themes." At the same time, as will be shown, both works demonstrate the continuing liminal status of the Mormons.

Legacy was produced in 1990 under the direction of the First Presidency, written and directed by Kieth Merrill, with an all-Mormon cast and the music performed by the Tabernacle Choir and the Utah Symphony. The narrative of the film starts in 1892 with the capstone-laying of the Salt Lake Temple and, after establishing a rudimentary frame narrative, continues with a flashback/memory of the woman narrator that covers the period from 1830 to 1847, and thus primarily the trek west. As the narrative emphasizes from the beginning, this trek was not simply a journey to new land but to the promised land of the new Zion. The movie makes a high claim to historical authenticity: the historical events are shown in their relation to composite characters; costumes, sets, and events are detailed and historically verifiable. As the director claims, most of the dialogue was taken from pioneer journals and letters, while everything that Joseph Smith says in the movie is "quoted from something that he actually said or wrote" (quoted in Gaunt 32). However, the primary aim of the movie is not only historical accuracy but transport and empathy: the director wanted to "capture the spirit of sacrifice, the spirit of faith" and to render a "journey of the human heart back through time" that allows the audience to be "totally swept away in time and space" rather than merely be informed of historical facts (Gaunt 32). In accordance with this professed aim, the genre of the movie is clearly melodrama, the suffering of innocence. A significant part of the movie is devoted to showing patient Mormons moving ever westward to escape tarring and feathering, if not killing, but also their extraordinary accomplishments in the face of adversity. In this regard, the film stands in several formal and thematic traditions. As *melodrama,* it works with the familiar repertoire of one of the most popular nineteenth-century entertainment forms, melodramatic plays, and their ideological investment of projecting a world clearly split into good and bad, where moral behavior was always rewarded in the end, even after an extended time of (frequently cathartic) suffering, and bad characters had to pay their due. Especially during the second half of the nineteenth century, with industrialization creating increasing inequality and social unrest, this ideology advocated individual rather than social and systematic responsibility for poverty, inequality, and injustice.

Tellingly, it had an influential renaissance during the Reagan and Bush era, the time during which *Legacy* was produced, and also the time during which Hollywood started churning out masses of films in one of its most popular and successful genres until today: melodrama. Indeed, the film often seems like a Mormon version of Reagan's *Morning in America* campaign commercials with their "vision" of America. The movie thus engages in at least two rhetorics familiar from the aforementioned presidents: individualism and family values. While the Mormon experience was communal, the individual had to recognize the true gospel and remain faithful in the face of adversity and suffering; on several occasions in the movie, the characters' faith and endurance are tested. At the same time, family values and social cohesion and conformity are shown as paramount to survival.

Visual style and mise-en-scène of the images showing the trek west in *Legacy* are arranged accordingly and remind us of the visual and structural characteristics of nineteenth-century melodramatic tableaux. Toward the end of the movie, in a kind of visual culmination, there are several minutes of extremely long shots accompanied by music, but without narration, showing the Mormon trek over the plains. Style and framing recall the landscape shots in the 1950s and early 1960s westerns of John Ford, Howard Hawks, and others. The trek is shown against the backdrop of a vast and impressive nature, and the music is dramatic and orchestral. Western film and melodramatic tableaux are merged in showing the individual at once reduced to insignificance in the face of the natural grandiosity of the nation and a larger scheme of things, and yet stubborn, resilient, and resourceful enough to conquer and settle this landscape and form the new nation.

Most important for the ideological work of the film, however, is what is not there. The movie starts in the early days of the LDS movement but does not present its actual beginnings, the visions of Joseph Smith or any of the other contested events that accompanied its inception, such as early testimonies and their rescinding. Tellingly, the film also ends before the group actually arrives in Utah and thus does not show the life there that was the subject of so much public, political, and legal (largely uninformed and ignorant) debate. It shows neither internal strife, leadership struggles, and schisms (of which there were plenty) nor the Mormons' own participation in conflicts with their neighbors and state leadership. None of the so-called Mormon wars are mentioned, nor are the Danites, a Mormon militia founded to protect them from mob violence. Also, the key bone of contention and most widespread cliché about the Mormons, polygamy, is not given so much as one word. In short, the history we see is homogeneous, unified, and teleological. The film renders, as an authorized version, the mainstream tale with its myth and legacy. But in blacking out anything beyond the pale, any outsiders within this group of outsiders, the film situates the Mormons right within mainstream American mythologies of the West and simultaneously conforms to its contemporary conservative agenda of enforcing at least the image of a unified stable identity where there is none, as noted in the beginning.

The Mormons are clearly shown as religious dissenters, as persecuted and marginalized; this is a necessary part of their self-styled identity. However, the movie's genre, visual code, and emphasis on their pioneer past simultaneously claim that this is exactly what makes them central to American history and that they may justifiably lay claim to a place in its future. Consequently, the movie paradoxically situates the Mormons simultaneously as outsiders and insiders. Yet the movie does not self-reflexively acknowledge the *continuing* liminality of the LDS Church; on the contrary, it seeks to move them right to the heart of conservative America: even before the first shot appears, white writing on a black screen announces that the times of conflict and strife have passed. Additionally, the frame narrative ensures that the film ends on a happy and consoling note that makes clear that Mormons are no longer outsiders. Considering the historical context of the movie, the approaching millennium, and the debates about Francis Fukuyama's thesis about the end of history, the Mormon *legacy* and teleology merges the secular and sacred into an extremely conservative vision of the future of the United States.

Angels in America would seem to be almost diametrically opposed to *Legacy*. The themes, content, and structure of the play make clear that there is no unified national story to be found here, that there is chaos, pain, suffering, and bare survival instead, and certainly no teleology that arrives at some kind of biblical or even secular millennium, neither Marxist nor Hegelian.

Given the length and formal complexity of the play, it can hardly be summarized, a fact that already makes a basic formal point: the play's episodic structure and its many plots and subplots make it impossible to talk of *one* story. Of the many plots and subplots, the one of most relevance here concerns the character Prior, who suffers from AIDS and receives a visitation by an angel who wants him as prophet. Prior is given (or rather forced to accept) plates to translate and a prophecy to disseminate. Thematically, the play offers analogies to the Bible, the Book of Mormon, historical records, and various other works.

For example, Prior wrestles with an angel just like Jacob did (II 117ff), and the book and the reading implements Prior is given resonate with Joseph Smith's visitation by the angel Moroni (II 43ff). Correspondingly, the angel bears a message for Prior, a revelation very similar to that allegedly experienced by Joseph Smith. However, all of the analogies are ironically undercut. The angels are powerful but stupid; God has left them, and now Heaven looks like San Francisco after the quake of 1906. Because every change and progression of humanity leads to further disruptions in Heaven, the angels have chosen Prior to make humanity stop moving. As an appropriate but nasty metaphor, Prior has AIDS, the terminal progression of which mirrors the angel's ultimate aim, stasis:

> YOU HAVE DRIVEN HIM AWAY! YOU MUST STOP MOVING!
> . . . Forsake the Open Road: Neither Mix nor Intermarry: Let Deep Roots Grow: If you do not MINGLE you will Cease to Progress: Seek Not to Fathom the World and its Delicate Particle Logic: . . . HOBBLE YOURSELVES! . . . STASIS! The END.   (II 49ff)

If Prior, and by extension humanity, did as bidden, there would be no change and no progression. Eventually, it would literally mean the death of all life, the END. But even before that, it would mean the *conservation* of all things as they are: no mixing and intermarriage that might lead to racial ambiguity, no increasing understanding of the complexity of the world that might lead to an insight into the workings of ideology, no moving to other, possibly foreign places that might bring about a more transnational, cosmopolitan attitude, and so forth. The prophecy thus quite literally propagates a conservative ideology that unabashedly reminds one of Reaganism taken to its extreme consequences. The fact that this conservatism comes through the channel of divine inspiration and revelation could, without much effort, be read as a sarcastic comment on the idea of America as God's nation and the president as the executive of divine will. Consistently, Prior—a WASP, homosexual, liberal HIV-positive intellectual very much aware of the implications of this divine order—refuses "his" prophecy.

The most crucial scene for the argument of this essay is the so-called diorama scene. It takes place in the diorama of a Mormon visitor center in Manhattan showing the Mormon trek west. In the course of the scene, the whole myth of the Mormon trek is dismantled as almost everything that *Legacy* has left out is brought to the fore. The tableau is a "classic wagon-train tableau;" the stage directions specify dramatic music as a voice tells the story of the trek: "In 1847, across fifteen hundred miles of frontier wilderness, braving mountain blizzards, desert storms, and renegade Indians, the first Mormon wagon trains made their difficult way towards the Kingdom of God" (II 65). Watching the scene are Prior, Harper (Mormon wife of Joe, who has started an affair with Prior's ex-lover Louis), and Hanna (Harper's Mormon mother-in-law, who has deserted Salt Lake City in order to help her valium-addicted and hallucinating daughter). Harper comments on the diorama and the narrative as the voice proceeds and the diorama figures talk:

> Harper: There's a dummy family in the diorama, you'll see when the curtain opens. The main dummy, the big daddy dummy, looks like my husband, Joe. When they push the buttons he'll start to talk. You can't believe a word he says but the sound of him is reassuring. (II 63)
> Harper: They don't have any lines, the sister and the mother. And only his face moves. That's not really fair. (II 65)
> Harper: It's a Promised Land, but what a disappointing promise! (II 66)
> Harper: This isn't a place for real feelings, this is just storytime here. (II 68)

As the scene continues, other characters add to the humor as they parody the earnestness of *Legacy* with comments such as "I thought you were all out west somewhere with the salt flats and cactuses" (II 68) or "I don't like cults. . . . Any religion that's not at least two thousand years old is a cult" (II 67). Harper brings the scene to a metadramatic point that can also serve as an illuminating reflection on *Legacy* by dryly explaining the rather fantastic events that follow (the diorama figures come alive) with the "magic of theatre" (II 68). Everything is an illusion, well staged perhaps, but an illusion nevertheless. The myth of the innocent Mormon pioneers with their trek west and the illusion of the one true story are deconstructed and shown as "a falsely promising vision of America as heaven on earth for latter-day saints" (Miller 69). In fact, were it not for the constant ironic and metadramatic undercutting, the dialogue of the diorama figures, highlighting the bright-spiritedness and innocence of the family, especially the children, would perfectly fit into a (western) melodrama, where the good and stalwart family is sure to be rewarded for its search of worldly and heavenly paradise. However, as Harper makes clear, the price is high and the actual reward questionable. In reality, many Mormons did not survive the trek and the first winter in the Utah desert.

The fact that the scene features a diorama adds another layer of historically contextualized irony. Dioramas and panoramas were rivals to melodrama for popular entertainment in the second half of the nineteenth century. They were supposed to transport the viewer to faraway or historically significant places, for example the American West or Gettysburg, by flawless visual illusion. They simultaneously served the ideological purpose of postulating and celebrating the grandeur of the nation in nature and history. In *Angels in America,* the illusion of the diorama is not only far from flawless, as the machinery does not work, but also reveals its ideological investment, in this case the myths surrounding the Mormon trek west. As the play unfolds into a complex welter of plots and subplots, microcosms, stories and histories, realities and fantasies, the illusion of an uninterrupted continuum of history and one teleology is rent. Consistently, the guiding metaphor, theme, and image of the play is Walter Benjamin's angel of history (see also Harris 185ff).[5]

Despite the criticism, the Mormons and their myths are not entirely denigrated. The play does repeatedly point at sexist, patriarchal, homophobic, and racist elements in the history and present of the LDS Church; it does show that while the Mormons may have been pioneers important in the settlement of the West, neither were they innocent then, nor is their conservative vision for the future of the United States wholly salutary now. More importantly, most of the Mormon characters in the play are so-called Jack Mormons, that is, outsiders within their church. Harper is an addict, Joe is homosexual, and Hannah is a chain-smoker. Thus, the play again reinforces the Mormons' liminality. On the one hand it emphasizes that the Mormons are an integral part of American history, one that contemporary clichés do not do justice to. Their story is one of the many "National Themes" as the subtitle has it. The play offers a grudging kind of respect for the Mormons' perseverance in the face of persecution and hardship, and for their insistence on their vision, even though it may be flawed.

On the other hand, the play shows us only Mormons that are outsiders, while the diorama scene ridicules the official church's attempt to situate itself at the center of American history. Correlatively, Kushner's references to the American West are rendered almost exclusively through the lens of the Mormon experience. The central national story here is thus told from the perspective of a group of religious outsiders, repeating the structural liminality.

*   *   *

In a sense, both film and play transport a structurally similar idea, namely the "central outsider" trope introduced in the beginning, demonstrating the liminal social, political, and cultural position of the LDS in the United States. The crucial difference lies in their ideological investment and their closure. Where *Legacy* tells *one* story that ultimately arrives at *one* side of the insider/outsider dialectic, *Angels in America* constructs different stories and new visions with no oppressive, finalizing teleology, because for Kushner's characters this would mean death. The two texts also show immense qualitative differences. *Legacy* is pure, serious, unironic melodrama without formal complexity, whereas *Angels in America* is ambitiously complex, self-reflexive, and highly ironic. The latter announces its ideological investment, whereas the former naturalizes its interests both in form and content. Given their thrust, these strategies do make sense: where the movie paradoxically confirms and downplays the Mormons' outsider status through its homogenization and appropriation of the national story discussed above, the play brings the outsiders closer to home by showing that they have always been there and by emphasizing the multiplicity of national stories. Both texts appropriate the past to secure their ideological investment in the future. For both, history bestows upon the present not only a heritage of the past but also a legacy for the future.

NOTES

1. The official name for the Mormon Church is the Church of Jesus Christ of Latter-day Saints (LDS). This is the largest and best known of the several Latter-Day movements that arose in the 1830s and 1840s, some of them still extant today. For brevity's sake, the term "Mormon" will be used to refer to this church. While the use of the single term "Mormons" might suggest group homogeneity, the Mormons are in fact very heterogeneous. More than 50 percent of them now reside outside the United States, with substantial growth rates in Middle and South America and Asia (Murphy 455). As Joanna Brooks notes, the "white English-speaking American westerners now constitute a minority of Mormon church membership" (291).

2. There are significant differences between the early and contemporary Mormons, not the least of which are mentioned in note 1. In addition, their "outsider" status is structurally different now from the 1830s and 1840s. The Mormons are no longer persecuted and no longer perceived as a threatening minority with ambitions to establish a theocratic state in the Utah desert. However, some key concepts such as a millenarian-tinged Manifest Destiny for the Chosen People and a New

Jerusalem remain at the heart of the official theology and doctrines, and the introductory discussion should have illuminated their perception by a wider public as an exotic, if no longer threatening, minority.

3. Some critics, however, maintain that Manifest Destiny is "inherently religious" (Loy 57).

4. This argument is based on the fact that a significant number of pioneers were actually recruited through proselytism in Great Britain.

5. In the ninth section of his "Theses on the Philosophy of History," Benjamin refers to a painting by Paul Klee called *Angelus Novus* in order to illustrate his conception of history. An angel is haplessly propelled forward by a wind we call progress with his back to the future and his face to a steadily growing, chaotic pile of rubble we call history. There is no teleology, no order, no system, merely destruction.

Works Cited

Abanes, Richard. *One Nation under Gods: A History of the Mormon Church.* New York: Four Walls Eight Windows, 2002.

Arrington, Leonard, and Jon Haupt. "Community and Isolation: Some Aspects of 'Mormon Westerns.'" *Western American Literature* 8 (1973): 15–31.

———. *The Mormon Experience. A History of the Latter-day Saints.* 2nd ed. Urbana: University of Illinois Press, 1992.

Austin, Michael. "Finding God in the Desert: The Landscape of Belief in Three Modern Mormon Classics." *Literature and Belief* 23.1 (2003): 39–54.

Bloom, Harold. *The American Religion.* New York: Simon & Schuster, 1992.

Brooks, Joanna. "'Genealogy is in our Blood': Terry Tempest Williams and the Redemption of 'Native' Mormonism." In *True West: Authenticity and the American West,* edited by William R. Handley and Nathaniel Lewis, 290–303. Lincoln: University of Nebraska Press, 2004.

Eliason, Eric. A. "Introduction." In *Mormons and Mormonism,* edited by Eric A. Eliason, 1–22. Urbana: University of Illinois Press, 2001.

Gaunt, LaRene. "Legacy." *Ensign* (July 1993): 32.

Givens, Terry. "Caricature as Containment: Orientalism, Bondage, and the Construction of Mormon Ethnicity in Nineteenth-Century American Popular Fiction." *Nineteenth-Century Contexts* 18.4 (1995): 385–403.

Grey, Zane. *Riders of the Purple Sage.* Oxford: Oxford University Press, 1995.

Handley, William R. "Distinctions without Differences: Zane Grey and the Mormon Question." *Arizona Quarterly* 57.1 (2001): 1–33.

Harris, Martin. "Flying the Angels of History." In *Approaching the Millennium: Essays on Angels in America,* edited by Deborah R. Geis and

Steven F. Kruger, 185–198. Ann Arbor: University of Michigan Press, 1997.

Jackson, Richard H., ed. *The Mormon Role in the Settlement of the West.* Provo, UT: Brigham University Press, 1978.

Kennedy, John F. "Address to the Greater Houston Ministerial Association." *InfoUSA,* U.S. Department of State, June 6, 2007. http://usinfo.state.gov/usa/infousa/facts/democrac/66.htm.

Kushner, Tony. *Angels in America: A Gay Fantasia on National Themes.* Part One: *Millennium Approaches.* New York: Theatre Communications Group, 1992.

———. *Angels in America: A Gay Fantasia on National Themes.* Part Two: *Perestroika.* New York: Theatre Communications Group, 1992.

Legacy. Directed by Kieth Merrill. Intellectual Reserve, 2004.

Loy, R. Philip. "Saints or Scoundrels: Images of Mormons in Literature and Film about the American West." *Journal of the American Studies Association of Texas* 21 (1990): 57–74.

Miller, James. "Heavenquake: Queer Anagogies in Kushner's America." In *Approaching the Millennium: Essays on Angels in America,* edited by Deborah R. Geis and Steven F. Kruger. Ann Arbor: University of Michigan Press, 1997. 56–77.

Moore, Laurence. *Religious Outsiders and the Making of Americans.* New York: Oxford University Press, 1986.

Murphy, Thomas W. "From Racist Stereotype to Ethnic Identity: Instrumental Uses of Mormon Racial Doctrine." *Ethnohistory* 46.3 (1999): 451–80.

Norton, William. "Competing Identities and Contested Places: Mormons in Nauvoo and Voree." *Journal of Cultural Geography* 21.1 (2003): 95–119.

Poll, Richard D. "Utah and the Mormons: A Symbiotic Relationship." In *Mormons and Mormonism,* edited by Eric A. Eliason, 164–79. Urbana: University of Illinois Press, 2001.

Stegner, Wallace. *The Gathering of Zion: The Story of the Mormon Trail.* New York: McGraw-Hill, 1964.

Twain, Mark. *Roughing It.* Edited by Harriet Elinor Smith and Edgar Marquess Branch. Berkeley: University of California Press, 1993.

CHAPTER 4

MIDDLEBROW READERS AND PIONEER HEROINES: WILLA CATHER'S *MY ÁNTONIA*, BESS STREETER ALDRICH'S *A LANTERN IN HER HAND*, AND THE POPULAR FICTION MARKET*

Melissa Homestead

In 1918, Houghton Mifflin published *My Ántonia,* Willa Cather's fourth novel and her second to make an immigrant woman from the Nebraska prairies its heroine. A decade later, in 1928, D. Appleton & Co. published Bess Streeter Aldrich's *A Lantern in Her Hand,* another novel of the pioneer era in Nebraska with a female heroine, this one a native-born child of Protestant Irish immigrants. Both novels have been in print continuously since. Initial sales of *My Ántonia* were modest, reflecting the small size of the first edition. Houghton Mifflin paid Cather royalties on sales of 3,261 copies in October 1918, a month after the novel's initial publication.[1] In the first few years after 1918, annual sales hovered at just over 1,000, but then they gradually began to climb to 2,000 and above, causing the editor, Ferris Greenslet, to remark with satisfaction in 1921, "'MY ANTONIA' seems to be settling into a very long stride." Promoted more aggressively by its publisher in a literary market much expanded in a decade, *Lantern*'s initial sales far exceeded those of Cather's novel—9,000 two months after publication, 16,000 within four months (Williams, Letters to BSA). Sales continued to increase, so that by the early 1930s, *Lantern* enjoyed the unusual distinction of first appearing on bestseller lists several years after its initial publication (Peterson, *Bess Streeter Aldrich* 88). Thus, like *My Ántonia*, *Lantern* had a "long stride," its steady-seller status attesting to its enduring appeal to ordinary readers.

Why, then, do these two novels so seldom appear together in literary history, and why have *A Lantern in Her Hand* and its author received so little sustained scholarly attention? Despite one scholar's recent analysis of what she calls the "resurrection" of *A Lantern in Her Hand* (Knight), the novel never "died" in the first place. Outside of the prestige economy of academia, the novel remained vitally alive. As Sharon O'Brien has observed, Cather, too, found herself outside of the canon from the 1920s on, as H. L. Mencken and other elite tastemakers who had championed her work in the teens dismissed her in gendered terms as backward-looking and minor. In the twenty-first century, however, Cather's canonical status is secure. Her works are widely taught in university classrooms, and a veritable scholarly industry publishes scores of articles on her works every year.

Along with repositioning Cather in a new reading context, this essay aims to bring Aldrich and her novel into literary history (and college classrooms) by putting her work into dialogue with Cather's. I do not, however, elevate Aldrich to the status of elite artist, a move that she herself would disavow. Instead, I seek to revalue the middle-brow as a mode of authorship, circulation, and reading for the literary history of the American West and to place *Ántonia* and *Lantern* together on that oft-scorned terrain. When Aldrich is taken note of in Western literary history, she receives only glancing attention after being categorized as "sentimental," a word seldom defined but seemingly associated with pandering to readers and their emotions.[2] What if, instead, we take seriously the "sentiments" of the legions of ordinary, nonacademic readers who have kept both Aldrich and Cather in print? Certainly, Cather's embrace of the literary market and the tastes of ordinary readers were more tentative and covert than Aldrich's. For instance, when she wrote to Mencken in 1922, prior to the publication of *One of Ours,* seeking (fruitlessly, as it turned out) to avert a negative review of her World War I novel, she reminded him that "they were both enemies of a debased, popular American literature" and were "both committed to overturning Booth Tarkington platitudes and raising American literature to a higher plane" (O'Brien 114).[3] Certainly, Aldrich's current critical reputation more closely resembles that of the best-selling Indiana novelist Tarkington than

Cather's, and Cather probably would have disavowed any connection to Aldrich as she did Tarkington. Nevertheless, locating *Ántonia* and *Lantern* together in the middlebrow recovers with more precision the terms on which Cather engaged the literary market and a popular readership. It also throws new light on the deep investment of a national readership in fictional depictions of Midwestern pioneering.

*   *   *

Although the terms "highbrow" and "lowbrow" designating zones of culture emerged in the nineteenth century, the term "middlebrow" first emerged in the 1920s. The middlebrow resides somewhere between the easily identifiable low of mass-circulated dime novels and pulp magazines, written up to plot outlines by nameless scribes, and the edgy *avant garde* of modernism circulated in little magazines and books in small editions as the creative emanations of autonomous authors. Because of this "betweenness," commentators have often criticized the middle as violating the proper boundaries between commerce (low) and art (high). Nevertheless, cultural historians and literary critics have attempted in the last fifteen years to give the middlebrow its due. Rather than identify a group of texts or authors as inherently middlebrow, Joan Shelley Rubin focuses on the middlebrow as a form of circulation and its accompanying critical apparatus "aimed at making literature and other forms of 'high' culture available to a wide reading public" (xi). In her study of the Book-of-the-Month Club (BOMC), Janice Radway likewise focuses on a business enterprise designed to distribute literary texts to a growing professional managerial class as a central institution of the middlebrow. In addition, she theorizes an associated set of reading practices in which readers identify intensely and empathize with characters they feel to be "real," leading to deep absorption in the imagined world of the book (*Feeling* 262, 282–84). Although some critics have damned the excluded middle in literary history because of its association with women, both as authors and as readers, feminist literary historians have recently reclaimed the middle, much as an earlier generation of scholars reclaimed popular women's writing of the nineteenth century (Radway 189–216; Botshon & Goldsmith). Focusing on the middlebrow as an authorial mode practiced by women writers, Jaime Harker explains that middlebrow women authors "depended, financially and artistically, on their relationship with their readers" (6). They thus avoided radical formal experimentation and did not claim alienation as a badge of artistic authenticity or attack the values of average readers.[4]

At times, Cather's aesthetic pronouncements mock the taste of average readers. In her essay "The Novel Démeumblé" (1922), for instance, Cather publicly professed scorn for the popular taste as she did privately to Mencken. Dismissing "the novel manufactured to entertain great multitudes of people" as being like consumable cheap soap, she asks rhetorically, "Does anyone pretend that if the Woolworth store windows were piled high with Tanagra figurines at ten cents, they could for a moment compete with Kewpie brides in the popular esteem?" (44). Placing herself on the side of "art" as against "amusement," she seems to turn her back on the market and most readers (44).

Despite this public posturing, she nevertheless quietly exploited middlebrow institutions, such as book clubs and mass-circulation women's magazines, as a way to reach and engage the common reader. No doubt her experience as an editor of *McClure's Magazine* gave her an understanding of the evolving middle zone of the market because *McClure's* was, as Radway explains, one of the magazines that "invented a new product—the audience's attention—and thus were absolutely crucial to the development of a nationally oriented consumer culture" ("Research Universities" 224). *My Ántonia* preceded the BOMC by nearly a decade, but as Mark Madigan has recently demonstrated, many more of Cather's books received the club's imprimatur than previously recognized. *Shadows on the Rock* (1931) and *Sapphira and the Slave Girl* (1940) were Cather's only books to be "main selections" of the club, but *My Mortal Enemy* (1926), *Death Comes for the Archbishop* (1927), *Obscure Destinies* (1932), *Lucy Gayheart* (1935), and even *Not Under Forty* (1936) (which reprinted "The Novel Démeumblé") were all designated "other new books recommended" that readers could choose if they declined to accept the main selection (Madigan 72–79). Notably, in 1929, the BOMC designated *My Ántonia* an "Outstanding Older Book" readers could receive instead of a main selection (Madigan 74). Selection committee member and novelist Dorothy Canfield Fisher (Cather's friend since adolescence) wrote the review in the *BOMC News,* telling readers that whenever she visited a public library, the "worn and shabby" appearance of copies of *Ántonia* testified "the lasting love of our people for that beautiful book. . . . The next step should be to move it from the public library shelf to the home shelf, to see it in every American's house as part of the stuff of life," so that people can reread and "live with" the novel and "grow up to" it (Quoted in Madigan 75). Even though Cather's fiction appeared in smaller-circulation, higher-prestige magazines earlier in her career, in the

1920s and 1930s, the women's magazines presented Cather's fiction to large audiences of middlebrow women readers and their families.[5]

Cather embraced not only middlebrow circulation, but the critical apparatus that promoted books and authors to middlebrow readers. Cather's correspondence with her family, especially her brother Roscoe, suggests that she saw her family members as model general readers and demonstrates her embrace of the middlebrow critical apparatus. Henry Seidel Canby, another BOMC judge and editor of the *Saturday Review of Literature,* defined the "average intelligent reader" as one "who has passed through the usual formal education in literature, who reads books as well as newspapers and magazines, who, without calling himself a litterateur, would be willing to assert that he was fairly well read and reasonably fond of good reading. Your doctor, your lawyer, the president of your bank" (qtd. in Radway, *Feeling* 296). Her brother Roscoe, a bank president in Lander and then Casper, Wyoming, fits this profile precisely. Cather delighted in reporting the critical and popular success of her works to Roscoe, sending him reviews and press notices. In 1918, self-consciously straddling the divide between approval from professional critics and common readers, she combined in her letter a report of reviews of *My Ántonia* with her delight at how many ordinary people, not just high-brow cultural arbiters, enjoyed the novel despite its apparent plotless-ness. Among the readers whose approval she reported with pleasure was her own father, Charles Cather, a small-town mortgage agent, who professed to like *My Ántonia* as much as any other book he had read. In a letter reporting his second reading of *Ántonia* to Willa, Charles Cather characterized both *Ántonia* and *O Pioneers!* (1913) as being "like old tried & true friends to me." As radio developed, Cather began reporting to Roscoe about radio broadcasts featuring her as a speaker or mentioning her and her works. Rubin has charac-terized the middlebrow critical apparatus, and particularly "book talk" on the radio, as combining critical evaluation with an awareness of the "news value" of books and authors to readers struggling to keep up with an ever-expanding print culture (42, 266–329). The critic and radio personality Alexander Woollcott is one of Rubin's central figures. In December 1933, Woollcott "toasted" Cather's birthday on the air. Delighted but perplexed because she did not know in advance, she went to the trouble of securing a transcript of the toast to send to Roscoe. Two years later, forewarned of Woollcott's intention to "serenade" her on the air, she made sure Roscoe had advance notice (Bloom).[6]

Cather's and Aldrich's market strategies placed their works on the same cultural terrain and made them available to the same readers, even if Aldrich's public embrace of the market was more overt than Cather's. In 1921, when Aldrich was a successful magazine writer but had not yet published a book, she bluntly told readers of the *American Magazine,* "You have to *work* to be a successful writer, just as you have to work to be a successful grocery-man, or to be a successful anything else" ("How I Mixed" 38). In a speech before the Nebraska Writer's Guild, she unapologetically explained, "I see no reason why art and checks should be considered oil and water . . . [W]e should write like inspired artists and sell like shrewd Yankees" (Untitled). Like Cather, Aldrich placed much of her fiction in women's magazines in the 1920s and 1930s. Aldrich's "I Remember" and Cather's *My Mortal Enemy* both appeared in *McCall's* in 1926, for instance, and Aldrich's "The Day of Retaliation" and "The Runaway Judge" and Cather's "Three Women" (the magazine title of "Old Mrs. Harris") all appeared in the *Ladies' Home Journal* in 1932. Cather initially expressed reservations about allowing the BOMC to make *Shadows on the Rock* (1931) a main selection, but Aldrich and her publishers enthusiastically sought status for *Lantern* as either a main selection or an alternate.[7] The attempt failed, but the logic of the attempt was clear in light of one of the BOMC's objectives—to get books to readers who lived outside of major metropolitan areas and had limited access to well-stocked bookstores (Radway, *Feeling* 190–91).

Aldrich's embrace of readers extended to inviting them into her creative process. As she was preparing to write *A Lantern in Her Hand,* she spoke on a radio station in Lincoln, Nebraska, about "The Pioneer in Fiction" and asked listeners to send to her "little *detailed* enlightening anecdotes" about the pioneer history of their own families and communities, "some dramatic thing which happened to you and which you recall vividly—or some humorous thing which still brings forth a smile as you remember." She explained that she could not pay them for material, "but . . . you might have the satisfaction later of seeing it worked into a novel and you would feel that *you* had helped to preserve the old pioneer days in fiction." In a speech given around 1929 to a Nebraska audience, she claimed, "There had been many gracious reviews [of *Lantern*], but nothing any clever critic has said has meant so much to me as the commendations of the children of the prairie. No New York or Boston or London review has pleased me as have the letters from the pioneer's [*sic*] sons and daughters which said 'You have written the story of my own mother,' or 'Abbie Deal [the heroine of *Lantern*] was just like my grandmother.'" In "Wild Critics I Have Known," published in *The Bookman* in 1930, she proclaimed that by "tabulat[ing]" opposing critical responses, she had rendered the critic "harmless" to her self-esteem as a writer (72). In sum, Aldrich publicly positioned herself as an ally of common readers and as a sometimes bemused spectator of professional evaluators of literature.

* * *

Aldrich's reference to readers writing her to proclaim that the fictional Abbie Deal was a realistic portrait of their mothers or grandmothers as pioneer women is literally true—scores of readers say exactly that in the nearly two hundred letters preserved in her papers. However, those letters tell only a part of the story of ordinary readers' deeply felt engagements with *A Lantern in Her Hand,* a kind of engagement also documented, but less extensively, in the few dozen letters to Cather that have survived.[8] I turn now to documenting and theorizing the middlebrow style of reading revealed by these fan letters, reading practices that allowed a wide variety of readers from across the United States to experience a deep and sympathetic engagement with the novels' prairie pioneer heroines.

As Radway first proposed and as Jennifer Parchesky has elaborated using the evidence of readers' letters to Fisher, engagement and identification are the central dynamics of middlebrow reading. According to Parchesky, middlebrow readers sought to "assuage anxieties about a rapidly changing and deeply disconcerting modern society" by seeking "in their reading a sense of meaning and community" (232). They identified and imagined themselves as part of a community comprising both literary characters and their creators, making "a sense of identification and community among cultural producers and cultural consumers" the "hallmark of the middlebrow ethos" (233). In the reading community constructed by the BOMC, as Radway observes, literature was not conceived of as something to be "appreciated" with a sense of aesthetic distance. Instead, BOMC readers were encouraged to see literature, including novels, as something they could use (*Feeling* 142). As Parchesky elaborates, fiction served middlebrow readers as "structures of feeling: epistemological structures for perceiving and interpreting certain experiences as significant, and psychological, affective and narrative structures for organizing and representing their own experiences" (245).[9]

One of the central tropes of reader letters to both Aldrich and Cather is literary characters as friends, a trope that Cather's own father deployed. For him, the characters in *Ántonia* were friends in a more literal sense, fictionalized versions of his friends and family several decades earlier. Other readers of *Ántonia* and *Lantern* constructed imaginative scenarios in which the characters were "real" and lived in their imaginations even after the temporally limited act of reading had finished.[10] A mother of high-school-aged children from Vincennes, Indiana, explained to Aldrich: "Your stories are so real, so fine your characters are so *alive,* that I live the book as I read it. I rejoiced with Abbie, I mourned with her, I *loved* her and at the close of the day as her spirit went forth with 'the lantern in her hand[.]' I cried as for a precious friend" (Wiseman). A traveling Chautauqua lecturer from Indianola, Iowa, wrote to Cather that he read all of her books, including *Ántonia,* "slowly—leaving intervals between them—I want them to last a life time." Conflating real and fictional places and characters in central Nebraska (a practice still very common in "Catherland"), he explained, "I know your Nebraska well—I have stopped at the hotel where Ántonia worked—I heard Blind Boone play in the parlor and I have seen his watch" (Winters). Implicitly analogizing the act of reading with a social interaction with a person, a young woman from Lakewood, Ohio, wrote to Aldrich that "Abbie Deal and I have become acquainted with each other about six different times" since she first checked *Lantern* out of a library six years before. She described herself as "grateful" to Abbie for the example she set of self-sacrifice (as a young woman, Abbie dreams of going to New York and becoming a singer or actress, but her marriage to Will forecloses this possibility, as well as her ambitions to paint and to write). Using language very much like Fisher's BOMC recommendation of *Ántonia,* this twenty-year-old reader also said that it would take her a "lifetime" of rereadings to "grow up to" Aldrich's novel. At the conclusion of her very long letter, she explained clearly the way that *Lantern* had provided her with a "structure of feeling" that helped her meet the challenges of modernity: "If ever I feel muddled up about the turn of events in my own life, Abbie Deal always helps me see straight again. If I ever need a jolt out of a rut of taking modern life for granted, Abbie will show me all the hard work in its beginning" (Walker).

Readers extended this construction of friendship and intimacy to include others they had never met in the flesh, Aldrich and Cather. As a fifteen-year-old girl wrote to Aldrich, enclosing a photo inscribed "Your devoted friend," "It seems funny—we have never seen each other, you didn't even know I existed and yet you are one of my best friends" (Brand). A nineteen-year-old man studying at a Catholic College in rural Wisconsin characterized himself as a classic middlebrow reader, but one frustrated by Cather's lack of an orthodox religious vision. When he read, he explained to Cather, he sought to "penetrat[e] the story to the heart of its creator in an attempt . . . to find the writer himself," seeking "companionship with another mind that lived beyond ink." Characterizing Anton Rosicky of "Neighbour Rosicky" and Ántonia as "the kind of people I would like to meet on summer evenings, walking through quiet fields to them, to look at them and listen to them," he complained that these literary friends did not bring him the "peace" he sought. He routed his frustration through an oblique reference to the most quoted passage in *My Ántonia,* in which Jim Burden characterizes the adult Ántonia as firing his imagination with the simple gesture of putting her hand on a crabapple tree, making him "feel the goodness of planting and tending and harvesting at last" (342). Ántonia "unconsciously found" a "deep peace," the reader complained to Cather, but "it was only that of a beautiful superior plant life; and I was sorry because (selfishly?) I thought I had come to the end of my friendship with you" (Curran).

These rural and small-town Midwesterners were not the only readers to claim Cather, Aldrich, and their characters as friends, and even as "family." Letters to both authors revealed a broad geographic diversity as well as class and occupational diversity. Not just lawyers and bank presidents, but housewives, farmers, teachers, students, ministers, manual laborers, secretaries, and clerks also wrote. Furthermore, even letters that proclaimed a family connection to prairie-pioneer subject matter often testified to a Nebraska diaspora, the movement of the children and grandchildren of women like Abbie away from the region of their birth or early migration. Although *Lantern* culminates with the triumphant full flowering of the state of Nebraska, with Abbie Deal's life synecdochally representing the state's history, postpioneer out-migration and depopulation were already a historical and demographic reality in the 1920s (Nugent 193, 244). Thus we find a New York lawyer born in Platte County, Nebraska, describing himself as "so much a plainsman that it was very difficult for me to read [*Lantern*] except with deep emotion—it is very real to me for I love the prairie country" (Matters). An older woman from Monterey, California, described her own experience homesteading near Lexington, Nebraska, in 1884, followed by a move to "the newer country—Oklahoma, but I have always felt that some part of me was left in Nebraska." Burdened with the care of a seriously disabled husband, she expressed her "unsatisfied yearning to return to my childhood home and tho I may never realize my desire, I know it will go with me to 'the End of the Chapter' unless I do." Nevertheless, she could travel to Nebraska in her imagination and

take inspiration from Abbie Deal's struggles (Campbell). A professor
of sociology at a theological seminary in the Philippines represented
a particularly revealing case. He first described his "homesickness" for
Nebraska after reading *Lantern* and placed his childhood and family
in relation to "the Nebraska county which Willa Siebert [*sic*] Cather
immortalized in some of her earlier books." He then described his
own journey away from a childhood "on a poor Webster county
farm" for education at the University of Nebraska, theological study
at Yale, a brief return to Hastings, Nebraska, as a minister, but then
his move half a world away. Finally, however, he protested the fact
that all of Abbie Deal's children move off the farm. "I love Nebraska,
and it is a matter of pride to me that my state has such writers as
yourself, Cather, and Neihardt to sing its worth," he wrote, but he
gently rebuked Aldrich for writing a novel in which "the kind of
success the children of Abbie Deal achieved consisted . . . in escape
from the farm" (Fey). This sociology professor was anxious to claim
Cather for Nebraska as a counterweight to this exodus, but Cather
was herself a Nebraska expatriate—she lived most of her adult life in
New York City. However, reading *My Ántonia* enabled readers from
everywhere to live through the Nebraska pioneer era, whether or not
they had direct experience of it.

Similarly, as Carol Miles Peterson suggests and Aldrich's fan letters
confirm, Aldrich "offered to her readers the feel of the country, the
best of their memories of rural homes known or imagined" (Introduction xiii). Because as middlebrow readers, they identified intensely
with characters, people with no "real" connection to the pioneer era
on the plains nevertheless acquired "memories" of "imagined rural
homes" through reading. That is, reading about Abbie Deal's life
became a means through which people from throughout the nation
experienced the same affective, emotional ties to the pioneer era
as those with familial connections to the pioneers. A woman from
Henrietta, North Carolina, who identified herself as "just one of the
plain mothers of America" who had "never known pioneer life on the
prairies" still thanked Aldrich for portraying "those same heart breaking struggles [and] thoughts" she experienced as a mother (Cain).
A young woman from an economically marginal family in New York
wrote Aldrich at length about her and her mother's intense emotional and imaginative engagements with Aldrich's fiction, especially
Lantern. After her mother finished "that epic of Nebraska," she told
her daughter, "Life would never have seemed so dull if I could have
known there were books like Abbie Deal's life to turn to." Writing
in 1935, the daughter reported that at times "the depression spreads

like a blanket over" the entire city of New York, and she herself felt "caught in the web that is depression" when she graduated high school and had trouble finding work. However, after reading *Lantern* and Aldrich's other novels, she would go to the rooftop of her building and imagine seeing the prairies or "standing in the doorway with Abbie Deal watching the sunset." She, like many of both Aldrich's and Cather's readers, reported first discovering Aldrich's books in public libraries, but she and her mother used scarce financial resources to buy their own copies, which her mother, "who is the soul of generosity in everything, refuses to put them out where careless friends may casually borrow them. Instead, they are carefully tucked away," lent only to friends who were "booklover[s] of the first order" (Brennan).

The intense affective ties Aldrich's readers express bring us back to dismissals of Aldrich's writing as "sentimental," charges that are often oddly paired with the "optimistic" or "romantic" as negative terms in the vocabulary of Western literary history. Certainly, in Aldrich's characterizations of her motivations for writing *Lantern* and the relation of it to previous depictions of similar subject matter, she proclaimed her own optimism. Acknowledging her own "audacity" in writing about "midwest women of the soil" in the wake of Hamlin Garland and Ole Edvart Rolvaag, she complains, "They had so often drawn these women as gaunt, hopeless despairing creatures . . . browbeaten women . . . women whom life seemed to defeat at the end. That was not my mother nor the mothers" of other Nebraskans (ellipses in the original). Instead, she characterizes her mother as an optimist who did not seek the "pity" of a later generation looking back on her hardships (untitled).

Nevertheless, Aldrich's novel is far grimmer and less optimistic than *My Ántonia,* which ends with Ántonia in vigorous middle age, surrounded by her healthy children and satisfied with the course her life has taken. Death, disappointment, and betrayal come early in Ántonia's life and in the novel, not at its conclusion. *Lantern* ends, instead, with its heroine's death after many years of loneliness and frustration because she has lost her husband's companionship to death and her adult children do not fully understand or value her. Her children succeed because of her willingly made sacrifices, but she still grieves for what she has lost. Even Abbie's role as a symbol of Nebraska's triumph as an agricultural state is far more ambiguous than it seems. As the Nebraska expatriate from the Philippines astutely pointed out, all of Abbie's children "succeed" by leaving the farm. Even more significantly, Abbie sells off her farm, piece by piece, to finance their education and eventual successes, leaving her a pioneer farmwoman without a farm, just a farmhouse.

Readers wrote to Aldrich to tell her that Abbie "inspired" them, but the long time span covered by the novel (1854–1927) and the length of Abbie's life allowed readers to draw very different lessons from it. Some readers found "inspiration" in Abbie's optimism in her early life, when she refused to let obstacles and failures beat her down, but others found "inspiration" in her later life as an exemplar of self-sacrifice and of resignation in the face of frustration, age, and loss. The New York lawyer from Nebraska, for instance, wrote not just about his Nebraska childhood, but about his non-Nebraska wife's death, sending a copy of *Lantern* for Aldrich's autograph "because it was the last book my wife, Amy L. Matters, read before her passing. I shall always recall the great joy this story of pioneer life afforded her" (Matters). A partially paralyzed invalid from Los Angeles wrote about how reading transported her imaginatively out of her sickbed, but she also recounted to Aldrich how *Lantern* and its sequel *A White Bird Flying* (which follows the life of Abbie Deal's granddaughter Laura) "helped me to become more reconciled to the recent death of a very beloved sister" (Chessman). Twenty years after the book's first publication, a recent widow from Girth, Idaho, suggested that years of reading and thinking about Aldrich's novel had prepared her for what she confronted in the present: "All through the years I must have known it would be this way. I've cried barrels of tears over THE LANTERN IN HER HAND. I'll try to be like Abbie Deal and not be a bother to my children but the years will be long without them" (Reid). Another widow, an uneducated Russian emigrant whose husband died when her two children were young, wrote fifteen years after that death. She thanked Aldrich for Abbie's story as an example that gave her the courage to open a small business (a bookshop) in Olympia, Washington, and to make sacrifices in order to educate her children, citing in particular Abbie's example as "this fine American Pioneer type who sold parcel by parcel of her valuable land to send her children to School" (Blom).

These remarks of the early twentieth-century readers suggest that the sentimentality of Aldrich's novel worked in precisely the way that Joanne Dobson theorizes in relation to nineteenth-century literary sentimentalism. Sentimentalism is "premised on an emotional and philosophical ethos that celebrates human connection, both personal and communal, and acknowledges the shared devastation of affectional loss," Dobson claims (266). Based on this ethos, sentimental writers respond in two primary ways to the threat of "violation, actual or threatened, of affectional bonds": by producing either "bleak, dispirited, anguished, sometimes outraged, representations of human loss" or "idealized portrayals of human connection or divine consolation" (267). The latter half of Aldrich's novel is not outraged, but it is often bleak, and Abbie is often dispirited and anguished. Readers responded to Aldrich's representations of loss by imagining their own idealized human connections to both Abbie and her creator. Likewise, one might classify *Ántonia* as sentimental in the optimistic mode, because it ends with an idealized portrait of the reclaimed and reconstituted human connection between Jim and Ántonia.

* * *

In reading *My Ántonia* and *A Lantern in Her Hand,* people throughout the nation came to possess the stories of Nebraska pioneer women as a familial inheritance through the practices of middlebrow reading, which privileged deep absorption and emotional engagement and identification with characters. How is it, then, that Aldrich's and Cather's novels have maintained a devoted following among ordinary readers, remaining continuously in print, while having very different fates in terms of the literary canon based on judgments by professional readers like us? Returning to the question of how each writer positioned herself in relation to the market, I explore how, over time, two classes of readers came to diverge in their judgments. I also argue that academic readers should take a cue from ordinary readers by taking Aldrich seriously and putting *My Ántonia* and *A Lantern in Her Hand* in dialogue in literary history and the classroom.

Although *My Ántonia* is now canonical enough to be included in its entirety in the *Norton Anthology of American Literature,* literary historians did not always grant Cather such high status. O'Brien lays the blame for Cather's noncanonical status during her late career and in the decades after her death on Cather's own actions, inaction, and temperament. Cather refused, O'Brien claims, to engage the "social and institutional forces that were increasingly structuring" the "writer/reader bond" in the 1930s and 1940s, turning instead for affirmation to a "view of the relationship between writer and reader" as "based on the private model of friendship" (122, 121). As O'Brien notes, Cather refused to allow most of her fiction to be anthologized or published in classroom editions that would allow "literary and academic institutions" to shape readers' interpretations (121).[11] In her late career, I would add, she also refused opportunities to circulate her works in ways that would have made them more broadly

accessible to readers outside of academic institutions. Although she
allowed Armed Services Editions of *My Ántonia, O, Pioneers!* and
Death Comes for the Archbishop during World War II, she refused to
allow a Viking Portable paperback edition of her works after the war
(Chinery 293–94).[12] And after an unhappy experience with a film
adaptation of *A Lost Lady* in 1934, she refused all further film adaptations and included provisions in her will directing her estate to do
the same (Schueth).

Despite these refusals of distribution channels that would have
made her works more accessible to ordinary readers, highbrow critics
nevertheless tarred her with the middlebrow brush. As Jane Waterman
notes, "'Best-seller,' 'magazine,' 'Hollywood,' 'women's clubs,' and
'well paid' all became synonymous and encoded middlebrow terms"
in the vocabulary of highbrow critics (76), and such critics deployed
this arsenal of what they considered to be insults against Cather. In his
review of *One of Ours,* for instance, Mencken complained that although
the first half of *One of Ours* "ranks almost with *My Ántonia*," which he
had championed, "the other [half] . . . drops precipitately to the level
of a serial in the *Ladies Home Journal*" (Scrhoeter 10). In 1937 in *The
Genteel Tradition,* Lionel Trilling likewise complained that Cather's
"mystical concern with pots and pans" in her "later books" was
"not . . . very far from the gaudy domesticity of bourgeois accumulation glorified in the *Woman's Home Companion*" (Scrhoeter 154–55).
Although these critics exempted *My Ántonia* from their scorn, Cather's
oeuvre as a whole suffered in terms of highbrow prestige.

In contrast, Aldrich's consistent public positioning of herself as a
market-oriented author openly invited such dismissals. She traveled
to Hollywood repeatedly, trying to interest producers in her works.
She was delighted with *Cheers for Miss Bishop,* the 1941 adaptation
of *Miss Bishop* (1933), and one of the great regrets of her career was
that *Lantern* was never adapted for film (Meier 86ff). She was also
enthusiastic about the Pocket Books paperback of *A Lantern in Her
Hand,* which was printed in an edition of 275,000 copies in 1947,
nearly twenty years after its first publication (Rapport) (she attempted
to use the sale of the Pocket Books edition to entice Hollywood, but
to no avail [Brown]). Cather's experiences as a teacher made her resist
circulation of her works in formats meant for students, but Aldrich's
teaching career left her with no such reservations. She embraced
the use of *A Lantern in Her Hand* in classrooms, authorizing an
educational edition and expressing pride that the novel served as
supplementary reading in Nebraska high school history classrooms
because of its historical accuracy ("Story Behind" ix). Tellingly,

however, Aldrich's novel found its way into high school, not college and university, classrooms.[13]

So what was the source of the eventual rise of Cather's stock in the prestige economy and the accession of *My Ántonia* into the canon of literary texts taught at the postsecondary level? Deborah Lindsay Williams has argued that Cather's refusal to affiliate herself publicly with women authors who were her contemporaries underwrote Cather's eventual reclamation for the canon. I believe Cather's public disavowals of the popular taste just as she first hit the bestseller lists with *One of Ours* similarly preserved her availability for recuperation because such disavowals have encouraged critics in the past two decades to read her as a literary modernist. "The Novel Démeumblé," her screed against commercialism and the popular taste, now appears in the *Norton Anthology* as one of a group of "Modernist Manifestos."[14] In contrast, Aldrich's avowed market orientation and her embrace of the tastes of a mass audience made it easy for academic readers to dismiss her as a sentimental hack.

As Pierre Bourdieu argues, in the field of cultural production the most prestige and cultural capital accrues to artists who position themselves as producing for the sake of art and refusing to compromise to the demands of a broad audience, while the least prestige accrues to "the 'popular'" that derives its "consecration" from "the choice of ordinary consumers, the 'mass audience'" (51). Behind the scenes, Cather was nearly as engaged with "ordinary consumers" as Aldrich, but her seemingly unambivalent disavowals *in public* appealed to the values of those who evaluate literature professionally.[15] Yet nonacademic readers imagined—and continue to imagine—the pioneer era through their deep attachments to Ántonia and Abbie as their "friends." What if academic readers conceive of these sentimental attachments of middlebrow readers to Cather's and Aldrich's novels as a source of value, a reason to "consecrate" both *My Ántonia* and *A Lantern in Her Hand* as meriting serious attention? Read the paeans to *A Lantern in Her Hand* posted by readers on Amazon.com, teach it to your students, take their sentiments seriously, and perhaps dare to let your own sentiments be engaged, just as you do with Cather's pioneer fiction.

NOTES

*Thanks to the staff of Archives and Special Collections at the University of Nebraska-Lincoln's Love Library and of the Nebraska State Historical Society. Thanks as well to the following scholars for their help and advice and for sharing resources: Jaime Harker, Molly O'Hagan Hardy, Mark Madigan, and Vicki Martin.

1. Sales figures are drawn from Cather's "Bank Book," in which she entered both the amount paid and sales numbers reported by publishers.

2. For typical dismissive characterizations of Aldrich as "sentimental," see Meyer (68–9, 200) and Western Literature Association's *Literary History* (652); Cather receives extended, laudatory treatment in both. Aldrich receives passing attention in broad thematic surveys (e.g., Fairbanks, Quantic, and Raub). Although I have sought out original materials, Peterson's biography was an essential guide in my research. In *Updating the Literary West,* the Western Literature Association notes in passing the availability of Peterson's biography and the Bison Books edition of *Lantern* (644, 674) while devoting an entire chapter to the most recent decade of Cather scholarship.

3. Because Cather's will prohibits direct quotation from her unpublished letters, I quote O'Brien's paraphrase.

4. Harker foregrounds the progressive politics of her subjects, which Aldrich and Cather did not share, but she makes clear that middlebrow authorship was not exclusively progressive (20).

5. For recent analyses of Cather in women's magazines and her negotiations with editors and agents, see Bucker and Roorda. For women's magazines as middlebrow, see Harker (chap. 1).

6. On Cather's friendship with Woollcott, see Chinery (286–89). Note, however, that she mischaracterizes Cather's opposition to being drawn into Woollcott's radio program (287)—Cather objected only to her works being *read aloud,* not to being the subject of comment.

7. On D. Appleton's enthusiastic pursuit of BOMC main selection status for *Lantern,* see Jewett. Lee documents main selections for the 1920s through the 1940s, but not alternates. A review of the *BOMC News* located no reference to Aldrich's books.

8. It is impossible to know whether Cather actually *received* fewer fan letters than Aldrich, or whether she saved fewer, or Edith Lewis or Cather's family preserved fewer after her death. During her lifetime, Cather seems to have *preserved* more letters related to *One of Ours*—in a letter to Carrie Miner Sherwood, Lewis describes letters from soldiers about *One of Ours* as having filled "one small suitcase" while Cather discarded other letters. Furthermore, in her memoir of Cather, Lewis briefly quotes from a number of reader letters including letters about *Ántonia* that do not survive (186–88). Likewise, clearly only a fraction of Aldrich's reader letters survive. Many letters reference earlier letters not extant, for instance. In June 2008, too late to be included in this study, more than seventy-five previously unknown fan letters to Cather were donated to the Susan J. Rososwski Collection at the University of Nebraska-Lincoln Archives and Special Collections.

9. Both Radway and Parchesky conceive of middlebrow readers in narrow class terms—for Radway, the professional managerial class (such as Cather's bank president brother Roscoe), for Parchesky the new middle class (especially teachers). Reader letters to Aldrich suggest that people from a much broader range of class positions employed middlebrow reading practices.

10. See Greer for the deployment of this same trope by working class women who studied in Bryn Mawr College's summer program, as well as the nineteenth-century precedents for it. See also Ryan for fan letters to Gene Stratton Porter, another regional novelist with devoted readers.

11. O'Brien also depicts Cather as "refus[ing] to allow her books to be adopted by book clubs" as part of her resistance to any force that would "force" readers to read her books (122, 121). However, Madigan's recovery of the range of Cather's engagements with the BOMC complicates this picture. I would also add that Rubin's and Radway's work on the BOMC and the middlebrow sharply distinguishes the judgments of middlebrow cultural authorities from academic ones.

12. As Chinery notes, this edition likely led to hundreds of fan letters to Cather about *Ántonia* that have not survived (293).

13. Dorothy Canfield Fisher and Pearl Buck shared the same fate, transformed into "adolescent literature" and "K-12 staples" (Harker 152).

14. Modernist antagonism toward mass culture has spawned a vast scholarly literature. See Botshon and Goldsmith for a summary and the implications for the middlebrow.

15. Even in private, Cather evidenced some ambivalence about popularity. Writing to her brother, she simultaneously embraced and distanced herself from her own popularity, saying that she didn't think a really good writer could be popular in his own lifetime.

WORKS CITED

Aldrich, Bess Streeter. "How I Mixed Stories with Doughnuts." In *Collected Short Works, 1920–1954*, edited by Carol Miles Peterson, 33–42. Lincoln: University of Nebraska Press, 1999.

———. *A Lantern in Her Hand*. 1928. Lincoln: University of Nebraska Press, 1994.

———. [The Pioneer in Fiction]. Ts of radio address, 1925. Aldrich Papers.

———. "The Story Behind *A Lantern in Her Hand*." 1952. In *A Lantern in Her Hand*, v–ix.

———. Untitled. "Nebraska History in Nebraska Novels." Transcript draft of speech, ca. 1929. Aldrich Papers.

———. Untitled. Ts. draft of speech to Nebraska Writers Guild [?], ca. 1931. Aldrich papers.

————. "Wild Critics I Have Known." *Bookman* November 1930: 72–73.

Blom, Anna. Letter to BSA. 19 May 1943.

Bloom, Sarah J. [Willa Cather's secretary]. Letter to Roscoe Cather. [14 Mar. 1935]. R & M Cather.

Botshon, Lisa, and Meredith Goldsmith. "Introduction." In *Middlebrow Moderns: Popular American Women Writers of the 1920s*, edited by Lisa Botshon and Meredith Goldsmith, 3–21. Boston: Northeastern University Press, 2003.

Bourdieu, Pierre. *The Field of Cultural Production: Essays on Art and Literature*. Edited by Ronald Johnson. New York: Columbia University Press, 1993.

Brand, Thelma Taby. Letter to BSA. n.d. [after 1935].

Brennan, Mary. Letter to BSA. 10 November 1935.

Brown, Ned. Letter to BSA. 11 September 1947.

Bucker, Park. "'That Kitchen with the Shining Windows': Willa Cather's 'Neighbour Rosicky' and the *Woman's Home Companion*. In *Willa Cather & Material Culture: Real-World Writing, Writing the Real World*, edited by Janis P. Stout, 66–112. Tuscaloosa: University of Alabama Press, 2005.

Cain, Mrs. Charles. Letter to BSA. 30 January 1935.

Campbell, Lola A. Letter to BSA. 18 March 1935.

Cather, Charles. Letter to WC (fragment). [1918]. Southwick.

Cather, Willa. Bank Book 1913–30. Rosowski.

————. Letter to Roscoe Cather. 8 December [1918]. R & M Cather.

————. Letter to Roscoe Cather. 11 January [1934]. R & M Cather.

————. *My Ántonia*. 1918. Willa Cather Scholarly Edition. Lincoln: University of Nebraska Press, 1994.

————. "The Novel Démeumblé." *Not Under Forty*. New York: Knopf, 1936.

Chessman, Hallie L. Letter to BSA. 16 January 1935.

Chinery, Mary. "Wartime Fictions: Willa Cather, the Armed Services Editions, and the Unspeakable Second World War." In *Cather Studies: History, Memory, and War*, edited by Steven Trout, 285–96. Lincoln: University of Nebraska Press, 2006.

Curran, John. Letter to WC. 18 February 1936. Rosowski.

Dobson, Joanne. "Reclaiming Sentimental Literature." *American Literature* 69.2 (1997): 263–88.

Fairbanks, Carol. *Prairie Women: Images in American and Canadian Fiction*. New Haven, CT: Yale University Press, 1986.

Fey, Harold E. Letter to BSA. 27 April 1931.

Greenslet, Ferris. Letter to WC. 27 October 1921. Rosowski.

Greer, Jane. "'Ornaments, Tools, or Friends': Literary Reading at the Bryn Mawr Summer School for Women Workers, 1921–1938. In Ryan and Thomas. 179–98.

Harker, Jaime. *America the Middlebrow: Women's Novels, Progressivism, and Middlebrow Authorship Between the Wars*. Amherst: University of Massachusetts Press, 2007.

Knight, Denise D. "'I Try to Make the Reader Feel': The Resurrection of Bess Streeter Aldrich's *A Lantern in Her Hand* and the Politics of the Literary Canon." In *Separate Spheres No More: Gender Convergence in American Literature, 1830–1930,* edited by Monika M. Elbert, 282–96. Tuscaloosa: University of Alabama Press, 2000.

Lee, Charles. *The Hidden Public: The Story of the Book-of-the-Month Club.* New York: Doubleday, 1958.

Lewis, Edith. Letter to Carrie Miner Sherwood. 19 December [195-]. Willa Cather Foundation, Red Cloud, NE.

———. *Willa Cather Living: A Personal Record.* New York: Knopf, 1953.

Madigan, Mark. "Willa Cather and the Book-of-the-Month Club." In *Cather Studies: Willa Cather as Cultural Icon,* edited by Guy Reynolds, 68–85. Lincoln: University of Nebraska Press, 2007.

Matters, Thomas H. Jrs. Letter to BSA. 6 April 1935.

Meier, A. Mabel. "Bess Streeter Aldrich: A Literary Portrait." *Nebraska History* 50.1 (1969): 66–100.

Meyer, Roy W. *The Middle Western Farm Novel in the Twentieth Century.* Lincoln: University of Nebraska Press, 1965.

Nugent, Walter. *Into the West: The Story of Its People.* New York: Vintage, 1999.

O'Brien, Sharon. "Becoming Noncanonical: The Case against Willa Cather." *American Quarterly* 40.1 (1988): 110–26.

Parchesky, Jennifer. "'You Makes Us Articulate': Reading, Education, and Community in Dorothy Canfield's Middlebrow America." In Ryan and Thomas. 229–58.

Peterson, Carol Miles. *Bess Streeter Aldrich: The Dreams Are Real.* Lincoln: University of Nebraska Press, 1995.

———. "Introduction." *The Collected Short Works, 1907–1919,* edited by Bess Streeter Aldrich, vii–xiv. Lincoln: University of Nebraska Press, 1995.

Quantic, Diane Dufva. *The Nature of Place: A Study of Great Plains Fiction.* Lincoln: University of Nebraska Press, 1995.

Radway, Janice A. *A Feeling for Books: The Book-of-the-Month Club, Literary Taste, and Middle-Class Desire.* Chapel Hill: University of North Carolina Press, 1997.

———. "Research Universities, Periodical Publication, and the Circulation of Professional Expertise: On the Significance of Middlebrow Authority." *Critical Inquiry* 31.1 (2004): 203–28.

Rapport, Samuel. Letter to BSA. 3 September 1947.

Raub, Patricia. *Yesterday's Stories: Popular Women's Novels of the Twenties and Thirties.* Westport, CT: Greenwood, 1994.

Reid, Agnes Just. Letter to BSA. 7 December 1947.

Roorda, Rebecca. "Willa Cather in the Magazines: 'The Business of Art.'" *Willa Cather Newsletter & Review* 44.3 (2001): 71–75.

Rubin, Joan Shelley. *The Making of Middlebrow Culture.* Chapel Hill: University of North Carolina Press, 1992.

Ryan, Barbara. "'A Real Basis from Which to Judge': Fan Mail to Gene Stratton-Porter." In Ryan and Thomas. 161–78.

Ryan, Barbara, and Amy Thomas, eds. *Reading Acts: U. S. Readers' Interactions with Literature, 1800–1950.* Knoxville: University of Tennessee Press, 2002.

Schroeter, James, ed. *Willa Cather and Her Critics.* Ithaca: Cornell University Press, 1967.

Schueth, Michael. "Taking Liberties: Willa Cather and the 1934 Film Adaptation of *A Lost Lady.*" In *Willa Cather and Material Culture: Real-World Writing, Writing the Real World,* edited by Janis P. Stout, 113–24. Tuscaloosa: University of Alabama Press, 2005.

Walker, Vivian. Letter to BSA. 10 February 1937.

Waterman, Jayne. "Louis Bromfield and the Idea of the Middle." *Midamerica: The Yearbook for the Study of Midwestern Literature* 30 (2003): 73–84.

Western Literature Association. *A Literary History of the American West.* Forth Worth: Texas Christian University Press, 1987.

———. *Updating the Literary West.* Forth Worth: Texas Christian University Press, 1997.

Williams, Deborah Lindsay. *Not in Sisterhood: Edith Wharton, Willa Cather, Zona Gale, and the Politics of Female Authorship.* New York: Palgrave Macmillan, 2001.

Williams, J. L. B. Letters to BSA. 5 November 1928 and 25 January 1929.

Winters, Emerson. Letter to WC. 2 November 1940. Southwick.

Wiseman, Mrs. Arthur. Letter to BSA. [1936].

In citations for letters, Willa Cather as recipient is abbreviated as WC and Bess Streeter Aldrich as BSA. All letters to Bess Streeter Aldrich are from the Bess Streeter Aldrich Papers, Nebraska State Historical Society Library, Lincoln, NE. The following abbreviations are used for other archival collections, all at the University of Nebraska-Lincoln Archives and Special Collections:

R & M Cather: Roscoe and Meta Cather Collection.

Rosowski: James R. and Susan J. Rosowski Collection.

Southwick: Philip L. and Helen Cather Southwick Collection.

PART II

INTERSECTING STORIES: THE WORKING-CLASS WEST

CHAPTER 5

INDIGENOUS WAYS OF
KNOWING CAPITALISM IN
SIMON ORTIZ'S *FIGHT BACK*

Reginald Dyck

just another worker,
just another Indian.

—*Simon Ortiz, "What I Meant"*

What other Native poet besides Simon Ortiz has more than glanced at the structural causes of poverty, looked closely at work culture, seen a connection between Indians and unions, and named both the causes and costs of economic exploitation? What other collection besides *Fight Back: For the Sake of the People, for the Sake of the Land* critiques capitalism as having values antithetical to Native survival? We need to read this text as a radical political document, powerful both in its language and vision. Imaginatively using a range of literary forms, Ortiz exposes capitalism's impact on workers, their families, the Acoma community, and the United States as a whole.[1] The poems and prose pieces depict the racial and economic exploitation Native peoples continue to experience, but they also celebrate the people's continuance. While addressing issues of identity and tradition common to much contemporary Native literature, *Fight Back* distinguishes itself by doing this with a structural critique of economic relations and work culture.

The original 1980 edition is regrettably no longer in print. Thankfully, the 1992 Sun Tracks edition of *Woven Stone,* a collection of three books, has kept *Fight Back* in bookstores, classrooms, and in readers' hands, even if it puts a glossy veneer on it. Missing, however, is the large-font dedication to the warriors of the 1680 Pueblo Revolt. Also left out is Roxanne Dunbar Ortiz's preface, which emphasizes connections between the 1680 resistance movement and contemporary struggles addressed by the poetry and prose that followed. Dunbar Ortiz exclaims, "The real heroes of Indian resistance are portrayed here, and, we believe, they would find Popé and other revolutionaries of 1680 very much like themselves, workers fighting for freedom, for liberation and for decent, healthy lives" (n. pag.).

The cover of the 1992 volume does seem appropriate for the collection's title, *Woven Stone.* The beautiful photograph of sinuous, sensuous canyon walls looks peacefully modernist, almost abstract in the manner of Edward Weston. Yet it calls to mind the Depression era quote by photographer Cartier-Bresson: "The whole world is going to pieces and people like Adams and Weston are photographing rocks." The photo naturalizes the title's reference to a wall properly built by ancient workers ("A Story of How a Wall Stands" 145). Hard labor and traditional skills, examples of the human efforts Ortiz emphasizes in these poems, are elided as the photo celebrates the beauty of natural processes.

The original cover of *Fight Back,* as well as the other jagged illustrations by the Acoma artist and activist Maurus Chino, suggests a different idea. The drawings offer rough folk-like depictions of people who suffer and struggle to fight back. The cover illustration sketches a miner bent over, deep in a mine shaft, digging into the earth. The dark red color of the cover evokes the Red Power of Native resistance or the Red of a revolution that challenges the economic structures and the alienated life capitalism has imposed on indigenous cultures. Rather than a poetry chapbook, the original edition feels like an instruction manual for an insurgency or a strategy document hammered out late at night and carried in a worker's back pocket to a picket line.

The new edition gives no original publication date to situate this poetic report. Also, leaving out the 1980 publication date along with the dedication elides the connection between the present call to action and the Pueblo Revolt of 1680. Rather, the record is gentrified through omission, as in the concluding biographical description: "[Ortiz] eloquently expresses the living story of his people, a story often marred by social, political and economic conflicts with Anglo American society." As the poems make clear, the Acoma people and the nation have been much more than "marred." Yet the Sun Tracks edition does keep *Fight Back* alive and available for readers, provides the context of Ortiz's two earlier works, and includes an introduction by Ortiz that offers a courageous account of his life and work. Ortiz here makes a major statement on language, history, art, and politics. Part of that statement, in a section called "Being and Reality," is a dialectical investigation of uranium mining, the immediate struggle that *Fight Back* engages. This mining, Ortiz notes, brought to the area modern corporate industrialism. Because so many were facing unemployment, Pueblo workers provided an inexpensive source of labor (22). Although wage work offered an antidote to poverty, the workers became dependent not just on wages but also on "purchasable satisfaction and comfort" (23). For the Acoma Pueblo, the powerful mining system left them feeling politically eviscerated, powerless to challenge its dominance. "As a young working man . . . I was angry," Ortiz explains (24). Many people were angry during this time of civil rights struggle, political assassinations, wars of liberation, and oppressed people's "demand for social, economic, and political changes" (25). Linking these struggles, Ortiz sees a long history of fighting back. For Pueblo peoples, that history is embodied in the Pueblo Revolt of 1680. Yet this history, too, is enmeshed in a broader, hemispheric process of challenging "the European urge for domination, compounded by capitalism's quest for profit, [which] overwhelmed and submerged everything and everyone not only with language, philosophy, behavior, economy, government but with violence and brute force when rhetorical persuasion failed" (29).

As a means of continuance, Ortiz in the new introduction calls for a broad vision for indigenous people: "Fighting back is fighting on. . . . It must be a part of every aspect of Native American life and outlook" (31). For his people, the United States is an inescapable context and responsibility because he hopes that Native writing can help the country "to go beyond survival" (33). This is the challenge of Ortiz's writing, *Fight Back* in particular.

* * *

In commemoration of the Pueblo Revolt of 1680
and our warrior Grandmothers and Grandfathers

With this dedication, the 1980 edition of *Fight Back* links the Pueblo Revolt to a continuance of resistance. The original preface by Dunbar Ortiz helps build the connection between the Revolt and the uranium mine workers' struggles of the 1960s and 1970s. Dunbar Ortiz also published a book on the Revolt's tercentennial, *Roots of Resistance: Land Tenure in New Mexico, 1680–1980.* Her introduction and conclusion offer a useful context for *Fight Back.* Dunbar Ortiz argues that although Spanish conquest had a deep impact on the Pueblos, it was U.S. capitalism that threatened their very survival. Land was the basis for the new U.S. form of colonialism (2). Having had their land turned into a commodity and sold to settlers, the Pueblo people as agricultural producers lost their means of providing for themselves. Instead, they began to serve outside agricultural interests as "a surplus, cheap labor force, dependent on capital for their existence" (5). Similarly, as Kerr-McGee and other corporations developed mines and processing plants, Navajo and Pueblo Indians, having few other options, became an important part of the uranium industry workforce.

Dunbar Ortiz recognizes that social and economic relations to the land are related. A people cannot maintain their culture without the necessary resources to sustain themselves economically. She adds that control of land and water "are related to both resistance to colonialism and cultural integrity" (*Roots* 128–29). This struggle against colonialism is a class struggle, Dunbar Ortiz argues: "The most powerful corporations in the world, often in collusion with elements in the federal and state governments, extract mineral and other natural resources, as well as the surplus value from cheap labor, reaping fantastic profits and destroying the delicate environment." The fight against this exploitation has significance not just for the Southwest, Dunbar Ortiz claims, but also for "the national socioeconomic development" (131).

Using a variety of forms, *Fight Back* makes a similar argument. Ortiz bluntly states that to create change, people need to grasp the underlying causes of injustice. Rather than shadowboxing with superficial manifestations, "they will have to be willing to identify capitalism for what it is, that it is destructive and uncompassionate and deceptive" (361).[2] Not surprisingly, his analysis of the 1680 revolt is in part economic. The people were "commonly impoverished" and "forced to submit to the control of the wealthy." Their "liberation struggle" successfully expelled "the destroyers and the thieves" (347). The thievery continued in Ortiz's father's generation as the railroads took water and land from the people. This forced a transformation in work and culture as people had to give up traditional agricultural production for wage labor. With the next generation, Ortiz's, the uranium mines and processing plants became the sites of alienated labor and the cause of the land's further destruction (343–44).[3] *Fight Back* comes out of Ortiz's own experience as a member of the Acoma people, as the son of a railroad maintenance worker, and as a blue-collar worker in the uranium industry. In considering this work history, Ortiz reaches a broad conclusion:

> The American poor and the workers and white middleclass, who are probably the most ignorant of all U.S. citizens, must understand how they, like Indian people, are forced to serve a national interest, controlled by capitalist vested interests in collusion with U.S. policy makers. . . . Only then will there be no more unnecessary sacrifices of our people and land. (361)

Only by having the courage to struggle against these exploiters "will we know what love and compassion are" (363). One of Ortiz's great strengths is that his work integrates the present experiences of the Pueblo people with both their own history and the dominant socio-economic structures that have impacted their history. Ortiz creates this poetic, political integration "for the sake of the people, for the sake of the land."

*   *   *

Another important strength of Ortiz's work is the serious attention it gives to work itself and the meanings particular cultures create for it. Focusing with sympathy and respect on working-class characters, Ortiz takes seriously the hardships they experience in changing work situations. Thus he strategically links the Pueblo revolt and the railroad work to the conditions of uranium mining and processing workers. In the preface, Dunbar Ortiz extends the connections even further: "How is it then, that Indians are rarely viewed as workers? . . . [T]he war dancer at the pow wow, the singers around the drum, the Navajo woman in velvet and silver, the AIM speaker, the wise medicine man or woman, all are workers most of their waking hours and most of their lives." *Fight Back* clearly presents this perspective of Indians as workers.

Ortiz opens *Fight Back* with an invocation, "*Hanoh Kuutsenaih/ Hahtse Kuutseniah*," "the People's fight back is critical" (287, see 293). What follows makes clear why. Yet, before the narrative poems and prose set forth the exploitative working conditions and land use, Ortiz offers a "Mid-America Prayer" (289–90). The title's reference is not to geography but to cultural values. The struggle is for the heart of the Acoma Pueblo nation, damaged by the economic values of another nation. Both nations need healing, which will only come by challenging the status quo. For Ortiz, fighting back means "standing again/within and among all things" and being responsible in that relationship (1–2, 21–22). At stake is "the continuance of life" (29). This prayer evokes a necessary cosmic context for daily struggles. Having offered this prayer, the poet rolls up his sleeves and gets to writing about work.

In the opening, Ortiz states, "The songs, stories, poems and advice will always remember/my father, mother, and my people" (287, 3–4). While the whole book can be read as advice about fighting back, the only overt advice given is the father's admonition that his sons should "never work for the railroad" (293). Ortiz followed his father's advice, instead finding work closer to home at a uranium mine and processing plant. The first and longest of the book's two sections, "Too Many Sacrifices," is interspersed with poems in which the son tells his father's story. These justify the advice against the railroad work and remind us that the uranium workers' stories are not isolated but part of a history of systemic exploitation. The fight back, as Ortiz concludes, needs to address more than just immediate grievances.

In recalling his father's experiences, Ortiz presents what Patricia Albers calls "the communicative context of labor and laboring" (112). Albers alerts us to the importance of understanding not only the material conditions of work but also the meanings people give to it; that is, individual experiences are shaped not only by the work conditions of their specific job but also by the ways their communities conceptualize work, consciously and unconsciously. The picture of blue-collar workers and their manual labor in *Fight Back* has little to do with what we usually see in beer or truck commercials. The "communicative context" does not focus on the camaraderie and authenticity of "real" work as opposed to white-collar office work. Characters do no talk about pride in a job well done or the masculine reassurance of physical strength. Instead, Ortiz opens the section "Too Many Sacrifices" with his father's advice against the "grueling labor" of railroad work.

This theme of alienated labor is picked up again as Ortiz returns to railroad work in "Final Solution: Jobs, Leaving" (318–20) midway through this section. Here too, physical work conditions are described as brutal, but the emphasis has changed because the point of view is no longer that of the workers themselves but of the family members left behind. Work here is a family and community affair. The poem's title and the opening leave-taking evoke the trains of Nazi Germany carrying racial outcasts to the death camps. This comparison makes a harsh indictment. The form of internment, however, is different here. "Surrounded by the United States," the men felt trapped by an increasing need to make money in order to survive (13–14). The poem describes the family consequences of wage labor as fathers traveled to "Utah/California/Idaho/Oregon" to make a so-called living. For the children, their fathers' leaving "seemed always, always, so final" (3). The paradoxical repetition emphasizes a child's limited perspective. Some, though, never did return as a result of work-related deaths or because of desertion when the silence and anger of those they left behind became too much to bear. The father's letter home teaches the lesson of "Mid-American Prayer," that the family should be "in a relationship that is responsible" (Fast 171). Yet the following lines of the poem about the father's failings make clear how difficult the separation makes this.

The poem's collage of voices and styles captures the range of emotions the wives experienced: hatred, hope, longing, and desperation—all registered in the silence of repression. "Final Solution" concludes with a short history lesson, the moral of the story: the women would wait again for weeks or months but never again for years. Ortiz brings up the theme of waiting again in *Fight Back*'s second and final section, "No More Sacrifices." Writing about the Pueblo Revolt of 1680, he states, "It took years of tolerance before it became crucial to organize resistance—a liberation struggle—against the oppressor" (347). Yet Ortiz's point is that the waiting needs to end; it is time to fight back. The people must depend on their own strength, the poem concludes: "The woman anger and courage risen as the People's voice again" (320), "again" because it has happened before.

Two poems near the end of "Too Many Sacrifices" offer alternative, generational responses to the call for action of "Final Solution." The poem "Mama's and Daddy's Words" (329–30) seems an earnest but muddled response. Mama's words, if we can find them, are certainly different from the "woman anger and courage" of "Final Solution." The poem reads more like the father's justification for his generation's strategy of resistance than an exhortation to the next. The list of jobs the speaker (singular) has done, combined with his words of wisdom, "But you have to fight/by working" (19–20), seem an easy and common criticism of the young for their unwillingness to work hard like their fathers. In response to "back breaking/. . . low pay[ing]" work and racist conditions, the speaker only offers more work as a solution

(12–24). The goal is "that they'll learn" (34). The "they," like the "them" earlier in the poem ("hard / to put up with them" 15–16), presumably refers to those who make the racist comments and create the harsh working conditions. By working responsibly, even if at bottom-level jobs, Indian workers will challenge stereotypes and teach people the positive truths about themselves, the poem suggests. Even if dressed up as "work[ing] for the People and the Land" (24), which the railroad job must have been for many Acoma workers, this seems a naive and passive strategy in light of the next generation's Red Power movement and AIM (American Indian Movement) confrontations. One might read "Mama's and Daddy's Words" as a gentle critique of the past generation. Yet the poem's use of the Acoma language and hortatory earnestness seems inconsistent with this interpretation. The poem's disjuncture may register Ortiz's respect for the sacrifices his family and many others had to make while also questioning their strategy of resistance. Doing your best at work and then waiting for change is not enough, yet we must recognize that the blame for waiting falls much more heavily on the system that entrapped their father's generation than on the men themselves. Nevertheless, Ortiz recognizes that more direct ways of fighting back are necessary.

The following poem, "Returning It Back, You Will Go On," does actively challenge economic exploitation by presenting a Native alternative (330–31). The broad indictment of land theft and abuse reaches from corporations and companies to the people who work in them, "all of them—all of America" (20). For Ortiz, they all are guilty. In contrast to U.S. exploitation of land and people, the speaker calls for a return to traditional relationships based on reciprocity. The theme of fighting back returns as the conclusion presents the consequences of failing to change exploitative practices. In warning us of the future, this conclusion suggests an explanation for present conditions. Jails are full of Indians because they have been exploited and excluded. The implicit solution is not merely individual responsibility—although one imagines Ortiz would not deny that—but a reversal of the theft perpetrated by all Americans (26–28). Systemic problems require systemic changes. In the last lines, the city jail becomes a metaphor for the repressive regimes that control American Indians. Echoing the biblical language of resurrection to new life and using the grammatical certainty of prophecy, the poem concludes, "They will have risen" (54). Risen, that is, from their oppressor's jails to fight back. That, rather than waiting, will save the people.

With this same confident spirit, Ortiz returns to his father in the next poem, "This Song: Beating the Heartbeat" (332–33). It is the last narrative before the final incantation of "Too Many Sacrifices." These concluding poems emphasize the economic exploitation, work abuses, family struggles, and loss of land that make the fight back an economic and cultural necessity. "This Song" places the struggle in a cosmic context. No longer struggling under oppressive work conditions, the father now faces something more elemental, his journey "back north." Through the modern technology of an oscilloscope, the speaker links his father's life to his own and to the "continuing earth life." The concluding lines of this poem and the next echo the prophetic certainty of the ending to "Returning It Back." Its repetition of "They will have risen" becomes, in these poems, "We shall know living." This link also gives the title, "Returning It Back, You Will Go On," a new personal meaning as the son anticipates his father's death.

The final poem, "It Will Come; It Will Come," asserts that "we shall have victory" (18). Opening with the sacrifices made by railroad workers, "Too Many Sacrifices" closes with a song of continuance that echoes traditional chants. The poems describing the father's generation focus less on the immediate experience of hard physical labor, low wages, or bad bosses than on the effects of leaving the Acoma community because their families must participate in a money economy. The work results in anger, but from the worker's wives rather than from the workers themselves. This is the background and context for the next generation's experience of work. Uranium mining and processing exacerbated the exploitation of the Acoma land and people as work became available, for better and for worse, much closer to home. Different work situations resulted in new meanings or conceptualizations for the Indian working class who earned their living at the bottom of the uranium industry. Although Ortiz himself spent eighteen months doing this work, these poems also seldom dwell on specific work conditions. Instead, they narrate changing cultural conditions that result from the impositions of this new industry. The social context is different for this generation as well. It witnessed the traumas and victories of the civil rights movement, registered the divisive impact of the Vietnam War, and experienced the dramatic shifts taking place in U.S. culture. Yet beneath these generational experiences and changing work conditions remained the Acoma culture, changing with the times yet rooted in its tradition and its land.

*   *   *

Ortiz provides social context for his generation in an autobiographical essay "Always the Stories," written four years after *Fight Back*. Like the other Acoma, Laguna, and Navajo uranium workers, he too was hired as "cheap labor" because his family was poor, the mines were on or near their land, and few other work options were available (67). Writing about his experience twenty years later, Ortiz explains, he created a book that "is a political statement in thrust, nature and intent. . . . Its viewpoints, perceptions, ideas are expressed in the spirit of the protest, resistance, political literature of the Civil Rights-Third World-Vietnam War years" (67). In *Fight Back* he fulfills what he later asserts is Native writers' "responsibility to advocate for their people's self-government, sovereignty, and control of land and natural resources" ("Towards a National Indian Literature" 68).

While the poems about Ortiz's father's work for the railroad give historical background for the political work of Fight *Back,* the ones about Native uranium industry workers make up the bulk of "Too Many Sacrifices." They engage two related issues, exploitation and resistance. Around each is a cluster of ideas addressed in the poems.

The narrative poems of "Too Many Sacrifices" link economic and social exploitation, or class and race, often through stories of individual actions embedded in social structures. "Ray's Story" is an example (299–303). By invoking the narrator rather than the protagonist, the title calls attention to its "communicative context" (Albers 112) and alerts us to the complexity of this seemingly straightforward account. In presenting within a layered narrative the details of the protagonist Lacey's job, Ortiz reveals the competing meanings different groups give to his working conditions.

Details make clear that Lacey is stuck in a bottom rung, dead-end job that is unhealthy, dirty, and dangerous. Ray has heard the story about Lacey and is retelling it to another Indian worker who doesn't know the details of ore processing but does understand exploitative work conditions. For example, Ray notes that the company report may or may not have stated Lacey's cause of death, yet either way, he assumes his listener knows the real causes. He is killed while operating an ore-crushing machine because the shift foreman is driven by production demands, the safety engineer is caught in a system of complicity, the company values profits above worker safety, and because Lacey is an Indian. To the foreman and the "guys on shift afterwards," Lacey is only identified as an Indian (152, 140). Actually he is not even that; to them he is just a good story. Their version comfortably reduces the exploitation and real suffering of Ray's story to a crude sexual joke.

These non-Indians' attitude toward an Indian worker's death ironically underscores the dehumanization they themselves experience as workers. Even if some receive better pay, work structures reduce them all to parts of a crushing machine ("appendages to the machine" is Karl Marx's telling phrase) that do the machine's bidding. Yet, by distinguishing themselves racially, rather than as workers with interests different from the corporation's, these non-Indian workers disguise their own oppression. Their easy racism makes it easier for them to justify their complicity and thus for the company to keep workers like Lacey at the bottom, the ones who get killed or more ruthlessly exploited.

Everyday racism, however, usually has less overtly destructive consequences in these poems. It grinds more finely. While not directly telling a story about work, "Out to Tsaile Lake" (304–6) shows that attitudes expressed at work are pervasive in society. It also suggests that Indian camaraderie can include worker solidarity. Ortiz masterfully uses ordinary details to capture everyday racism. When the speaker asks a friendly question of a couple, the woman builds a racial barrier as she calms down the "little white dog" by saying that "it's just an Indian" (5, 8). The man then abruptly states that they saw "a turrible wreck" on the way to the lake. Assuming it was only "some Indians," the man had felt no obligation to help, although there was "no ambulance in sight" (14, 16). "Don't fret yourself" (23), the woman tells the dog as they continue fishing on this reservation lake.

The speaker of "Out to Tsaile Lake" recognizes the conventional racism of the couple; he has apparently heard it all before and makes no response. His silence is his form of resistance. The Indian speaker in "First Hard Core" (306) experiences silence differently because he still has lessons to learn about confronting this country's racism. He has no answer to the racist assertions of his fellow worker Herb. He concludes his monologue by saying, "I just felt powerless to answer. / I just said I didn't know" (59–60). Knowledge, however, is not the speaker's problem since he knows that he wants to tell Herb that their mining jobs depend on his people's land having been stolen. Rather, the speaker is silenced, Ortiz implies, because behind Herb's hard-core racism is a whole system to be attacked. The racist and exploitative structures that give Herb the unconscious confidence, the assumed sense of superiority, to ask his questions are the forces that silence the young Indian speaker.

We see manifestations of the same cultural assumptions in "To Change in a Good Way" (308–16), which links Kerr-McGee's "screw[ing] those folks in New Mexico" to colonialist stories about folks in the past doing their duty "fighting off Indians to build

homes/on new land so we could live the way/we are right now,
advanced and safe" (286, 262–67). The resistance against corporate
exploitation is complicated by the fact that the folks back home do
not see the connection between racial and economic exploitation,
just as the non-Indian workers at the uranium processing plant
didn't in "Ray's Story." In fact Indians too, Ortiz acknowledges, can
be blinded by stereotypes. "Stuff: Chickens and Bombs" makes this
clear as the narrator is smartly awakened from his assumptions about
backcountry whites (320).

One of the most powerful poems in the book, "What I Mean" also
engages the struggle to express oneself while facing racial and economic exploitation (326). "Agee. I don't mean that Agee," is Ortiz's
sly opening line. With it he brings in the irony of James Agee's title
Now Let Us Praise Famous Men, along with the memory of Walker
Evans's photographs of destitute Alabama sharecroppers, trapped and
exploited by a different version of the same economic system. Maybe
because the Agee of the poem is a dropout from a "real American
way" high school (18) and so did not have his spirit crushed by it, he
is not afraid to speak out in the heart of white working-class country.
Innocuously named Grandma's Café, this place is avoided by the
speaker, an apparent high school graduate. To him the café was not
a safe place for Indians. With a sharp jab at an old stereotype, Ortiz's
speaker states:

> We didn't talk much.
> Some people say Indians are like that,
> Shy and reserved and polite,
> But that's mostly crap. Lots of times
> We were just plain scared
> And we kept our mouths shut.   (48–53)

They had a lot to say about stolen Acoma land, the poem explains,
but they feared for their safety.

In the introduction to the 1992 Sun Tracks edition, Ortiz offers
a biographical explanation of this silence: the power of the dominant
society's hegemony to silence the people it exploits. Eviscerating the
resistance of the oppressed, this hegemony creates in them a belief
that they lack control over their lives. Ortiz returns to this problem
of control throughout the essay. As a young person, he found the
outside world intimidating. "It was a Mericano world where people
were well off and in control," while the Acoma people were poor and,
so they were told, had to be taken care of by the government (11). An

outsider to the world of power and plenty, Ortiz grew up dreaming of "being respected and looked up to, being successful and rich" (16). He came to know the colonizing society better than his own colonized, indigenous culture (20); it was the only way of satisfying "this hunger for a semblance of control" (23). The speaker's fear in "What I Mean," his avoidance of the non-Indian workers at Grandma's Café, results from this systemic repression: "In an America . . . overwhelmingly present every day, in every social, political, cultural, economic psychological way, it's hard not to feel as if you're *confronting* a reality that's so powerful you can't expect it to recognize you" (26).

And yet as Agee's experiences suggest, hegemonic power is not absolute. Ortiz situates the poem during the uranium workers' strike of 1961. The "hero" is talking to the workers in the café about a union contract. Agee is the one who sees beyond the individual job that pays the bills. Because this makes him dangerous to the company, "they" have him killed. This is an Indian version of the Joe Hill story, and the message is similar. "What I Mean" becomes "what we mean" (105, 114) as the speaker sees a common structure of exploitation in workers' and Indians' struggles, in the resistance of "just another worker, / just another Indian" (101–2).

Similar to "What I Mean," many of the poems about uranium workers recognize that Indians are part of a larger workforce caught up in a common struggle. However, Ortiz does not minimize differences. "Starting at the Bottom" exposes the economically useful discrimination that keeps Indians in that position, just as "Ray's Story" did. Ortiz also recognizes that unions did not care any more than the company about Indian workers or issues (8–12). Yet, if that alienation leads to arrests for drunkenness and disorderly conduct so that the city jails become full of Indians, "Affirmative Action" suggests that the problems have broadened to oppressed workers from many ethnic groups (303). "Indians Sure Came in Handy" (296–97), Ortiz explains, as the mining corporations, in collaboration with the legal system, used jailed Indians to beat the unions and avoid the expense of creating safe working conditions. These Indians are part of the workforce Agee tries to organize during the strike of 1961. Without worker solidarity that included Indians, the town "just kept on booming" while workers were trampled.

Agee's death, or murder one might say, suggests the difficulty of creating organized, multiethnic resistance to the dominant power. Yet "To Change in a Good Way" offers hope for solidarity on a personal level, which is a beginning. Based on friendship, support, and respect, this solidarity develops further as white and Indian working-class characters come to see their common exploitation by the U.S. military establishment. Its imperialist war against Vietnam that kills an "Okie" mine worker's brother is linked to the Indian wars as well as to their present legacy of uranium mining, which exploits Indian land and greedily sends workers into unnecessary danger. The conclusion about "breaking up that clay dirt" suggests that a broader than just personal healing is possible (354).

In this poem and elsewhere, the concept of "The People" is extended without losing its specific tribal meaning. Ortiz develops a strategy that includes both nationalism and a broader Native solidarity. Indian beliefs, represented by white corn and a cornhusk bundle (189), hold an Acoma couple to their people, but traditional practices can be shared with non-Indians who need the same protection as they face related injuries. As part of the changing social context of work, Indian uranium industry workers experienced broader solidarity in a more confrontational struggle than the previous generation of railroad workers did. Facing continuity in the structures of economic and racial exploitation, the people find continuance in resistance as they extend into the future a struggle that goes back to the Pueblo Revolt of 1680.

*   *   *

In the second main section of *Fight Back,* "No More Sacrifices," Ortiz links personal and community history by interweaving the story of a pilgrimage up Srhakaiya, Mt. Taylor, with accounts of changing water and work conditions for the Acoma people. The narrative charts the transformation of a traditional, self-sufficient society into one experiencing dependency and poverty, water scarcity, colonial political relations, and other hardships. Yet the struggle to maintain traditions and resist exploitation also developed. This section powerfully continues the fight back.

Focusing on "Our Homeland, a National Sacrifice Area," the first piece in the second section, Tim Libretti's essay "The Other Proletarians: Native American Literature and Class Struggle" explains a double alienation Native people experience. It recognizes their demand that the land be returned as the desire exists for both "a nonalienated labor and a disalienated relationship to the land" (166). Ortiz's speaker uses the term "otherness" for this double-edged alienation (337). Both spiritual and material losses are embodied in the deterioration of the Pueblos' water. The struggle Ortiz advocates is not merely for a more equitable capitalism offering a higher economic standard of living. Libretti explains, "Here we can see the overlap of Marx and Ortiz in their valorizing of a qualitative wealth over quantitative monetary wealth and in their focus on imagining a world that genuinely serves people, in a way capitalism clearly does not, by recognizing their connection with both the land and others" (177). Both Marx and Ortiz help us imagine alternatives to the status quo. Native people, too often unrecognized as part of the working class, can offer others "the historical memory of an unalienated relationship with the land." Ortiz provides this in the poem's descriptions of the "material well being and spiritual integrity" of traditional Acoma society (Libretti 183). This vision is not an ideal projected into the future but a historical memory. Ortiz's presentation of that memory offers a "catalog of what the American poor and working class need to see, understand, and do" (183).

In presenting histories of water and of labor that represent a double-edged alienation, "No More Sacrifices" offers an elaboration of the narratives making up the first section of *Fight Back*. It provides historical analysis of the changes Acoma people have experienced. Structural causes are presented for the more individualized experiences described earlier. The "otherness" the speaker feels has its source in a series of representative social dislocations: foreign geographical names mark outsiders' claims to Indian land, museums and parks colonize Indian culture, natural springs that are now dry wells represent the depletion of life-sustaining resources, and strangers welcomed to the community have exploited the hospitality offered.

In the face of these different forms of destruction, Ortiz courageously raises the troubling question: Why haven't the people revolted against the U.S. intruders as they did against the Spanish (348)? Since change has always been part of Acoma culture, why have "the people [become] bewildered and often helpless and, at best, [are] only able to cope inadequately" with this new colonial power (351)? Ortiz explains that instead of revolting, they "blamed themselves" (347). The problem is that the people "could not name an enemy" (348). He, however, does name names as he analyzes this new colonialism: "The Aacqumeh hanoh [Acoma people] had never seen thieves like the Mericano before. They were so shrewd, talkative, even helpful, and so friendly they didn't look like thieves. . . . [T]he Aacqumeh hanoh like other Indians across the nation were in the hands of a ruthless, monopolistic U.S. empire" (347–48).

Similarly, Dunbar Ortiz states, "The US was the first and perhaps the only state ever formed for the sole purpose of capital accumulation" (*Indians* 278), and that this "accumulation" was dependent on land as a commodity (Dunbar Ortiz, *Roots* 2). The reservation system, the Allotment Act, and the Indian Wars were all part of the process of "claim[ing] eminent domain," Ortiz writes (350). The economics of land as a commodity, embedded in capitalism's relentless drive for profit, has been the basis for expropriation and exploitation of Indian land. Whether it was the railroads, the Atomic Energy Commission, or the mining corporations who took the land, the U.S. government has been in collusion with them (354–55). This continuing appropriation of Indian land and resources left less and less room for traditional subsistence agriculture and the culture it sustained. As a result wage labor became increasingly necessary for the Acoma people, with far-reaching, disorienting, and destructive consequences (351). The earlier poems offer specific examples of these consequences. Here Ortiz generalizes the personal and communal consequences of taking jobs in the uranium industry (357–58). In the *Woven Stone* Sun Tracks edition of *Fight Back*, Ortiz extends this story by a decade; as the uranium market dropped, workers were laid off. Downstream from the mines, people lacked water for the little agriculture that remained and had only contaminated drinking water for themselves (363).

The lesson Ortiz presents is not just for the Acoma people or Southwest Indians. The same system of "economic, social and political forces" that threaten Indian survival and quality of life "will surely destroy others" (360). In a sense, Indians are canaries in the U.S. mine.[4] Because their widespread poverty and special political status make them particularly vulnerable, Native peoples provide an early warning of a broader systems failure. Thus, as Ortiz asserts, all U.S. people need to understand that their own fate is bound up with the fate of Native peoples. In order to fight back, all must recognize the economic structures of capitalism, "destructive and uncompassionate and deceptive," with their profound social and cultural effects They must see that so-called national interests are actually capitalist interests that exploit rather than support them (361). For recognizing this, Native people's historical memory is crucial in providing both a lesson in what our capitalist system can do to all of us and an example of a lived alternative. By understanding and then accepting responsibility for our understanding, Ortiz insists, we make the decision to fight back (363).

*   *   *

While *Fight Back* has been recognized as Ortiz's most overtly political work, its politics have received little specific attention from critics.[5]

Their analysis has tended to do for the book what the *Woven* Stone edition does—make it more respectable and less provocative. Recognizing the political limits of much criticism of Native literature, Eric Cheyfitz uses Robert M. Nelson's essay in the *Handbook of Native American Literature* as an example of critics' failure to see Ortiz as an "anticolonialist" writer. Nelson "explicitly separate[s] the political from the cultural, centering the latter while marginalizing the former" (97). This typical strategy begins with the false contrast Nelson creates between Dunbar Ortiz's preface, "an ideologically Marxist reading," and Ortiz's resistance, which Nelson sees as "maintaining and promulgating the old ways, of preserving life in the oral traditional way" (Nelson 486). Cheyfitz rightly argues that Nelson is separating (and thus distorting) "two forces that Ortiz unites, oral tradition and contemporary politics (98).

Reacting against Nelson's type of criticism, Craig Womack states in *Red on Red*: "I will seek a literary criticism that emphasizes Native resistance movements against colonialism, confronts racism, discusses sovereignty and Native nationalism, seeks connections between literature and liberation struggles, and, finally, roots literature in land and culture" (11). This criticism refuses to draw a line between Native traditions and politics: "[S]pirituality without politics appropriates belief systems without taking responsibility for human liberation" (53). Robert Warrior makes a similar demand, explaining that while Indian literature has engaged the wider world and "continues to push the boundaries of creativity, . . . criticism has remained, by and large, content with the narrowest, most parochializing foci" (xx).

Fight Back exemplifies that expanded literary horizon. Our reading must engage the political themes Ortiz addresses through narratives, analysis, self-reflection, and prophetic pronouncement. The struggle for the land and the people is, Ortiz explains in his next book, "very spiritual and its manifestation is economic, political, and social" (*from Sand Creek* 54). In *Fight Back* Ortiz emphasizes economic structures. As Dunbar Ortiz explains in her work on land tenure, "Without economic viability there is no assured social and cultural integrity" (*Roots* 28). It is a necessary part of the "our struggle . . . for the continuance of life" ("Mid-American Prayer," *Fight Back* 290).

NOTES

1. Ortiz in this work uses "Aacqu" rather than "Acoma." The biography at the end of *Woven Stone* describes him as "a native of Acoma Pueblo." In *Acoma: Pueblo in the Sky,* a semiofficial history, Ward Alan Minge explains, "the elders claim that the word 'Acoma'—along with

other spellings that are equally correct and historically applicable, including *Akome, Acu, Acuo, Acuco,* and *Ako*—all denote a 'place that always was'" (1). For the sake of simplicity, I use the most common term "Acoma" throughout the article.

2. Unless otherwise noted, references to *Fight Back* are from *Woven Stone,* the most readily available edition of this work, and are cited by page number in the text.

3. Richard Nafzinger's "Transnational Energy Corporations and American Development"; Peter H.Eichstaedt's *If You Poison Us: Uranium and Native Americans;* and Ward Churchill's "A Breach of Trust: The Radioactive Colonization of Native North America" are useful sources of information about Native Americans and the uranium industry.

4. *Indian Country Today* ran an editorial on Felix Cohen's "famous comparison of American Indians to 'miner's canary.'" Cohen wrote, "It is a pity that so many Americans today think of the Indian as a romantic or comic figure in American history without contemporary significance. In fact, the Indian plays much the same role in our society that the Jews played in Germany."

5. Another exception, along with Libretti's essay, is Norma C. Wilson's chapter on Ortiz.

WORKS CITED

Albers, Patricia. "Marxism and Historical Materialism in American Indian History." In *Clearing the Path: Theorizing the Past in Native American Studies,* edited by Nancy Shoemaker, 107–36. New York: Routledge, 2002.

Cheyfitz, Eric. "The (Post) Colonial Construction of Indian Country: U.S. American Indian Literatures and Federal Indian Law." In *The Columbus Guide to American Indian Literature of the United States since 1945,* edited by Eric Cheyfitz, 3–124. New York: Columbia University Press, 2006.

Churchill, Ward. "A Breach of Trust: The Radioactive Colonization of Native North America." In *Perversions of Justice: Indigenous Peoples and Angloamerican Law,* edited by Ward Churchill, 153–200. San Francisco: City Lights, 2003.

Dunbar Ortiz, Roxanne. *Indians in America: Human Rights and Self-Determination.* New York: Praeger, 1984.

———. "Preface." In *Fight Back: For the Sake of the Land, For the Sake of the People,* by Simon Ortiz, n. page. Albuquerque: INAD—University of New Mexico Press, 1980.

———. *Roots of Resistance: Land Tenure in New Mexico, 1680–1980.* Los Angeles: Chicano Studies Research Center Publications and American Indian Studies Center—UCLA, 1980.

Eichstaedt, Peter H. *If You Poison Us: Uranium and Native Americans.* Santa Fe, NM: Red Crane, 1994.

Fast, Robin Riley. *The Heart as a Drum: Continuance and Resistance in American Indian Poetry.* Ann Arbor: University of Michigan Press, 1999.

Minge, Ward Alan. *Acoma: Pueblo in the Sky,* revised and edited. Albuquerque: University of New Mexico Press, 1991.

Nafzinger, Richard. "Transnational Energy Corporations and American Development." In *American Indian Energy Resources and Development,* edited by Dunbar Roxanne Ortiz, 9–40. Albuquerque: Native American Studies—University of New Mexico Press, 1980.

Nelson, Robert M. "Simon Ortiz." In *Handbook of Native American Literature,* edited by Andrew Wiget, 483–89. New York: Garland, 1996.

Ortiz, Simon. "Always the Stories: A Brief History and Thoughts on My Writing." In *Coyote Was Here: Essays on Contemporary Native American Literature and Political Mobilization,* edited by Bo Scholer, 57–69. Aarhus, Denmark: English Department—University of Aarbus SELKOS, 1984.

———. *Fight Back: For the Sake of the Land, For the Sake of the People.* Albuquerque: INAD—University of New Mexico Press, 1980.

———. *from Sand Creek.* Tucson: University of Arizona Press, 1992.

———. "Towards a National Indian Literature: Cultural Authenticity in Nationalism." In *Critical Perspectives on Native American Fiction,* edited by Richard F. Fleck, 64–68. Washington, D.C.: Three Continents, 1993.

———. *Woven Stone.* Sun Tracks Series. Tucson: University of Arizona Press, 1992.

Warrior, Robert Allen. *Tribal Secrets: Recovering American Indian Intellectual Traditions.* Minneapolis: University of Minnesota Press, 1995.

Wilson, Norma C. *The Nature of Native American Poetry.* Albuquerque: University of New Mexico Press, 2001.

Womack, Craig. *Red on Red: Native American Literary Separatism.* Minneapolis: University of Minnesota Press, 1999.

CHAPTER 6

LOUIS OWENS'S REPRESENTATIONS OF WORKING-CLASS CONSCIOUSNESS

Renny Christopher

Very little has been written about Native Americans and social class,[1] and even less about contemporary Native American writers' relationship to social class. Louis Owens is a Native writer of working-class origin whose work can be seen as working-class writing as well as mixedblood writing, and an examination of his work from the critical perspective of Working-Class Studies can illuminate aspects of his writing that have not yet received the attention they warrant.

Owens is a mixedblood Choctaw/Cherokee/Irish writer and also a mixed-class writer. Owens came from the working class and, as a professor of literature, entered the middle class; his writing reflects a working-class, or perhaps better, a mixed-class consciousness in that his works refuse to celebrate the possibility of upward mobility. Working-class writers frequently question the middle-class values that underlie most of canonical American literature—values of individualism, materialism, ambition, and movement. Owens's work fits in a genre of working-class literature that I call "unhappy narratives of upward mobility," which questions or rejects outright all those values in favor of working-class values of community, interdependence, and connectedness.[2] Owens has said that he feels "like I live in the world I grew up in, my parents' world, and that out of that world I deal with this other one. The result is that I feel like a foreigner in the academic world" (personal communication, August 1999). The world of his parents was a working-class one; the university world is often an unwelcoming one for academics from the working class, because of the difference in value systems.[3]

This aspect of Owens's life has been well documented, but not in the context of working-class consciousness. This is not surprising. As Martha C. Knack and Alice Littlefield note in their introduction to *Native Americans and Wage Labor: Ethnohistorical Perspectives,* even scholars studying North American Indian economic life have not paid attention to Native Americans as participants in wage labor, as members of the working class, although for at least a century large numbers of Native American individuals have been wage laborers. Knack and Littlefield cite as a reason for this neglect "[a]nthropological fascinations with the 'traditional,' or compulsions to salvage the 'aboriginal' before it became hopelessly contaminated by the 'modern.'" This infatuation with the past combines with the tendency to "study" Native communities as separate from the non-Native and create "theories [that] are too narrow to account for the phenomenon of Indian wage labor, which of historical necessity has existed along the contact zone between Indian and non-Indian communities and cultures," (3) the contact zone that forms a focal point in much of Owens's work.

The majority of American Indians are now part of the working class, but they occupy a particularly exploited sector of that class, with "higher turnover of jobs . . . more dependence on temporary or seasonal work, greater dependence on public employment, and below average incomes" (Littlefield and Knack 15). And while she does not address the issue of class directly, Joane Nagel reports that in 1990, only 68.7 percent of Indians were high-school graduates (98). Class is implied in such figures, since most non-high-school graduates are held within the lower levels of working-class economic and social status, and holding a bachelor's degree is usually the minimum entrance requirement into the middle class.

Class oppression is intertwined with racial oppression. Richard Jarvenpa writes that the "development of reservations and reserves has perpetuated racial segregation, administrative paternalism and lower-class status for Indian people" (29), and that "three-quarters of all Indians in the U.S., and over half of all Canadian Indians, have incomes below official poverty levels. Half of all U.S. and Canadian Indians tallied in the labor force are unemployed" (35). At the other end of the social scale, affluent, urban people with Indian ancestry "may not identify themselves as Indians, except under advantageous circumstances, while expressing contempt for and distancing themselves from less affluent Indians in ghettos and on reservations" (36).

Between the extremes of poverty and affluence, Jarvenpa notes the existence of a "relatively stable" urban Indian working class. Jarvenpa also examines cultural movements and adaptations, concluding that "self-determination, with its emphasis upon group rights, stands in opposition to the concept of individual rights embedded in Western law and institutions" (44). This is not far from working-class culture's emphasis on community, collectivity, and interdependence (as opposed to bourgeois culture's emphasis on individualism), suggesting that a Native consciousness, or more specifically a *mixedblood* consciousness, might not be incompatible with a working-class consciousness.

Owens's autobiographical writing places him clearly as a working-class writer, and his fiction consistently expresses not only a mixedblood Native American perspective but also an identifiably working-class perspective. His work needs to be viewed in the context of Native American Studies but also, simultaneously, in the light of Working-Class Studies, because Owens himself has noted the existence of a working-class dimension in mixedblood writing. In one instance he points out that Mourning Dove wrote "in a tent after working as a farm laborer all day" (*MM* 39). He has written that the "Native American novel is the quintessential postmodern frontier text, and the problem of identity at the center of virtually every Native American novel is the problem of internalized transculturation" (*MM* 46). The lines that Owens's own work crosses are lines not only of racial identification but of class experience and consciousness.

In novels such as *Wolfsong, Bone Game,* and *Nightland,* Owens writes directly about class experience as well as about ethnic experience. Because American culture in general, and literary studies in particular, have very poorly developed vocabularies with which to discuss class experience and the representation of it, it is easy to discuss literary works in terms of race /ethnicity and gender/sexuality, for which we have developed vocabularies that have come not only out of academic discourse but out of social movements and activism. With the birth/rebirth of Working-Class Studies over the past decade or more, a focus on writers' representations of class experience has once again (following the period of class consciousness aroused in the 1930s) become possible. It is important to look at writers of color in terms of their representation of class as well as of race, so that not only white working-class writers count as "classed" (instead of also "raced") and so that writers of color count as "classed" (instead of only "raced"). An incident in *I Hear the Train* illustrates the way in which something that is really a factor of class can be misascribed to race.

Describing how his older brother, Gene, ran cross-country races in high school barefoot, Owens writes that "people who knew our family sometimes attributed his barefoot running to the fact that he was 'Indian.' The reality was, of course, that he simply couldn't afford cross-country shoes. The money we made from summer and after-school jobs went for clothes and food, not frivolous things like running shoes" (5–6). A white working-class boy in similar circumstances might also have run barefoot, but people who knew the Owens family saw "Indianness" where they should have seen poverty, thus making race stand in for class, of which there is much less consciousness in the United States than there is of race.

In writing about how he felt about the family's mixedblood identity when he was a child, Owens says that he thought no one but a Choctaw "could be as beautiful as my father's mother, or as great a hunter as my father, and though in California I was embarrassed by our poverty and bad grammar, I was nonetheless comfortable with who we were" (*MM* 176). What he seems to be expressing here is a complicated matrix of comfort and discomfort related to ethnicity and class: While he is "comfortable" with what he understands about his family's ethnic composition, he is "embarrassed" by the markers of the low-class status they inhabit. In *Mixedblood Messages* he writes of his ability to pass for white: passing "was easy, something I did not really have to think about very much. The hard part was being poor in a small town where people knew everyone. Dirt poor, shit poor, offal poor, embarrassing poor" (196). For the young Owens, ethnicity apparently posed far less of a problem in identity formation than did class. Low-class status, for members of all ethnic groups, is a source of shame in this culture, which blames the poor for their own poverty.

Owens is of particular interest in terms of Working-Class Studies because mixed-class experiences are common and crucial in the discussion of class in America, and Owens is not only a person of mixed blood; he is also a person of mixed-class background, having been born into an impoverished working-class culture and having become, eventually, a college professor. Owens writes that those

> of us who write, teach, and critique Native American literatures, whether we identify as American Indian, Euramerican, both, or neither, face the complex challenge of attempting to mediate without violating, and, above all, to facilitate an awareness that the literature we call Native American is indeed an "other" literature that nonetheless—in keeping with trickster's ubiquitous and uncontainable presence—participates profoundly in the discourse we call American and World literature. (*MM* 56)

One of the ways Owens's work participates in American and World literature is by being part of yet another "other" literature—working-class literature, that is, works by writers of working-class origin who exhibit working-class consciousness in their writing.

Owens writes in *Mixedblood Messages* of the simultaneously alienating and encompassing effects of a mixedblood identity; he does not address class directly, but the following passage comes at the end of a section in which he has carefully documented the extreme poverty of his Mississippi childhood, the place in the lower levels of the working class his family occupied once they moved to California, and his own alienation from them through his education and entry into the white-collar world. He writes,

> I am descended from those people [Choctaws], *but I am not those people,* just as I bear the blood of the Trail of Tears and of an enormous Owens clan that reunites periodically . . . but I am not those people either. The descendant of mixedblood sharecroppers and the dispossessed of two continents, I believe I am the rightful heir of Choctaw and Cherokee storytellers and of Shakespeare and Yeats and Cervantes. Finally, everything converges and the center holds in the margins. This, if we are to go on. (177)

By stressing "sharecroppers" along with "mixedblood," and "dispossessed of two continent"—meaning the Natives forced along the Trail of Tears and all the paths of displacement and genocide as well as the poor of Europe who came to do that displacing because of their own exploitation on that continent—Owens is indicating not only his ethnic ancestry, but also his working-class ancestry. By making claim as a Choctaw/Cherokee/European mixedblood to Native and European traditions, he is also making claim *as a working-class man* to those traditions. The feeling of not being "of those people" is one that is common to narratives that chronicle upward mobility.

Owens's autobiographical writing, *Mixedblood Messages: Literature, Film, Family, Place* and *I Hear the Train: Inventions and Reflections,* set the class context in which to understand his fictions. He describes a process of writing family history that is common in working-class literature, when writers try to recover the family histories and lives of people who have lived outside the web of documentation:

> Uncle August and all the rest are particles scattered, the chaos of invasion, coloniality, deracination, and removal embedded in their blood and photographs. Like Uncle August, we are all between the tracks, framed by a vanishing point but satisfied and defiant to the end. . . .

> [O]n the back of a postcard photo of mainstreet Muldrow, Oklahoma, in 1913, also addressed to his mother, he writes, "I her the train so Bee good tell I see you." I, too, hear the train. Unseen, it rushes along shining tracks bracketing Uncle August in memory that arrives out of the dark and disappears at the vanishing point of convergence in a photograph. My inheritance, it leaves in the air a trace out of which I will construct history, mirroring consciousness. . . . Like that dollop of sourdough left behind in the bowl to double indefinitely into another loaf, it becomes stories that birth others. And, as Vladimir Nabokov knew and showed us so brilliantly in his novel *Pale Fire,* we make stories in order to find ourselves at home in a chaos made familiar and comforting through the stories we make. (*Train* xiii)

Owens demonstrates his mixed-class consciousness as well as his mixedblood consciousness here, putting together the semiliterate Uncle August and Vladimir Nabokov. Owens quotes Uncle August's postcard, with original grammar and spelling intact, not to exoticise or humiliate him, but to lovingly preserve him as he was and to bring him into a highly literary work, filled with literary allusions, in order to mix that semilegendary, uneducated figure of Owens's Native and working-class history with his educated and middle-class present. He does so to insist upon and demand the respect and recognition of that heritage—one usually invisible, erased in the world of letters—just as the very well-educated, professorial, and professional writer Owens will insist that his earlier blue-collar self, a firefighter, is equally his true self, and perhaps his preferred self.

In *Mixedblood Messages* Owens reprints family photographs and tells family stories. He writes about the criminals in his family, including Uncle Bob, who "spent more than half his short life in prison," describing how "more than once we watched Uncle Bob walk away in handcuffs" (137), and tells how he himself was born in prison. He describes the rural poverty of Mississippi, in which he spent his childhood "in a two-room cabin a stone's throw from the Yazoo River," without electricity or plumbing (152). He notes that it is not his "habit to write or talk in public about my family's everyday pathos or to quote various family members, for after all, each of us has a saga of our own to tell. However I think this personal history has some bearing on the subject of mixedblood identity as it is articulated in literature" (147). I would argue that it also has a bearing on his working-class consciousness, and further note that such reticence about talking (or writing) about family things in public is something that working-class writers suffer across ethnicities.

Revelation of a past that may be unpalatable, inexplicable, or unacceptable to middle-class readers is also a common element of working-class literature, exemplified by Owens's revelations about his criminal uncle and his defiant announcement that he himself was born in prison. (His father was working as a guard, and he was born in the prison infirmary; his mother was incarcerated only in the sense of being married to a man with a particularly ironic and unpleasant blue-collar occupation.) But Owens expands on this theme in a chapter of *I Hear the Train* called "My Criminal Youth," in which he describes the curriculum of bicycle theft and breaking-and-entering he followed under the influence of a cousin when he first moved to California from Mississippi at the age of eight. "California, I saw at once, was made of desirable objects and those who possessed such objects," he recounts (77). As he describes it, it is the first time he has lived among more affluent people, "on the periphery of a quasi-middle-class community on the edge of a great city. We were the bottom rung, of course" (78). Again, the feeling of shame imposed on those of lower-class status in this society emerges.

But here theft functions as a metaphor as well as a literal reality of his past, as it sometimes does in working-class literature, especially in descriptions of education, when upwardly mobile working-class students feel that they are stealing what they are not entitled to have. Owens describes a particular incident in which he peers through the living-room window at a family whose bicycle he is about to steal from their front porch. The family is sitting around a television (Owens's family doesn't have one, and there are too many of them— nine siblings—to sit around it if they did have one). Owens envies a perceived (and possibly, even probably, false) sense of stability that this middle-class family possesses. "There was a wholeness about the scene, a kind of completeness that I had never imagined in a family before. In my experience families were in constant flux, coming and going, messy and uncontained" (81). He takes off with the bike, and reflecting upon it, he still feels "the awfulness of the moment in which I broke into that perfect order, violated whatever it was inside the house that I could not understand. . . . At the time I knew it marked a point of departure, like a ticket bought and punched for a journey to a place I didn't even suspect existed" (81–82). And he did indeed embark on a journey, out of the working-class world in material terms even if he never left it in spirit, thus feeling divided along class lines. Working-class writers often describe getting an education as a form of theft, and sometimes describe their very presence in the middle class as writers as a form of theft. Owens uses theft as a metaphor in a way similar to that used by white working-class writers such as Jack London and Dorothy Allison.

Owens's brother was the first person in the history of the family to receive a high-school diploma, Owens himself was the second, and he alone went on to college. He writes of his own educational destiny—that he "drifted" into a junior college "and then, to my amazement and the astonishment of the few who paid attention, on to the University of California at Santa Barbara. So that now for more than twenty years I have lived in a world incalculably different from that of everyone else in my family" (*MM* 176). Noting this, Owens describes how his contact with his family makes him feel "sometimes like a time traveler beamed into an awkward past" (*Train* 7), a feeling recorded by working-class writers who have left their family of origin and received an education, from Jack London to Agnes Smedley to Anzia Yezierska to Richard Rodriguez.

He also documents his own blue-collar work history. Owens started "by hoeing beans at nine years old and graduating to weeding and thinning sugar beets by the time I was thirteen and fourteen," working side by side with braceros, using the infamous short-handled hoe (19). While working in the fields, he fantasized

> about the perfect job. Someday someone will pay you as much money as you can possibly imagine, say three-fifty an hour, to backpack in a mountain wilderness with meadows and streams and snow fields, like the pictures you've seen. But the men and women in the rows beside you don't think like that. They think of their families across the border, babies and kids in school, and they imagine working many years in the fields. (19–20)

As is the case with many working-class kids who have later undergone upward mobility, he knows himself to be an outsider all along.

He writes about working at a mushroom farm, describing in detail the conditions of work and talking about the owner's son, who was one of the part-time workers. "Unlike the rest of us, who were not thought to be college material, he knew he would be successful. . . . Our older brothers and friends were already part of a war in a place called Vietnam, a war that had not become ugly yet for most of us, and we looked forward to our turns at such excitement as soon as we graduated" (30). Even while he had dreams of better work and a better life, he knew where his class position placed him in the hierarchy of life chances.

Nonetheless, against the odds, he did go to college (he notes that in 1968, the year he entered the university, his father's income was $3,000 [*Train* 44]), but as is the case with many working-class college graduates, his education did not lead him immediately to a white-collar job. Instead, he worked for the Forest Service first on a trail crew, with a gang of MAs and PhDs working for love of the wilderness, next as a wilderness ranger, and then—the job he writes about with the greatest joy—as a member of a "hotshot" firefighting crew. He notes the falsity of media images that portrays this work as "miserable" and "dangerous," and writes that

> [j]ust off camera are a bunch of men and women having the time of their lives and making good money to boot. . . . [I]t's dangerous, and people have died, including some of my friends, but that's not what it's all about. As a sawyer I was up front, cutting the first swatch of line while a puller stood behind my shoulder pulling away the cut brush and limbs and tossing them to the side for someone else. . . . We could cut a ten-foot line down to mineral earth in minutes, working in controlled mania. We were efficient, good at what we did, young, excited. (58)

What he describes is a blue-collar job that has what few blue-collar jobs have: A chance to use one's skills in a situation allowing a great deal of autonomy and exercise of judgment and a chance for heroism, for a sense of achievement. "And all these many years later, in a different life, I find myself dreaming of dark forests that crown-out in racing flames, of small oak trees that explode like comets into the night sky, and of alpine ridges a million miles from the world" (63). In this blue-collar world where the mythology of blue-collar work is really true, where workers can do something well in a sort of journeyman-craft situation with a dash of danger and romance thrown in, Owens seems to have found a satisfaction unrivaled in any white-collar work except, perhaps, in writing itself.

As a novelist, Owens has produced some extraordinary works that perform both mixedblood consciousness and mixed-class consciousness. In *Wolfsong* the Joseph family has a history of working in logging. According to Knack and Littlefield, logging is one of the areas that were sometimes known as "Indian jobs." These "were often unskilled or at best semiskilled jobs. Some involved large-scale resource extraction, such as timbering and harvesting. . . . Few, however, involved control of material or financial resources, highly paid skills, or decision-making control over the worker's economic future.

In most cases there was explicit segregation of work crews and super-visory functions by ethnicity" (29). The work crews in Forks, Wash-ington, the setting for *Wolfsong,* are not segregated, perhaps because it is a small and sparsely populated place, the logging companies we see in operation are small, local companies (although there is a refer-ence to Weyerhaeuser working "over the mountain"), and, owing to an apparent labor shortage, it is not possible to segregate work crews. It is true, though, that we see no Indian supervisors in the Forks log-ging industry as Owens portrays it. And although the crews are not segregated at work, one telling scene shows their social segregation: Jimmy silently leaves the Red Dog tavern when Jake Tobin begins making racist remarks (*Wolfsong* 98).

Patricia C. Albers, in "From Legend to Labor: Changing Perspec-tives on Native American Work," notes how

> popular stereotypes place Native Americans in a double bind when it comes to realizing a sense of personal and/or social identity through their own labor. As an example, when Native Americans manufacture dream-catchers, even on an assembly line, their ethnic identity is vali-dated. When they rebuild an engine block as part of a pattern of reciproc-ity among kin, or when they do this as a wage laborer in a commercial garage, their ethnic identity is denied. In the first instance their work is associated with a legendary "traditionality" emblematic of the American Indian; in the second their labor occupies a liminal space because it lacks the cultural boundaries that stereotypically associate Native Americans with particular economic activities. Imagemaking of this kind reaches beyond the realm of identity because it influences the very character of the labor Native Americans perform, encouraging them to pursue spe-cific types of jobs while excluding them from others. (249)

The additional layer of difficulty in *Wolfsong* comes from the fact that in logging, the full-blood men of the Joseph family are helping to destroy the natural world. Uncle Jim ultimately becomes a monkey wrencher, taking shots at bulldozers to protect that natural world by preventing the construction of a road through a wilderness area that will provide access to an area where an open-pit copper mine will be dug. The family, as well as all the Native inhabitants of Washington State who are caught up in the logging economy, are trapped in a complicated web: economic necessity, pride in the quality of their work (Uncle Jim is called one of the best loggers ever, and Tom himself is told by his boss that he could be the best choker-setter he ever had), and recognition of capitalism's destruction of not only the natural world but also the very resources that provide the jobs that give economic sustenance and identity. The unresolvability of these paradoxes is recognized in the novel's unresolvable ending, which leaves Tom running (or floating, perhaps, if he is dead or dying) into an indeterminate future because there is no place for him either in Forks or at the University of California. Tom's sense of belonging nowhere and with no one echoes Owens's own feelings, described in his autobiographical writings.

Tom is uncomfortable at the university, and the history of forced acculturation through schooling is emphasized by Uncle Jim's memory of boarding school, where "they had cut out the tongues of Indians, sewing in different tongues while the children slept" (5). Uncle Jim only reconciles himself to Tom going off to university by promising that he will provide a countereducation when Tom comes back. He says that the university would be bad for Tom's brother Jimmy, "and for a lot of the other kids in the valley, not just Indian kids neither, it wouldn't be too good. But for you it'll be fine. When you come back we'll go for a long walk . . . we'll walk clear over the mountains to Lake Chelan and I'll tell you all the stories . . . and I'll teach you all them things you ain't learned yet" (88). But it is not fine for Tom. At the university he meets intellectually sophisticated, upwardly mobile Native American students and, comparing them with his uncle and brother, thinks of his family as "Indians not Native Americans." This seems to represent for him not only a different stance toward the issue of ethnicity but also a class difference (161). Tom says, "They built that campus on top of an old Indian burial ground. Sacred ground. Nobody else seemed to notice it, but I could feel those people there all the time" (65).

But it is not only this that makes Tom uneasy. He is the first kid, white or Indian, from Forks to get a scholarship to any university. He comes from the rural working-class to the urban, middle-class university. He has refused the more homey destiny that might have been his—he could have married Karen: "She would have worked while he went to junior college. They would have lived a familiar story" (73). Instead, he has chosen the unfamiliar, and rather than embracing the material values and ethical code required by the university path to upward mobility, he has returned home, feeling like an outsider even there. He also rejects the one path he might have been able to reconcile himself to—that of wilderness ranger. That job has been offered to him more than once, but he chooses instead to "range the wilderness" (207) in his own way, rejecting both a middle-class and a working-class life—either of which might have been available to him—in an attempt to opt out of the entire system.

Of all Owens's novels, *Wolfsong* is the one that focuses most on work itself, with the kinds of detailed descriptions of labor that appear rarely in American literature, including a consciousness of the dangers of blue-collar work.

> At the bottom of the tower, the yarder's diesel engine farted out noise and fumes, while in a cage above the engine a man grabbed levers and caused a steel cable to run in a wide triangle from the top of the tower back down to the base of the tower. The mainline cable ran up the slope thirty feet from the ground and passed through a block at the tailhold and angled off to a second stump before sliding back down to the tower, and from the mainline hung two choker cables which two men were frantically wrapping around a pair of logs, the men's shiny hardhats bobbing and sinking out of sight in the tangle of fallen trees. Finally the two jumped free, scrambling out of the narrowing vee of the cable triangle that the logger called the jaws of death and leaping behind a stump just as a third figure shrilled three short blasts on a whistle and the man in the cage jerked levers to start the haulback. . . . Tom watched the small men in the unit wrestle with the forest. There was something heroic in those puny figures working to move trees, and something disastrously out of proportion. (138)

When Tom himself takes his brother's place in the logging crew after the fight with Buddy and Jake, his presence disrupts the unity of the workforce, because his coworkers blame him for Jake's injury. They threaten him simply by not working with him as a team, and this could result in his death. A good deal of blue-collar work requires cooperation to ensure the safety of all the workers, and thus represents that larger ethic of interdependence that I identify as a core working-class value. When Vern fires him, he says, "A guy's got to be careful if the guys he works with don't look out for him, and some of these boys ain't going to be looking out for you any too much" (153). The logging crew stands as a metaphor for the lack of solidarity among the workers, a solidarity that might be able to oppose the oppression under which they all labor.

Tom remembers stories he has heard of the Wobblies, and specifically of the Everett massacre, in which sheriff's deputies killed 500 workers. "And so he became aware that they killed everyone, these whites, not only Indians but everyone, each other" (140). Of course, the insight that Tom doesn't quite get to is that they don't kill each other at random: those deputies are in the paradoxical position of being workers hired by the bosses to kill other workers for the benefit of the bosses. Thinking of the workers, Tom recognizes part of the paradox: that these "good, desperate men were the enemy too . . . men who would destroy their mother earth" (140). But the workers, the "good, desperate men," include not only whites but his brother Jimmy as well, and even Tom himself while he's working on the logging crew. He reflects on the job he takes, setting chokers, that it "was a job intent on destroying you, ripping your hands off with jaggers of frayed cable or flaying you with the electric lash of a broken mainline" (141). This job can serve as a metonymy for the exploitation of all blue-collar workers.

Tom's brother Jimmy is focused solely on economic concerns. "With the mill damned near shut down and logging almost dead, people need the jobs that mine'll bring in," he says (32). Even J. D. Hill, the big businessman in town, has some regard for the destruction being wreaked: "I feel a little bad about cutting that road into the wilderness area. But it's going to happen whether we like it or not, and I'm going to make sure that the multinational company doesn't just come in here and take everything. I'm going to see to it that some of that money stays in the valley" (67). In his own, inadequate and collaborationist way, Hill is trying to do good for his community, but he, like everyone else, is caught in the web of capitalism, and there is no way out. This "no way out" is voiced repeatedly by Jimmy, the most defeated character in the novel. He says Uncle Jim "never saw that we have to live here, the way it is right now" (112). Tom, though, knows that Jimmy's real economic outlook will not save him or anyone else. When Jimmy insists that their uncle's monkey wrenching was pointless, Tom counters, "Instead you want to help them dig a big fucking hole in the middle of the last country around here that isn't clearcut. So a few people can go another ten or twenty years swilling beer and buying four-wheel drives" (120).

The way the working class is valued by the bosses is made clear in a scene in which a representative of Honeycutt Copper comes to sell the idea of the mine at a town meeting. "He was proud of the fact that he didn't have a racist bone in his body, but still the word 'logger' kept reminding him of the word 'nigger.' Logger-nigger, nogger-ligger" (115). And in this is perhaps one clue to a way out. If workers could recognize their true interests—preservation and sustainability—across race lines, perhaps together they could fight the classist, racist, profit-maddened bosses. But as ever, racial conflicts divide working-class people. Jake, Buddy, and two others jump Tom and Jimmy, because Buddy knows or suspects that Tom has been seeing Karen again. Jake says, "We don't want woods niggers bothering white girls" (131). Juxtaposed with the Honeycutt Copper representative's conflation of all loggers—that is, all workers—with "niggers," Jake's characterization of Indians as "woods niggers" pointedly shows the bosses' divide-and-conquer strategy. And indeed, as a result of the broken arm Jake sustains in the fight, his own class status is reduced from proud logger to that of disabled security guard, over which he is bitter and from which he finds "no way out."

Grider, the white ranger who tries to talk Tom into becoming a ranger himself, talks about what is necessary to save the wilderness. He says, "You . . . have to figure it's all your country now, just like it's all mine. White and Indian don't matter any more" (173). What matters to Grider is saving the wilderness, saving the earth. Thus, Owens gives a piece of the truth to Uncle Jimmy, a full-blood, uneducated Stehemish, and another piece of the truth to Grider, the white, college-educated ranger. Ab Masingale, an old logger, also has a piece of the truth. He notes that the valley is mostly clear-cut, crisscrossed by roads, and the game is gone, and "it's a crying shame. And it was fellas like me that done it . . . and you all know it ain't gonna stop. There ain't no way it can stop" (185). Buddy objects that maybe all the old loggers did all that, but they had to make a living. Ab, then, has no way out to offer except to note that Buddy's generation is going to be stuck with the results: "Hell, someday a man won't be able to breathe any more" (185). Tom already cannot breathe, and so he tries to go for the walk all the way to Canada that his uncle promised him when he returned from the university. But his uncle is dead, and Tom does not make it. As someone who has crossed class lines through his education, he cannot find a place for himself in the world. The novel gives pieces of truth to various characters, but Tom cannot bring those pieces together for himself, from either a race-based or a class-based perspective.

Nightland also expresses an oppositional working-class consciousness that rejects bourgeois values as destructive. This consciousness is allied with the indigenous consciousness represented in the novel by the figure of Siquani, the possibly 400-year-old grandfather who converses with ghosts and who reads the signs to know that evil is coming.

Siquani represents one pole in the novel, a consciousness opposed on ethnic cultural grounds to the avariciousness and destructiveness of white bourgeois culture, but other characters—notably Will, the mixedblood protagonist, and his white wife, Jace—are characters who move to a less-assimilationist stance in regard to bourgeois culture through the course of the novel. While Will's turning away from that culture is partially influenced by his Native roots—he always respected Siquani's ways, although he doesn't completely share them—Will is a mixedblood working-class man, and part of his rejection of bourgeois values derives from his rootedness in alternative, pan-ethnic working-class values. For Jace, a member of the white world by heritage (although, like Will's and Billy's mothers, set somewhat in opposition to it through her marriage to an Indian), her return from bourgeois ambition to rejoin her husband in more humble surroundings than those she has sought in the city represents a return to working-class values.

Will and his childhood friend Billy are economic refugees. Their parents fled Oklahoma along with the other dustbowl refugees to seek a better living in New Mexico, but now that land, too, has dried up, and despite the fact that Will still owns his parents' ranch free and clear, he can barely make a living from it. Will and Billy, though they are both mixedbloods raised in working-class circumstances, have different relationships to the core bourgeois values of acquisition and upward mobility; Billy embraces them recklessly, which ultimately leads to his death, while Will regards them with caution and suspicion. Billy has always rejected Siquani's worldview: "Now don't start in with Cherokee superstition. I get enough of that from Grampa," he says to Will (11). Billy is destroyed not only because he rejects Native tradition, but because he adopts materialist, bourgeois values, buying a fancy new truck with the money that he is supposed to be keeping secret.

Will's equilibrium is thrown off by the acquisition of the drug money. When he returns home with his half, "the home he'd been born and grown up in seemed suddenly distant and strange, a dark stone set down in the night" (31). Will has not succumbed to materialist values; he "could buy a new truck, but that wouldn't make much of a dent [in the found money] and besides, the idea didn't appeal to him. He could rebuild the Chevy instead. He didn't need a new house. He didn't want a television or new clothes" (79).

Odessa, like Billy, is corrupted by materialist, bourgeois values. "I have a Ph.D. in genocide," she says. "When I was young and innocent I thought I could get a white education and fight back. But I was stupid. Now . . . I'm going to have the American dream. Almost a million dollars" (303). Higher education in America is not only white but also middle class—higher education is usually the gateway to the middle class, and in the course of higher education, values such as individualism and acquisitiveness are inculcated into students. For Odessa, the combination of a white education and a bourgeois education has corrupted her so that she is going to be an imperialist herself—she plans to go to South America—making her no better than those she blames for displacing her people.

When Will checks the hiding place of the money at the end of the novel, the money has vanished; there is water in the well instead, in which Will sees a crowd of faces reflected. The temptation—which Will was not very tempted by—toward the material values that destroyed Billy and Odessa is removed from Will's world, seemingly removed by the spirits of the land, and replaced by water in the well, symbolizing a healing of the land. But the faces in the water also suggest community, which is a working-class value as well.

Analyzing the class positioning and attitudes of a writer such as Owens can help uncover dimensions of his work that do not emerge through other analytical approaches. Bringing writings such as his into Working-Class Studies and literary theory can help expand that theory to encompass a more complex and therefore more useful vision of the working class, working-class literary production, and the intersections of race/ethnicity and class. As Albers writes in her conclusion to the volume *Native Americans and Wage Labor,* studies need to focus on situations that allow Native peoples "to construct an identity as wage workers without destroying basic cultural values." She further notes that in the "study of relationships among capitalism, wage labor, and ethnicity, the lived-in experiences of the workers must take center stage because it is at the point of their labor that ethnic heritage intersects with capitalism and the workplace" (258–59). By reading autobiographical and fictional works of writers such as Owens who write both out of a Native/mixedblood consciousness and a working-class consciousness, the dimensions of understanding that Albers calls for within sociology and anthropology can be further enlarged. Both working-class autobiography and fiction can be regarded as a form of testimony, and that testimony can help unlock the usually hidden dimension, the frequently silent term of the trinity of race, class, and gender: class.

NOTES

1. For the few studies that have been done, see Barsh; Biolsi; Brockmann; Christopher and Whitson; Faimann-Silva; Littlefield and Knack; McLaughlin; Moore; and Nagel and Rosier.

2. See Christopher.

3. See Dews and Law; and Tocarczyk and Fay.

WORKS CITED

Albers, Patricia C. "From Legend to Labor: Changing Perspectives on Native American Work." In *Native Americans and Wage Labor,* edited by Alice Littlefield and Martha C. Knack, 245–73. Norman: University of Oklahoma Press, 1996.

Barsh, Russel Lawrence. "Plains Indian Agrarianism and Class Conflict." *Great Plains Quarterly* 7.2 (1987): 83–90.

Biolsi, Thomas. *Organizing the Lakota: The Political Economy of the New Deal on the Pine Ridge and Rosebud Reservations.* Tucson: University of Arizona Press, 1992.

Brockmann, Thomas C. "Correlation of Social Class and Education on the Flathead Indian Reservation, Montana." *Rocky Mountain Social Science Journal* 8.2 (1971): 11–17.

Christopher, Renny. "Rags to Riches to Suicide: Unhappy Narratives of Upward Mobility: *Martin Eden, Bread Givers, Delia's Song, Hunger of Memory.*" *College Literature* 29.4 (2002): 79–108.

Christopher, Renny, and Carolyn Whitson. "Towards a Theory of Working-Class Literature." *Thought & Action* 15.1 (1999): 71–81.

Dews, C. L. Barney, and Carolyn Leste Law. *This Fine Place So Far from Home: Academics from the Working Class.* Philadelphia: Temple University Press, 1995.

Faimann-Silva, Sandra. *Chocktaws at the Crossroads: The Political Economy of Class and Culture in the Oklahoma Timber Region.* Lincoln: University of Nebraska Press, 1997.

Jarvenpa, Richard. "The Political Economy and Political Ethnicity of American Indian Adaptations and Identities." *Ethnic and Racial Studies* 8.1 (1985): 29–49.

Littlefield, Alice, and Martha C. Knack, eds. *Native Americans and Wage Labor.* Norman: University of Oklahoma Press, 1996.

McLaughlin, Castle. "Nation, Tribe, and Class: The Dynamics of Agrarian Transformation on the Fort Berthold Reservation." *American Indian Culture and Research Journal* 22.3 (1998): 101–38.

Moore, John L., ed. *The Political Economy of North American Indians.* Norman: University of Oklahoma Press, 1993.

Nagel, Joane. *American Indian Ethnic Renewal: Red Power and the Resurgence of Identity and Culture.* New York: Oxford University Press, 1997.

Owens, Louis. *I Hear the Train: Inventions and Reflections.* Norman: University of Oklahoma Press, 2001.

———. *Mixedblood Messages: Literature, Film, Family, Place.* Norman: University of Oklahoma Press, 1998.

————. *Nightland*. New York: Signet, 1996.

————. *Wolfsong*. Norman: University of Oklahoma Press, 1991.

Rosier, Paul C. "'The Real Indians, Who Constitute the Real Tribe': Class, Ethnicity and IRA Politics on the Blackfeet Reservation." *Journal of American Ethnic History* 18.4 (1999): 3–39.

Tocarczyk, Michelle M., and Elizabeth A. Fay. *Working-Class Women in the Academy: Laborers in the Knowledge Factory*. Amherst: University of Massachusetts Press, 1993.

CHAPTER 7

THE AMERICAN WEST IN RED AND GREEN: THE FORGOTTEN LITERARY HISTORY OF SOCIAL JUSTICE ENVIRONMENTALISM*

Steven Rosendale

The man sitting in the iron seat did not look like a man; gloved, goggled, rubber dust mask over nose and mouth, he was a part of the monster, a robot in the seat. . . . He loved the land no more than the bank loved the land. He could admire the tractor—its machined surfaces, its surge of power, the roar of its detonating cylinders; but it was not his tractor. Behind the tractor rolled the shining disks, cutting the earth with blades. . . . Behind the harrows, the long seeders—twelve curved iron penes erected in the foundry, orgasms set by gears, raping methodically, raping without passion. . . . The land bore under iron, and under iron gradually died; for it was not loved or hated, it had no prayers or curses.

—*John Steinbeck*, The Grapes of Wrath (49)

John Steinbeck's notorious description of the bank's raping tractor offers a remarkable concatenation of elements, as the central image closely links several of the legacies of pioneering in the American West: the industrial development of Western agriculture under capitalism, the exploitation and displacement of farming families like the Joads, and the despoliation of the environment. Steinbeck's explicitly ecological worldview, developed with biologist Ed Ricketts and most clearly articulated in *Log from the Sea of Cortez,* embraced the idea of interrelation itself as a fundamental concept, an emphasis that made him perhaps the best suited of all writers on the American left to record how environmental and human exploitation converge in the postfrontier West. But while *Grapes of Wrath* is sometimes regarded as a text almost unique in its participation in both proletarian and environmentalist traditions in American literature, in fact a surprising number of proletarian novels written during the first half of the twentieth century also included a strong environmental emphasis. In this essay, brief analyses of several proletarian novels will reveal the literary left's unexpectedly deep investment in discourses of the environment and demonstrate that the idea of nature, and particularly Western nature, played a central conceptual role in the work of many writers on the left. For, like Steinbeck, many proletarian novelists identified the destruction of natural environments as a principal feature of working-class oppression and featured the renewal of suitable working-class relations to nature as an important element of social change. Proletarian novels set in the urban East (Mike Gold's *Jews Without Money* will serve as a primary example) often pictured the solution to the urban working-class's wretched conditions in terms that tended to idealize earlier pastoral and frontier relations to nature. After considering both the figurative power and the ideological problems of Eastern proletarian imagination of nature in these two tropes, I will suggest that a variety of Western proletarian novels, particularly Arnold B. Armstrong's neglected *Parched Earth,* developed a more sophisticated approach akin to Steinbeck's own: with a healthy skepticism regarding the legacy of pioneering, these novelists developed an analysis of the interrelatedness of environmental and human exploitation that anticipates the emphases of recent New West history.

What did the environment mean to U.S. writers on the left in the early decades of the twentieth century? The question is likely to strike many readers as an unusual one for several reasons. Because the growing field of ecocriticism has tended to regard ecocentric and interhuman concerns (like class struggle) as conceptual opposites, it has not fostered attention to traditions like the proletarian novel. But in the profession more generally, the historical reception of proletarian literature has also seriously delayed attention to many of its most interesting features. As critics like Barbara Foley and Alan Wald have argued, many of our received notions of U.S. radical fiction stem from a "legacy of anticommunism," which has distorted the literary history and critical analysis of the movement. Much critical energy has of necessity been expended on correcting these distortions, especially the widely disseminated notion that the class-critique agenda of left literature was somehow intrinsically inimical to its aesthetic success. Only in the last few decades has serious work been devoted to discovering what *else* might have been at stake in the proletarian literature of the period, and studies like Foley's *Radical Representations* and Wald's *Exiles from a Future Time* have begun to revise our notions of the movement's actual aesthetic features, as well as its treatment of issues like race and gender. The environmental dimension of left literatures in the United States has not been widely explored, however.

Recent work in ecocriticism, historiography, and philosophy suggests that this kind of attention is needed. T. V. Reed and others have urgently called for an "environmental justice ecocriticism" that might save modern environmentalism from the "sad history of environmentalism generally, wherein unwillingness to grapple with questions of racial, class, and national privilege has severely undermined the powerful critique of ecological devastation" (145). This call echoes New West historiography's emphasis on previously unacknowledged or forgotten interrelations between the human and environmental costs of Western development. John Bellamy Foster has challenged the notion that Karl Marx was an "anti-ecological" thinker in *Marx's Ecology,* concluding that ecology was actually a central constituent of Marx's historical-materialist analysis. Other scholars have suggested that the rhetorical resources for left-green alliance might very well be evident in the left's own cultural history. In *Remaking Society: Pathways to a Green Future,* the libertarian social ecologist Murray Bookchin, for example, observed that the left has a long-established terminology in which the "denaturing of the environment has always been seen as *inherent* to capitalism, the product of its very law of life, as a system of limitless expansion and capitalist accumulation" (13).

We tend to think of these ideas as very contemporary developments in left thought, but even a cursory look at the literary left during the early decades of the twentieth century reveals that a variety of left writers emphasized both class and environmental critiques of industrial production under capitalism. Emerging during the same decades that saw the rise to ascendancy of Frederick Jackson Turner's enthusiastic appraisal of American "westering," proletarian novels exhibit a range of responses to the idea of pioneering and its results, some of them surprisingly critical and attuned to the connections between environmental and human exploitation. In the March 1930 issue of the *New Masses,* titled "Ford Plant, River Rouge," Robert Cruden offered a succinct articulation of the basic idea:

> *The crimson skies of night proclaim it.*
> *The roar of a thousand presses intone it.*
> *The bellow of furnaces echo it.*
> *The hum of machinery chants it.*
> *Power.*
> *Power of man over nature.*
> *Power of man over man.*   (8)

Cruden's articulation of the simultaneous domination of nature and the working class was part of a tradition that had begun well over a century earlier. As Lee Clark Mitchell has demonstrated in *Witness to a Vanishing America,* a significant number of nineteenth-century American writers felt an "undercurrent of apprehension" about both the human and environmental costs of pioneering and development (xiv). Leo Marx's well-known *The Machine in the Garden* established nineteenth-century American literature's preoccupation with the obtrusiveness of industrial society, symbolized again and again in the image of the locomotive disturbing peaceful pastoral scenes. Later left novelists faced a different situation and described settings in which the industrial machine had already not only interrupted, but overrun and replaced the pastoral American garden.

This idea found its most important early twentieth-century articulation in Upton Sinclair's 1905 *The Jungle,* a novel that introduced the resonant image of the urban jungle or city wilderness as a figure for the interconnection of environmental despoliation and worker oppression. Sinclair's novel featured an extended consideration of Chicago's Packingtown as a landscape utterly transformed by industrial capitalism, an arena of environmental destruction so extensive that virtually no vestige of nature's formerly provident functions remained for the wretched slaughterhouse workers. Ironically, Sinclair's "jungle" is an overgrowth mainly of the predatory survival struggle, without any of the nurturing features of its natural namesake.

A number of urban proletarian novelists seized on the rhetorical possibilities of the "urban jungle" metaphor. In Mike Gold's autobiographical novel of turn-of-the-century proletarian life on New York's Lower East Side, *Jews Without Money* (1930), Gold is at pains to depict his proletarian neighborhood as an "urban wilderness," a "tenement canyon" where cops and rival "brave and savage tribes" threaten his friends; the skies pour forth bricks, dead cats, and garbage instead of rain; and the tenements themselves function as a "generous garden," producing bumper crops of clients for doctors, settlement workers, pharmacists, and undertakers (36, 57, 235). The streets are full of prostitutes, whose exploitation is figured as the urban wilderness's perversion of fecund nature: "Earth's trees, grass and flowers could not grow on my street," Gold explains, "but the rose of syphilis bloomed by night and day" (15). "Never would we walk without fear through the East Side," Gold writes. He continues, "Now we knew it as a jungle, where wild beasts prowled, and toadstools grew in poisoned soil—perverts, cokefiends, kidnappers, firebugs, Jack the Rippers" (60).

In *Jews Without Money,* as in Sinclair's novel, the figure of the urban wilderness serves a dual purpose: while the jungle metaphor critiques the competitive struggle of industrial life, it does so in explicit contrast to a healthier relation to nature itself. Recounting the insult of the weekly "Nature Study" hour in school, Gold tells of the "banal objects" fetched from the teacher's dark closet: "Cornstalks, minerals, autumn leaves, and other withered corpses. On these she lectured tediously, and bade us admire Nature. What an insult!" (60). Gold's point, of course, is that the artifacts are poor substitutes for the viable presence of a living nature. In the same sketch, the narrator tells of the gang's excitement at the discovery of some grass struggling to grow between sidewalk cracks. "We guarded this treasure, allowed no one to step on it. Every hour the gang studied 'our' grass, to try to catch it growing. It died, of course, after a few days" (41). "No grass is found in this petrified city," Gold explains, "not big living trees, no flowers, no bird but the drab little lecherous sparrow, no soil, loam, earth; fresh earth to smell, earth to walk on, to roll on, and love like a woman. . . . Seven million animals full of earth-love must dwell in the dead-lava streets" (60).

Other proletarian novels set in industrial cities follow suit. In William Attaway's 1941 *Blood on the Forge,* the contours of the industrial landscape in the Monongahela Valley again testify to the massive displacement of nature. As the trio of protagonists, African American brothers escaping the hardships of the sharecropping South, first glimpse the steel mill where they'll work, it appears to them "as big as creation." The banks of the river are lined not with silt or grasses, but with great heaps of ore, limestone, and coke. The Valley itself appears as the product not of nature, but of an encroachment on nature: it is, the narrator suggests, as if a giant had "planted his foot on the heel of a great shovel and split the bare hills" (51). Garbage heaps and ash-piles substitute for mountains and hills, machine-mules have replaced the real beasts of burden, the clank of the millworks mixes with the sound of rain, and smoke pervades the atmosphere. As in *Jews Without Money,* Attaway's critique of industry's transformation of the landscape is directed at both its human and its environmental costs. "None of this," the narrator intimates, "was good to the eyes of men accustomed to the pattern of fields": "It's wrong to tear up the ground and melt it in the furnace," a prophetic character balefully comments on the environmental price of production, "Ground don't like it" (63).

In addition to the basic observation that the domination of worker and environment are intertwined under industrial capitalism, many urban proletarian novels affirm the importance of nature itself in conspicuous pastoral interludes. In *The Jungle,* the protagonist's grinding existence in Packingtown is temporarily relieved by a season on the tramp in which nature restores his physical vitality and prepares him for his later conversion to socialism. In *Jews Without Money,* the Gold family finds respite from the deadly struggle in the tenement canyon on an afternoon trip to Bronx Park that nourishes body and spirit in a manner never found within the city wilderness. Tillie Lerner Olsen's widely read unfinished novel of the 1930s, *Yonnondio,* features two similar pastoral moments: an afternoon in a wealthy, green suburb and a temporarily nourishing season on a Western rent-farm provide contrasts to the filthy urban and mining-camp environments of the rest of the novel. In *The Cultural Front,* Michael Denning identifies the genre associated with moments like these as "ghetto pastoral," and suggests that the genre "constituted a subaltern modernism and became the central literary form of the popular front" (231). The recurrence of these pastoral interludes makes it clear that, for many left chroniclers of the urban working-class experience, environmental degradation was an integral part of working-class oppression. The pastoral idyll implied that renewed contact with nature had potential to provide some form of redress and reinvigoration.

Gold and other Eastern proletarian novelists seldom recognized the deeper history of the American pastoral idyll, which was itself the product of human and environmental exploitation on the frontier. Gold, for example, frequently used pioneering as simply another metaphor for revitalizing contact with nature. Curiously, when pioneering rather than pastoral metaphors were used, the city wilderness was figured in enthusiastic Turnerian terms without any apparent awareness of the exploitative nature of the pioneering past or of the irony of using pioneering as an antiexploitative metaphor. In *New Masses* articles like "Go Left, Young Writer," Gold imposed the left-right spectrum of political ideology directly on the national map, a convention that he had employed in an editorial statement in the first issue of the *New Masses* in 1926. The statement, titled "Let It Be Really New!" explicitly figured the mission of the communist writer as a form of pioneering. Declaring that "American writers in general and *New Masses* writers in particular ought to set sail for a new discovery of America," Gold elaborated on the initial stages of the pioneer's journey in terms that represented the urban scene of working-class experience as an unspoiled wilderness, contact with which could inject an American cultural scene characterized by bourgeois "pessimism, despair . . . and fundamental chaos" with new life:

> Yes, let us explore this continent. Let us lose ourselves in this dangerous and beautiful jungle of steel and stone. Let us forget the past. Shakespeare, Dante, Shelley and even Bernard Shaw—for here are virgin paths their feet could not have trod in time and space. A gorgeous fresh adventure waits for us—no one has been this way before!   (20)

Gold's analysis of the frontier motif did extend beyond the simplistic literary pioneering advocated in his editorial work. In *Jews Without Money,* for example, the lure of Western nature and the frontier myth is strong for the children of the slum, but Gold's point in representing the lure of the frontier myth is ultimately to debunk the heroism of the pioneering past. Mikey, for example, identifies deeply with Buffalo Bill and enacts cowboy fantasies amid the ghetto ruins. Gold clearly represents the boy's enthusiasm for the frontier idea and is attuned to the power of the pioneering trope in his own development, but ultimately offers a skeptical analysis of the pioneering myth. As a model of power and transcendence over a hostile environment, Buffalo Bill provides an instructive but ultimately insufficient model to contrast with the helplessness of the young Gold against his East Side environment; even the solidarity of "cowboy" and "Indian" gangs in the slumdwellers' fantasy wars come to figure as incipient but insufficiently inclusive models of class consciousness. Gold's goal in *Jews Without Money* is to move toward the abandonment of such myths and fantasies in favor of the more genuine freedom and power they can only simulate: Mikey's conversion to revolutionary politics at the novel's end signals his rejection of the immature and narrow notion of freedom implied in frontier myth. The novel ends with a paean to the workers' revolution, and signals Gold's preference for the pastoral idyll: Gold's closing line predicts the destruction of the East Side slum and its replacement with a "garden for the human spirit" (309).

Gold's much-discussed ending reveals both the importance of the pastoral trope and its major limitation in many urban proletarian novels: while it served as a potent symbolic contrary to the denatured environment of industrial oppression, the ghetto pastoral also seemed to indict industrial production itself rather than its capitalist organization as the source of both environmental destruction and class oppression. For the landscape of the preindustrial past resurfaces as Gold's most plausible figure for the socially harmonious future, which he idealizes as a "garden for the human spirit" rather than providing a detailed portrait of how industrial life might be improved after the revolution. Nor, it should be noted, does Gold ever explicitly recognize the irony of his symbolic reversion to the image of pastoral America, which was itself in part a result of pioneering exploitation of nature and the labor of indigenous populations.

* * *

THE WESTERN PROLETARIAN NOVEL

Western proletarian novels generally succeeded in resisting the ghetto novel's tendency to rest in idealized notions of pastoral and pioneering relations to nature. In texts like Robert Cantwell's *Land of Plenty,* published in 1934 and reissued in 1974, a return to the pastoral and frontier conditions is barred because the aftermath of pioneering itself has depleted the natural landscape. The northwestern veneer mill that serves as the setting for most of this strike novel is set in a mythic space at the end of the frontier trail, wedged, as Cantwell describes it, "at the edge of the last great forests between the mountains and the Pacific," where natural forces no longer provide renewal and abundance. Rather, they seem to cooperate in their own destruction, as "the fires starting in the logged-off land" quickly spread to the remaining stands of green timber, creating "great glaciers of smoke" that spread over the town and pervade its very atmosphere with a reminder of the depletion of the once-endless seeming resources of the West (5). Nature provides little refuge for the embattled strikers in the novel: although the mill workers are better than their managers at negotiating the dangers of both the mill and the ruined landscape surrounding it, nature itself no longer serves as either a material or symbolic resource for the strikers.

Agnes Smedley's *Daughter of Earth,* first published in 1929 and reissued by the Feminist Press in 1987, presents another skeptical left critique of the West's pioneering past. For protagonist/narrator Marie Rogers, being a "daughter of earth" carries few of the pastoral connotations that appear in Eastern ghetto pastorals; instead, it directly equates with working-class struggle. "We are of the earth and our struggle is the struggle of earth" (8), she intones early in the novel. On one level, the equation is meant quite literally because of the physical labor represented in the novel. Marie's father, for example, works in mining, farming, and digging ditches: "He kept his eyes, not upon the stars, but upon the earth; he was of the earth and it of him. He dug in the earth, he hugged the earth, he thought in terms of the earth" (106). But in addition, *Daughter of Earth* thoroughly analyses the consequences of "westering" for the working class and its relationship to the environment. Fully the first half of *Daughter of Earth* describes the bankruptcy of the older pioneering dream, as the young protagonist's family struggles without success to regain the "security of life on the soil" all over the American West (34). Although the novel includes several passages devoted to the aesthetic beauty of various Western landscapes, the contrast between the myth of a beautiful pioneering life on the land and its reality is persistently used for ironic effect. Indeed, throughout the novel, the aesthetic potential of the natural landscape functions, not as an indication of the idyllic countryside, but rather as an ironic sign that Western nature no longer provides a usable ground for a good life, as when the narrator describes one place "where defeat came in a setting of unparalleled beauty" (84). While idealized relations to nature tend to prefigure and even nurture class-consciousness in Eastern proletarian novels, *Daughter of Earth* offers an interesting examination of how the ideology of American westering can actually inhibit the development of class-consciousness in the laboring class: in an extended passage describing the range of attitudes regarding a mining strike, Smedley offers a pointed critique of the aftermath of American westering that anticipates New West historiography's skepticism regarding the Turnerian notion of "progress" by half a century. While Marie's mother's experience of losing a farm and joining the ranks of the unskilled proletariat leads her to sympathize with the striking miners, the ideologies of "Americanness" and faith in economic progress turns her father's allegiance away from his fellow workers: "As a native American himself, with hopes of becoming an employer, he tried to identify himself with the sheriff and the official of the camp against the strikers, who were foreigners" (119), Marie laments. For other workers, pioneering ideology also impedes union solidarity: "During strikes, their sympathies seemed whole-heartedly with the miners, but as ex-cowboys they were individualists and did not understand the struggle" (119–20).

The texts mentioned above have all enjoyed unusual degrees of visibility and attention as compared with other proletarian novels; all have either been continuously in print or have been reissued for later generations. But perhaps the most striking and sustained fictional developments of a left critique of Western development can be found in a proletarian novel that has been largely neglected. The novel *Parched Earth* was published by Macmillan in 1934 under the pseudonym Arnold B. Armstrong (the identity of the author has never been discovered). Upon publication, the novel briefly made an impression on the literary left and garnered some critical praise, including a positive review by Granville Hicks in the *New Masses*. Hicks's review, like most critical attention to the novel, focused upon its potential status as a model of certain technical advances in proletarian fiction, but the novel failed to find an audience in later generations. Aside from brief treatments by later commentators that largely focused on its aesthetic failings, the novel has been largely ignored, and has not been reissued since its initial publication.

Nevertheless, *Parched Earth* deserves reconsideration because, while certainly not a novel of the stature of *Grapes of Wrath* in an aesthetic sense, it is one of the literary left's most sustained treatments of the interrelation of class oppression, racism, and Western development's environmental consequences. In addition to its noteworthy attention to this interleaving in its own historical moment, *Parched Earth* also features a dimension of explicit historical analysis that is lacking in many proletarian texts, tracing the roots of human and environmental exploitation deep into colonial history.

Although the bulk of *Parched Earth* details the struggles of the residents of the fictional Tontos Valley in California in the 1930s, the novel begins with a remarkable introductory section that fictionalizes both the human and the environmental history of the place beginning with its aboriginal inhabitants. Titled "Cyclorama," the chapter is remarkable for its explicit emphasis on the intertwining environmental and human costs of development in the Valley at each of four stages of social and economic development: aboriginal hunting culture, the development of a feudal ranch after Spanish conquest, the incursion of white settlers and development of agricultural society, and finally, the consolidation of capital and development of a complex agricultural industry.

The Indian way of life in the valley is described in idyllic terms that implicitly serve as the measure of all subsequent social and economic relations. Described as "a wiry, dark-skinned people living in mud wickiups and cellars roofed with tule fiber," the original inhabitants of the valley "conceive of existence in terms of love and leisure and laughter" (1). The people supply their congenial life by hunting and fishing, along with rudimentary forms of agriculture practiced by the women of the tribe who "in some miraculous way extended their fertility to holes toe-scraped for native seeds." The basic religious and ideological habits of the people betoken their reliance on nature for their way of life: Armstrong reports that they "thanked their God for the deer that fell meekly to their arrows, and for the fish avid to bone hooks in Tontos Creek . . . they remembered appreciation for the richness of the soil." The Indians appreciate nature aesthetically, too. "Now was happiness," Armstrong writes of the tribe's concept of mortality. "Here in the Valley were good, fat foothills affording view and plenty. Let Indian feet rustle in the softness of green grass, catch the stain of orange poppy. Let Indian eyes take pleasure in the sere brown of the changing season and learn from nature the gallant way to die" (2).

Whether or not Armstrong's benign description of the Indians' relation to nature is historically accurate (or subject to critique for a problematic romanticism), he is at pains to emphasize that the Indian relation to nature will be privileged in his account of Valley history precisely because it is nontransformational. "Hundreds of years they lived in the Valley and changed it not at all," he writes. The creek itself "marked the land by vexed cutting through the plain more than the human overseers of it"; the local trees "grew more than the Indians," who are described as "content with living, adding nothing" (2).

When a Spanish missionary arrives in 1769, accompanied by soldiers, the developments in social relations that ensue are described in terms that again emphasize the interlacing of environmental and human histories. The natives are decried for "ignoring the natural wealth of their heritage" (2), given the name "Tontos" or "fools," and set to work building a mission on the banks of upper Tontos Creek. When they prove recalcitrant to the appeal of Catholicism, the Spanish soldiers undertake a military campaign, not directly against the Indians themselves, but against the ecosystem that has sustained them for hundreds of years. They systematically slaughter the deer in the area and net Tontos creek upstream of the Indian village, completely disrupting the tribe's dependent relation to nature. The stratagem provokes some of the valley Natives, who "believed it an outrage to their God who had committed the game into their keeping" (5), but covert attacks against the mission only provoke concerted and brutal retaliation from the soldiers, effectively ending the traditional way of life in the Valley. Scarcity brings converts to the church for food, and these are put to work transforming the Valley into a grassland ranch for a Spanish settler named Don Miguel Vasquez. The feudal relations between the Indians and the settlers are cemented in the second major transformation of the Valley environment, as Vasquez pays the mission for Indian workers to build a dam across Tontos Creek. With both cheap labor and water supply for his cattle now secured, Vasquez soon grows wealthy: ironically, he gains a life of leisure on the backs of the Native Americans, whose own leisurely life had provided the pretext for dispossession by the Spaniards in the first place.

The simultaneous and interleaved transformation of social relations and environment intensifies with each successive cycle of development. Within three generations, white settlers have displaced the Vasquez family entirely. Dispossessed by a wealthy lawyer who will become the namesake of the Valley's town, Caldwell, the Vasquezes fall into the working class, and their downward mobility includes the two conspicuous features that marked their own dislocation of the Valley's original inhabitants: racism and environmental alteration. The Vasquez clan, now denigrated with the rest of the Spanish inhabitants of California as "greasers," is denied fair access to justice, and the family's ability to ranch is taken from them piece by piece as the Valley is first mined for gold, then planted in wheat, and finally turned into a massive fruit plantation.

With the deep social-environmental history of "Cyclorama" established, the narrative skips ahead a generation to the 1930s; as in previous cycles, changes in social relations are accomplished and signified by further transformations of the environment. The town, presided over by Everett Caldwell, has most of the expected, significant features of modern Western development. The Caldwell family has fully developed most of the Valley and controls an industrial fruit-packing corporation located near the town itself; the location of their mansion on a prominent hilltop signifies the consolidation of the Valley's capital. The town's middle class lives in an ersatz mission-style real estate development called "Floral Heights" that has contributed a large sum to the Caldwell family coffers. On the other side of the railroad tracks that split the town, and hidden from view by a series of strategically placed billboards, is "Workers' Rest," a tarpaper village on the remnant of Tontos Creek that houses migrant workers and Belle Vasquez, the town prostitute and descendant of the Valley's former ruling family. The topography of the town thus mirrors its class striation—a perhaps predictable symbolic gesture—but the layout of Caldwell also carries an important reminder of Armstrong's social-environmental thesis. The novel persistently develops the idea that the Caldwell's wealth is built on their continued exploitation of workers in a depressed economy, but Armstrong is at pains to emphasize too that their capital ultimately derives from the control of nature itself. Despite the seeming complexity of the town's economy, it is essentially a water economy ruled by a single family: the Caldwells' concentration of capital is accomplished by their concentration of basic resources of the environment, for they have erected a massive dam, the town's most visible structure:

> Only one thing on The Hill was more commanding than the mansion. Two hundred feet behind, monumenting the summit, reared the structure of the dam—a concrete plug for Tontos Creek spewing from its gap of hills. Pent up behind the dam were all the seasonal waters which once had meandered freely through the Valley for irrigation. Now that water was for sale. (39)

Much of the novel is devoted to describing rising tensions in the Valley as Caldwell mechanizes his packing operation and depresses wages for migrants and local workers alike. Throughout the narrative, the novel's revolutionary themes are consistently developed in terms that continue the critique of the Valley's pioneering past in "Cyclorama." In a memorable episode, Armstrong contrasts the poverty of the Valley's remnant pioneers and workers with the gaudy recasting of pioneer history during the town's fiesta: the celebration comes to an abrupt end when Wally, the idiot bastard son of Belle Vasquez by Everett Caldwell, exposes himself to the crowd, effectively undermining the town's paean to its pioneer past. As the narrative builds toward a large-scale confrontation between Everett Caldwell's forces and his increasingly agitated workers, led by Dave Washburn, a communist organizer, the town's last remaining pioneer holdouts, now reduced to seasonal work in the canning plants, struggle with a conflict between the rugged individualism of their pioneer past and their urgent need for solidarity with the militant workers. As one character counsels, it is imperative to recognize that pioneers' individualistic relation to environmental wealth was itself intrinsically flawed and needs to be supplanted by class consciousness:

> Maw, you're living way back in a time that's outlived itself. You ain't progressed. Organization's the thing that does it. They ain't no getting'

away from it. You got to organize. The frontier's gone, they ain't no more of it to be got 'less you dredge off part of the ocean. Yore frontier's right in your own front yard from now on. You can't hike off to a new country no more, when things don't go right. You got to stick and fight it out. You got to git together with yore fellow man. (150)

As in other Western proletarian novels, for Armstrong's characters, radicalization entails rejection of the pioneering paradigm. As Hattie, the daughter of one of the early white settlers, moves toward class consciousness, she still feels the restorative "wooing of nature" (204) on regular hikes in the countryside, but when she articulates her new revolutionary spirit, she does so in terms that recognize the depletion of pioneer values: "You had to fight! There wasn't any of the old frontier left. The new frontier was here—in your own front yard! It was girdled by machinery in the hands of soulless men who would kill you if you didn't fight back" (166). Just as the capitalist's appropriation of the labor's surplus value comes increasingly to be understood as exploitation, the concentration of environmental wealth must be understood as a usurpation of a community value as well. Because of this, evolutionary action must be directed toward the transformation of not only the workers' relation to production but also of society's relation to nature itself.

Both of these requirements are addressed in *Parched Earth*'s surprising conclusion, when Wally Vasquez dynamites the dam, flooding the town and destroying Caldwell's forces, while Dave Washburn and his proletarian comrades escape to the top of a water tower. Thus, the capitalist relations of production based on the manipulation of environment conceived as property are destroyed in a single stroke, symbolically suggesting both nature's revenge and the possibility of renewal: "It sure looks like a rich harvest for us," one of the escapees remarks in the closing line of the novel. With the exception of Granville Hicks, who thought this finale to be an interesting technical advance over the unsatisfying conclusions of other strike novels, most commentators on *Parched Earth* have disparaged Armstrong's ending, and clearly, the episode departs from the social realism of the rest of the novel in favor of a symbolic denouement. Surely, Barbara Foley is right in calling the conclusion a "somewhat bizarre narrative overdetermination" (408), for in the closing scene, nearly all of the capitalist water baron's sins (Wally, strikebreaking, the damming of the creek) come together without warning to destroy him. It must be acknowledged, however, that the episode is also rather extraordinary in its anticipation of what would, decades later, become one of environmental activism's most emblematic motifs; indeed, the dam-busting finale of the novel is arguably more sophisticated than later uses of the motif by ecocentrists like Edward Abbey because, in Armstrong's book, it offers a symbolic protest of social-historical as well as environmental problems.

Indeed, the aesthetic flaws of the novel notwithstanding, *Parched Earth* ought to be reckoned as an important document of its era and our own for it belongs to the literary prehistory of contemporary efforts to synthesize class, racial, and environmental analysis. Like *Grapes of Wrath, Parched Earth* offers a view of the American West in which environmental destruction and the abuse of human communities are intertwined with the legacies of pioneering and capitalism. If *Parched Earth* and the other proletarian texts discussed above seem uncannily prescient—more the sort of thing we might expect from recent New West cultural historians or social-justice ecocritics than from radical novelists of the 1930s—it is only because the left's investment in environmental issues and discourses has never been adequately acknowledged. Proletarian literature can supplement the tradition of American nature writing as a cultural resource, a basic model from our cultural past that may be instructive. For here is a genre that, decades before the New West supplanted Turnerian historiography, developed some of its most scathing criticisms of the social order by pointing to the degraded environments created by capitalist production and with surprising consistency imagined class, economic, and political freedom as manifest, not only in the transformed life of the proletariat, but also in the improvement of the American environment.

NOTE

*Portions of this essay also appear in Steven Rosendale's *City Wilderness: US Radical Fiction and the Forgotten Literary History of Social Justice Environmentalism* (Iowa City: University of Iowa Press, forthcoming).

WORKS CITED

Armstrong, Arnold B. *Parched Earth*. New York: Macmillan, 1934.

Attaway, William. *Blood on the Forge*. New York: Doubleday, 1941.

Bookchin, Murray. *Remaking Society: Pathways to a Green Future*. Boston: South End, 1990.

Cantwell, Robert. *Land of Plenty*. New York: Farrar and Rinehart, 1934.

Cruden, Robert. "Ford Plant, River Rouge." *New Masses* (March 1930): 8.

Foley, Barbara. *Radical Representations: Politics and Form in U.S. Proletarian Fiction, 1929–1941*. Durham, NC: Duke University Press, 1993.

Foster, John Bellamy. *Marx's Ecology: Materialism and Nature*. New York: Monthly Review, 2000.

Gold, Michael. *Jews Without Money*. New York: Carol and Graff, 1984.

———. "Let It Be Really New!" *New Masses* (1 June 1926): 20, 28.

Mitchell, Lee Clark. *Witnesses to a Vanishing America: The Nineteenth Century Response*. Princeton, NJ: Princeton University Press, 1981.

Olsen, Tillie Lerner. *Yonnondio: From the Thirties*. New York: Delta, 1974.

Rideout, Walter B. *The Radical Novel in the United States, 1900–1954: Some Interrelations of Literature and Society*. Cambridge, MA: Harvard University Press, 1956.

Reed, T. V. "Towards an Environmental Justice Ecocriticism." In *The Environmental Justice Reader: Politics, Poetics, and Pedagogy*, edited by Joni Adamson, Mei Mei Evans, and Rachel Stein. Tucson: University of Arizona Press, 2002.

Smedley, Agnes. *Daughter of Earth*. 1929. New York: Feminist, 1987.

Steinbeck, John. *The Grapes of Wrath*. New York: Penguin, 2002.

PART III

TRANSNATIONAL WESTS: ENGAGING THE HEMISPHERE, CROSSING THE OCEAN

CHAPTER 8

HELEN HUNT JACKSON'S
RAMONA: A TRANSNATIONAL
READING OF THE OLD WEST

Robert McKee Irwin

"Helen Hunt Jackson . . . ha escrito quizás en *Ramona* nuestra novela" (In *Ramona*, Helen Hunt Jackson perhaps has written our novel) (Martí, *Ramona* 204).[1] José Martí proposed this idea in 1887 upon the publication of his translation of Helen Hunt Jackson's best-selling 1884 novel of race and culture clash in the U.S. Southwest, now a classic of Western American literature. However, there is no doubt that the great Cuban poet and independence activist already had in mind the notion of "nuestra América" (our America) as a strategy of Latin American resistance to mounting U.S. imperialism in the Western Hemisphere, though he would not articulate the concept until his classic essay "Nuestra América" was published in 1891.

As a Mexicanist I have been excited to see *Ramona* given new attention by an American studies that calls itself "post-nationalist" by reflecting a new focus on issues of marginalized groups, including the Native Americans and Mexican Americans who are protagonists in Jackson's novel. Indeed, this anthology provides evidence that American studies and Western American studies alike are rapidly repositioning themselves for critical dialogues that do not constrain themselves in national terms. However, to date, I have been dismayed to discover that this notion of "post-national" does little to challenge linguistic borders and global hierarchies of knowledge.[2] While I find one Americanist rereading of *Ramona* as a border text to be exemplary of the new direction American studies—and Western American studies—should be taking because of its thoughtful consideration of Martí's translation (I refer here to Susan Gillman's provocative article "*Ramona* in 'Our America'"),[3] I will dispute an important idea that it brings to light: Martí's contention that *Ramona* is "nuestra."

My rereading of *Ramona* refutes that of Martí by showing that in 1887, *Ramona* was in several important ways not a Latin American novel; more importantly, it challenges Western American studies to let go of its nationalistic and monolingual defining principles in order to make itself truly capable of interpreting the complexities of the literature of the West, much of which is constituted as the multicultural borderlands of the United States and Mexico. This essay is meant to demonstrate why Western American studies work on the borderlands must engage actively with the cultural context of the Mexican side of the border. Furthermore, it must learn to dialogue with Spanish language scholarship, particularly that articulated and published in Mexico or elsewhere in Latin America. A U.S. centric and monolingual Western American studies contributes negatively to what Walter Mignolo calls "the geopolitics of knowledge." Western American studies must also, when it does produce "transamerican" work, avoid reducing Mexico or Latin America to a uniformly monolithic other.

A case in point: Martí's *Ramona* may have offered a representation of Latin American racial harmony that appealed to his objectives of Latin American unity in the face of Yankee imperialism; in that sense it may have been *nuestra novela* for Martí, but it was not so for Mexicans of the northwestern borderlands. In the late nineteenth century, Mexicans of the northwestern borderlands not only were at odds with imperialist interventions of their northern neighbors, but also were engaged in their own projects of colonization in Mexican territories controlled by as yet unconquered, unassimilated indigenous groups. The historical inaccuracy seen in the tropes of racial harmony employed in Martí's rhetorical strategy of Latin American unification has much in common with American studies' reductive understanding of the region; but Martí's anti-imperialistic politics are at odds with American studies' intellectual imperialism—unintentional though this may be.

I will reread *Ramona* specifically from the historical context of the northwestern Mexican borderlands of Sonora and Baja California in the late nineteenth century in order not only to rebut Martí's arguments but also to point to the importance of the Mexican borderlands, so often ignored both by American studies and Western American studies, as well as Latin American studies, in forming a postnational vision of race and intercultural relations in the Americas.

* * *

NUESTRA NOVELA

Ramona is the story of a lovely blue-eyed girl raised in the wealthy home of Mexicans in late nineteenth-century Alta California (known in the United States as simply California). She is the daughter of a Scottish sailor and a Native American woman. Her father had been in love with a Mexican woman, Ramona Orteña, who married someone else while he was off at sea.[4] Years later, still in love, he asks this woman to adopt his daughter, whom he has named after her. Childless, Ramona Sr. agrees, and he goes back off to sea. When she (Ramona Orteña) dies, the younger Ramona is adopted into the Moreno family, headed up by Ramona Orteña's sister, who raises Ramona along with her own son, Felipe.

Ramona, then, is a mestiza, but is raised as "white" in a well-to-do Mexican family (made Mexican American by the 1846–48 U.S.-Mexican War in which Alta California became part of the U.S. West). All is relatively peaceful until Ramona falls in love with Alejandro, a Luiseño Indian employee of her adopted mother's ranch. When she finds out about this romance, the racist señora Moreno drives Alejandro away. She then reveals to Ramona that she is half-Indian, leading Ramona to jubilantly and defiantly renounce her Mexican American white identity and run off to marry her Indian lover and live with his people. She even goes so far as to take up a Native American name, Majela.

The couple faces numerous problems, mostly from racist white Americans, one of whom eventually murders Alejandro. Finally, Felipe, who has loved Ramona all along, finds her and marries her. They try to build a life for themselves in California, but become fed up with anti-Indian and anti-Mexican prejudice. In the end, they move to Mexico City where they live happily ever after.

Jackson's most important publication prior to *Ramona* had been *A Century of Dishonor*, a report denouncing the U.S. government's injustices to Native Americans in the Southwest. However, it had not achieved the impact she had hoped it would. Jackson meant to follow the inspiration of Harriet Beecher Stowe and use a novel to provoke her readers into taking action on behalf of the Indian cause. The fact that *Ramona* was set in the multicultural borderlands of the

U.S. Southwest inevitably complicates things a bit. Its plot cannot be broken down into conflicts between black and white, or even white and nonwhite. Ramona is the mestiza daughter of white Anglo and Native American parents and is raised as a Mexican American criolla[5]; as such she is not a simple character to interpret in any framework of racial or national allegory. It is perhaps not surprising, then, that the novel, despite its enormous success, did not achieve precisely the effect that Jackson had intended.[6]

Carl Gutiérrez-Jones writes, "What actually took place was far from Jackson's intention. Instead of provoking an outcry over treatment of Native Americans, the novel won the affection of many faithful readers for its romantic plot" (57). The plot, focused around mestiza Ramona and not Native American Alejandro, both opens and closes in a Mexican American context. Moreover, the setting of the novel is a California nostalgic for an idyllically peaceful past of Spanish colonial mission culture. The California historian Kevin Starr sees *Ramona* as a "culture defining romance." He writes, "Jackson collapsed American Southern California back onto the Spanish past. There, she suggested, in the days of the Franciscan missions, Southern California could find spiritual foundations with which to upgrade the crass vacuity of the present" (61). Not only did the book popularize a revised Southern Californian heritage for Jackson's English-speaking readers, but it also inspired many of them, particularly Californians, to incorporate her ideas into the landscape: "When the wealth and culture of the American race began to wake up to the picturesqueness and appropriateness to the landscape of these Mission structures— awakened perhaps more by the warm-hearted but discerning descriptions of Helen Hunt Jackson than any other cause—bold and daring souls determined to appropriate some of the distinctive features of the architecture to their own dwellings," giving birth to so-called Mission Revival architecture (James 307). Interestingly, a popular vision of California history emerges that links Hispanic California not to pre-1848 Mexican culture but to Spanish colonial culture.

However, *Ramona* does not ignore Mexico by any means. The mistreatment of Native Americans by white Anglo settlers is compared not just to this idyllic Spanish colonial past but also to a Mexican past. For example, the Mexican government allotted to indigenous groups land that was unceremoniously confiscated by the U.S. government after 1848. Alejandro's cousin Isidro's land deed, "que era el decreto de fundación del pueblo, donde el gobernador de California, cuando era de México, reconocía a los indios tantas y tantas leguas, por este lado y por aquél. Aquello era bueno cuando California era de México; pero los americanos eran ahora los dueños, y la ley de los otros no era cosa de respetar: ahora todo se hacía por la ley americana" (Martí, *Ramona* 417) (from the Mexican Governor of California, establishing the pueblo . . . and saying how many leagues of land the Indians were to have; . . . that was all very well when the country belonged to Mexico, but it was not good now; . . . the Americans owned it now; and everything was done by the American law now, not by the Mexican law any more) (Jackson 257). The Mexicans had allowed indigenous peoples to coexist with them in peace, while the U.S. settlers and government strove to drive away or even annihilate Native Americans.

Moreover, at the time in the novel when Ramona, listless and nearly suicidal after the death of Alejandro, might likely die, Felipe appears, marries her, and finally whisks her off to Mexico City. There Felipe is welcomed as his father, a general in the U.S.-Mexico War, is remembered as a national hero. Mestiza Ramona and a surviving daughter (also named Ramona), whom she had conceived with Alejandro, are not victims of racial scorn. The mixed-race family goes on to live a comfortable life among the Mexicans, south of the border (where it would seem they had belonged all along). The novel promotes not only the cause of indigenous America, but also what would become the Latin American ideal of *mestizaje*—as part of Latin American, but not U.S., culture. The latter point is perhaps the most important for Martí in his designation of Jackson's novel as "nuestra."

Regarding Latin American views on mestizaje and nation in the era, Doris Sommer's reading of the nineteenth-century romantic novel in the Americas (her highly acclaimed study *Foundational Fictions*) is telling. For example, according to Sommer's critical vision, José de Alencar's *Iracema* (1865) promotes a racially integrated Brazil by romantically joining indigenous princess Iracema with Portuguese conquistador Martim Soares Moreno.[7] Their son, Moacir (whose name means "son of suffering"), is the first modern American (note that Iracema is an anagram of "America"), "a new breed, where an unmistakably Brazilian past blends with an unpredictable future; he is the answer to Brazilianness" (Sommer 171). This allegorical integration of diverse components of national culture by means of cross-cultural romance is typical of the Latin American novel of the nineteenth century. However, national romance in the United States differs in that it does not permit mestizaje. Cora, in James Fenimore Cooper's *The Last of the Mohicans* (1829), does not represent a new American identity. Cooper's America cannot tolerate an impure bloodline: "Cora is a woman marked by a racially crossed past that would have compromised the clear order Cooper wanted for America. And that is precisely why, tragically, he has to kill her off" (Sommer 52).

Ramona was a new kind of national romance, going beyond the racially segregating schematic of *The Last of the Mohicans* and the simple integrating allegory of *Iracema*. It is a border novel whose cultural context exceeds a white/indigenous dichotomy. The adoption device allows Jackson to complicate the standard bicultural marriage allegory to include the three most prominent cultural groups of California in the 1880s. The allegory is perhaps more regional than national, but for Martí it became something much more. *Ramona* is a novel whose protagonist, "la mestiza arrogante" (the arrogant mestiza), speaks directly to "nuestros países de América" (our countries of America) and to "nuestra raza" (our race) (Martí, *Ramona* 203–4). Gillman affirms that such a reading continues to carry weight a century later when the Cuban cultural critic Roberto Fernández Retamar cites Martí in locating *Ramona* within a genealogy of nineteenth-century romantic novels by reformist woman intellectuals such as Stowe's *Uncle Tom's Cabin* (1852), Cuban Gertrudis Gómez de Avellaneda's *Sab* (1841), and Peruvian Clorinda Matto de Turner's *Aves sin nido* (1889) (Gillman 93–97).

Similarly, Americanist Anne Goldman aligns *Ramona* with María Amparo Ruiz de Burton's *The Squatter and the Don* (1885) against typical U.S. novels of the era for looking at postwar California from Mexican (or more correctly, Mexican American) points of view. For Goldman, Jackson and Ruiz de Burton represent "two exceptions to the willful amnesia that characterizes much late nineteenth-century fiction" (39) with regard to the cultural conflicts of the era in the West. In a slightly different vein, David Luis-Brown performs an interesting Martí-inspired comparison of *Ramona's* and *The Squatter and the Don*'s implications with regard to racial politics, finding that "Jackson's project of white-Indian national reconciliation sharply contrasts with the intercultural but racially homogeneous national reconciliation of Ruiz de Burton" (828). Romantic liaisons in *The Squatter and the Don* are about uniting white Mexican criollos with white Anglo Americans, while excluding nonwhites from the mix. Margaret Jacobs also looks at a pair of Jackson and Ruiz de Burton novels, *Ramona* and *Who Would Have Thought It?* (1872), finding both to be about the politics of a culturally defined whiteness that Ruiz de Burton believed should include bourgeois *californios* (whom she saw as distinct from "the undifferentiated mass of 'non-White' Mexicans and Indians") (228). Jackson, on the other hand, presented a more ambiguous view of racial definition and hierarchy but ultimately excluded elite *californios*, including those who would have seen themselves as white in a Mexican context, from the privilege of white identity in the United States.

Martí must have read the novel as Goldman and Luis-Brown do, but not as Jacobs does. For this reason, he translated it, had it published (in New York and Mexico City), and enthusiastically circulated propaganda promoting its distribution throughout Mexico (see Fountain 44–50). Notwithstanding the content of the novel, it must be remembered that Martí's project of Americanism (his "*nuestramericanismo*") was not really concerned with Mexico, and even less with the U.S. Southwest. Martí's interest lay in contesting U.S. imperialistic attitudes toward Latin America in general, but most particularly toward his home country of Cuba. In its quest for independence from Spain, Cuba risked tying itself problematically to the United States. Martí himself lived much of his adult life "inside the monster" in New York. He dreamed, like Simón Bolívar before him, of a Spanish America that would unite and share three goals: to ground itself in a local culture and history strong enough to resist Eurocentric hierarchies of knowledge; to protect itself from encroaching Yankee imperialism; and most immediately, to join forces so that internal disarticulations do not invite incursions by stronger enemies, whoever they may be (see Martí, "Nuestra América" 121–26, "Our America" 295–300).

Martí's strategies are complex and his views on race in particular sometimes seem contradictory. For example, it might seem paradoxical that the author of the line "No hay odio de razas, porque no hay razas" (There is no hate among races because there are no races) ("Nuestra América" 126, "Our America" 301) also published a seminal essay entitled "Mi raza" ("My race"). It must be taken into account, of course, that Martí was not so much developing a theory of race as reacting against the many racist theories of his age. Writes Fernando Ortiz, "En ese huracán de encontradas ideas e intereses, movido por los vulgos, las clerecías, los filósofos, los científicos y los políticos, tuvo José Martí que enfrentarse con los problemas de las razas y los racismos; en el pensamiento, en le palabra y en la acción" (In that hurricane of conflicting ideas and interests, provoked by the common people, clergy, philosophers, scientists and politicians, José Martí had to confront the problems of races and racisms, in thought, in word and in action) (12). His writing on the topic never coalesced into the focused volume of work he intended one day to write, such as *Los indios de hoy: Estado actual de las razas indias en América* and

Mis negros (Ortiz 15), but it instead was "una producción fragmen-
taria, casi siempre dispersa" (a fragmentary, nearly always dispersed
production) (Ortiz 13).

Nonetheless, Martí appears to follow a general trajectory in his
writings on race that took on a lucid form, according to Jeffrey
Belnap, around 1884, the year in which *Ramona* was published by
Jackson. Belnap writes, "Martí rejects a biologically based model of
identity formation in the name of a cultural/geographical one" (204).
The races are indistinguishable except by their history: indigenous
Americans are kept down not by inherent inferiority but by material
circumstances, justifying his symbolic use of them in his constructions
of Latin American identity. According to Belnap:

> Although the notion of "playing Indian" may appear condescending
> when taken out of context, Martí's notion of returning to "nature" by
> identifying with the native peoples of America couples the nationalistic
> rhetoric of his naturalistic age with a more complex intuition as to what
> it might mean to reverse the negative sociocultural forces that govern
> racialized hierarchies in America's nation-states.   (208)

More specifically, Martí's antiracist views on American indigenous
cultures seem to take on two repeating motifs in his writing. The first
is typified in his letter to the editor of *La Nación* dated October 25,
1885, usually reprinted as "Los indios en los Estados Unidos." In
the letter, he lauds the U.S. Indian reform movement and promotes
policies of practical education for Indians and notions of racial equality. Problems of apparent laziness and drunkenness among Native
Americans can be addressed by carefully supervised land reform based
on individual and not collective ownership, and an education policy
designed to teach indigenous Americans about farming and about
their own culture; in other words, "Aquellas reformas prácticas que
pueden convertir una muchedumbre costosa de hombres agobiados
e inquietos en un elemento pintoresco y útil de la civilización americana" (Those practical reforms that may turn a costly crowd of over-
burdened and unsettled men into a picturesque and useful element of
American civilization) (Martí, "Los indios" 326). While this attitude
may seem patronizing by twenty-first-century standards, Martí's idea
was to better the life of indigenous Americans and thereby make way
for the advancement of the nation: "Hasta que no se haga andar al
indio, no comenzará a andar bien la América" (Until the Indian is
impelled forward, America will not begin to move smoothly ahead)
("Autores" 337). Mexico's indigenous president Benito Juárez is a

great symbol of nuestra América thoughout Martí's oeuvre (Estrade 232).[8] Martí's rhetoric in this regard sometimes tends toward the assimilationist as he wishes to "garantizar que no se le niegue a la mayoría rechazada el acceso más amplio posible a la dirección del país y por consiguiente a la lengua unificadora dominante" (ensure that the excluded majority is not denied the greatest access possible to the ruling of the country and therefore to its dominant unifying language) (Estrade 243).

His second strategy comes out in a series of articles published in *La América* in 1883 and 1884 on subjects such as "Mexican antiquities," "aboriginal art," "primitive arts of ancient American man," and similar topics.[9] Martí, in brief, promotes indigenous American culture, or more specifically, ancient American culture as a viable subject of intellectual inquiry. This is an essential project for Martí since contemporary citizens of "our America" must understand their land. Martí wrote:

> Viene el hombre natural, indignado y fuerte, y derriba la justicia acumulada de los libros, porque no se la administra en acuerdo con las necesidades patentes del país. Conocer el país, y gobernarlo conforme al conocimiento, es el único modo de librarlo de tiranías . . . La historia de América, de los incas acá, ha de enseñarse al dedillo, aunque no se enseñe la de los arcontes de Grecia. Nuestra Grecia es preferible a la Grecia que no es nuestra.
>
> (Martí, "Nuestra América" 123)

> [Along comes the natural man, indignant and strong, to overturn the justice accumulated in books, because it has not been administered in accordance with the patent necessities of the country. To know, then, is to resolve. To know the country and to govern it in accordance with this understanding is the only way of liberating it from tyranny. . . . The history of America, from the Incas to present, must be taught hands-on: even at the expense of the archons of Greece. Our Greece is preferable to the Greece that is not ours.]
>
> (Martí, "Our America" 297)

Moreover, Martí's incorporation of indigenous American literature, art, and theater into American culture serves to show that indigenous peoples are not inherently barbarous or culturally inferior to Americans of European ancestry.

Martí has been criticized for his rather impersonal, idealizing view of indigenous cultures. He was personally acquainted with very few indigenous people during his lifetime and as a result had a tendency to represent them as an amorphous mass (Estrade 227, 231). None-theless, the evolution of his thinking is seen in his rhetoric, which early in his career often employs the term *indios salvajes* (savage Indians) (Estrade 242), a phrase that disappears from his writings once he arrives in the United States, where he is appalled by this country's apparent policy of annihilation. Indigenous Americans quickly become part of his liberating cause to define America as racially inclusive, and racial justice for all Americans becomes a major concern of his work (Estrade 238–39). It is during this epoch that Martí becomes inter-ested in the writings of Jackson.

*   *   *

RAMONA AND MEXICO

There is no doubt that Martí had carefully read *Ramona* before translating it to Spanish and endorsing it as "nuestra novela." His vision is based upon the reality of Latin America that he knew better than most any intellectual of his day. It is also based upon his vision of Latin American unity, a noble vision meant to strengthen Latin America in the face of the cultural, political, economic, and military imperialism of Europe and the United States, but a vision born of assumptions not necessarily in line with the reality of day-to-day life throughout Latin America. In particular, I will argue that Jackson's (and Martí's) *Ramona* as a borderlands novel—just like the field of contemporary American studies, including Western American studies, that has rediscovered both versions of the novel in recent years—is limited by a focus on the cultural conflicts occurring within the geographical limits of the United States. A rereading of *Ramona* from the point of view of the nineteenth-century northwestern bor-derlands of Mexico shows the novel's context to be hardly "nuestra." Furthermore, such a reading lays bare a particularly troublesome element in Martí's project of Latin American unity: the place of the indigenous American. More than anything, though, this analysis is meant to demonstrate the need for Western American studies to transcend linguistic and geopolitical borders of critical analysis that confine cultural inquiry to a closed Anglo-U.S. context. *Ramona* in particular has made numerous incursions into Mexico (the first being Martí's translation of the novel) and should not be read from a multicultural perspective that limits its "Mexican" point of view to that of Mexican Americans and Chicana/o studies scholars writing in English in the United States.

The first element of *Ramona* that might seem out of place if not utterly ridiculous to the Mexican reader of the nineteenth century is Jackson's (and Martí's) portrayal of race relations in Mexico. Not only was Mexico shown to have treated the indigenous peoples of California justly, unlike the nasty gringos, but it also turned out to be a welcoming haven for mestiza Ramona at the novel's end. Perhaps in Mexico where mestizaje was part of everyday life, race relations between white and indigenous Mexicans might have been less conflictive than those of the United States in some ways. The common reductive view that Mexico assimilated its indigenous population, while in the U.S. racial purists chose to annihilate theirs is not entirely without foundation. Moreover, Mexico's most popular president of the century (Juárez) and its leading figure of literary nationalism (Ignacio Altamirano) were both indigenous. Meanwhile, no indigenous man or woman in the nineteenth-century United States could have dreamed of achieving such mainstream prominence.

Still, on the whole, Mexico, despite its large mestizo and indigenous populations and despite the distinction achieved by a handful of national leaders, defined itself as a criollo nation, and its policies toward indigenous groups were, by twenty-first-century standards, largely racist. As the Mexican historian Moisés González Navarro summarizes, "In the nineteenth century, the country was ruled by the criollos, liberal or conservative, who sought . . . to 'whiten' the population" (González Navarro 154). Despite an official liberal enlightenment rhetoric of equality, the need to "destroy peculiar Indian institutions, especially the agrarian ones" (González Navarro 146), and to put down numerous indigenous revolts led to the implementation of policies that were brutally anti-indigenous. Referring specifically to the violent racial conflicts of the Mexican northwestern borderlands in the 1880s, Martí critic Paul Estrade wonders, "¿Ignora entonces lo que está ocurriendo realmente . . . en los territorios Yaquis del Estado de Sonora?" (Is he then ignorant of what is really going on . . . in the Yaqui territories of the State of Sonora?) (Estrade 238).

Moreover, to the extent that intermarriage was acceptable in Mexico, it tended to be portrayed following certain well-known paradigms. The common trope of mestizaje is played out in numerous Mexican (and non-Mexican) novels of the nineteenth century that feature the character of la Malinche. Examples include the anonymous *Jicoténcal* (1826), *Guatimozin* (1853) by Cuban Gertrudis Gómez de Avellaneda, *Los mártires de Anáhuac* (1870) by Yucatecan Eligio

Ancona, and *Amor y suplicio* (1873) and its sequel *Doña Marina* (1883) by Mexican Ireneo Paz (see Cypess 41–97). La Malinche, of course, is frequently seen as a national traitor for aiding and abetting the invading Spanish during their conquest of the Aztec empire. Her sexual (and political) linking to Hernán Cortés also provides the founding allegory for mestizaje in Mexico: the rape of the indigenous maiden by the conquering Spaniard. Modern Mexicans, defined according to Octavio Paz (following the tradition of his grandfather, Ireneo) as "los hijos de la Malinche" (sons of la Malinche), are the bastard children of this violation (59–80). González Navarro notes that "the term *mestizo* became synonymous with bastard, a stigma that was to disappear only after the Revolution of 1910 rehabilitated Indian culture" (González Navarro 145).

While Ramona's mestizaje is somewhat similar to la Malinche's (her white father procreates with and then abandons her indigenous mother), the interracial bonding explored in the novel is quite different. Ramona is not an Indian maiden sexually assaulted by a more powerful white man. Raised as a wealthy criolla, she is the girl who abandons her privileged culture to marry a lowly Indian. She personifies the rejection of racist Mexican criollo culture.

Meanwhile, Alejandro, although mission educated, articulate, and talented as a European-style violinist and singer, remains true to his indigenous heritage. He does not abandon his people and assimilate totally into criollo culture, and in fact he is not permitted to enter it on comfortable terms. He identifies instead as a Luiseño Indian and remains deeply attached to his culture. When he marries Ramona, he does not join her culture; she joins his.

Alejandro stands in stark contrast to the protagonist of the novel that would come to be Mexico's greatest early model of racial integration, Ignacio Altamirano's *El Zarco* (1901), a book Doris Sommer cites as a major Latin American "foundational fiction."[10] Nicolás of *El Zarco* is Mexico's first major indigenous literary hero. Yet, unlike Alejandro, his indigenousness is only skin deep. Nicolás, like Altamirano himself, is fully acculturated into mainstream criollo culture. This can be seen in his dress, in his speech, in his habits, in his aspirations. While the female protagonist, Manuela, is not attracted to him physically for his dark skin, he is otherwise at least as desirable as any criollo suitor. His marriage at the end of the novel to Manuela's adopted sister, Pilar, is an allegory of racial integration by assimilation. Nicolás, unlike the blond *bandido* el Zarco is a model of good Mexican citizenship and for that reason, regardless of his racial heritage, deserves to be welcomed as a member of mainstream Mexican society. Altamirano is bold in his promotion of dark-skinned Nicolás as a heroic figure of a national novel, but mestizaje for Altamirano is about acculturation and whitening.

Once again, *Ramona*'s mestizaje is quite different from that of the Mexican national literary tradition. It involves, like *El Zarco*, the romantic pairing of an indigenous man and a presumably criolla woman, but in a much more threatening way. *Ramona*'s interracial romance is not a whitening move of assimilation of the indigenous male into mainstream white criollo culture but the opposite. Ramona gives up her criolla identity and assumes an indigenous one, abandoning her upper-class lifestyle to live the "primitive" life of an Indian bride.

Discomforting as this representation of mestizaje may have been to readers of Ireneo Paz and Altamirano in central Mexico, it would likely have elicited a much more pronounced negative response in the northwestern borderlands, where multiple indigenous groups remained hostilely unassimilated into Mexican culture. But before looking at *Ramona* from a northwestern borderlands perspective, it is worth noting just how original this approach is. The borderlands are, after all, a popular node of inquiry in the contemporary academy (in American studies, Western American studies, Chicana/o studies, Native American studies, and Latin American studies). And yet, ever since Herbert Eugene Bolton's early border studies project,[11] there has been a tendency for inquiries into the U.S.-Mexico borderlands to limit themselves at the border, confining themselves to the United States.

This is particularly evident in recent projects of nineteenth-century border studies initiated in the United States. The recent flurry of interest in texts such as *Ramona,* the works of Ruiz de Burton, and Yellow Bird's *The Life and Adventures of Joaquin Murieta* (1854) is a case in point.[12] There is an unarticulated geographical limit to much nineteenth-century border studies that coincides with the United States's national border with Mexico. Even worse, there is a linguistic limit in this body of work to English language bibliography. As I have previously shown in the case of writings on Joaquín Murrieta, including the study by Western Americanist Noreen Groover Lape, while Mexican-based studies typically feature a bilingual bibliography, most U.S.-based studies cite only English language scholarship (see Irwin "Toward"; Lape). As another example, Goldman's book on the Southwest, including its analysis of *Ramona,* lists only a handful of nineteenth-century Spanish-language magazine articles and no critical works in Spanish. It ignores Martí's translation of and commentaries on the novel. Even texts that label themselves as examples of "post-nationalist" American studies fail to cross linguistic and geopolitical borders to dialogue with Latin American border scholars. An important example of this shortcoming is John Carlos Rowe's edited collection *Post-nationalist American Studies* in which chapters on Murrieta and border autobiography occasionally cite U.S.-based Latin Americanists (such as Luis Leal, Mary Louise Pratt, and Ruth Behar), but virtually ignore the wide range of Mexican scholarship on the topics at hand.

Another common problem with U.S.-based border studies is that when it does look at Mexico, it reduces Mexican culture practically to a cliché. For example, when Gloria Anzaldúa's seminal border studies text *Borderlands / La Frontera* does turn from U.S. Chicana/o to Mexican culture, it tends to focus on representative texts that reduce Mexican culture to Mexico City–based nationalist/centralist symbols and fails to recognize Mexico's enormous regional diversity.[13] While it might not be expected that Anzaldúa would seek out texts from every region and subculture of Mexico, it is surprising how little attention she pays to Mexico's northern borderlands. For example, her Mexican indigenous culture is Aztec, not Yaqui, Seri, or Tarahumara. While it is unfair to attack Anzaldúa, a veritable border studies and Chicana/o studies pioneer, the fact is that her breakthrough book has taken on monumental importance. Walter Mignolo has cited its "new *mestiza* consciousness" as exemplary of "border gnosis," a deserving designation in many ways (Mignolo, *Local* 5–6). But it would certainly be a better example had it not marginalized and subordinated Mexican culture in relation to U.S. Chicana/o culture.

Even more troubling is a recent review article in *Latin American Research Review*. Benjamin Johnson reviews six recent studies of the U.S.-Mexican borderlands, none of which focuses on the Mexican side of the border. When even Latin Americanists view the borderlands as the U.S. Southwest, then it is clear that some sort of metacritical intervention is necessary.[14] A U.S.-Mexican border studies that limits itself to the U.S. side of the border reinforces hierarchies of knowledge favoring the United States by marginalizing Latin Americanist and Spanish language critical research. Moreover, it leaves out a crucial aspect of critical inquiry: what goes on in non-U.S. territory?

A look into Mexican borderlands history brings to light a series of insights into U.S.-Mexican intercultural and political relations that U.S. Southwest focused investigations do not address. Whether the goal of the investigation is to obtain a better understanding of U.S. imperialism or of race relations or of migration, and so forth, a view

of the borderlands that includes attention both to what goes on in
Sonora or Baja California and to what Mexican or Latin American
(or Mexicanist/Latin Americanist) scholars have to say provides more
complete evidence from which to draw conclusions.

* * *

MEXICO'S NORTHWESTERN BORDERLANDS

So, what went on in Mexico's northwestern borderlands in the late
nineteenth century that does not come to light in reading Jackson's
and Martí's *Ramona*? Despite the fact that Jackson "con la más
sensatez y ternura ha trabajado año sobre año para aliviar las desdichas
de los indios" (with the greatest sensitivity and tenderness has worked
year after year to alleviate the misfortune of the Indians) (Martí, "Los
indios" 321), and that Martí too was dedicated to eradicating racial
injustice, neither of them showed any interest in the particular problem
of groups such as the Yaquis, Mayos, and Seris in northwestern Mexico.
Unlike the Luiseños of *Ramona* or the ancient Mayas, whose art and
literature Martí admired in "Antigüedades mexicanas," the Seris and
Yaquis in the 1880s remained utterly unincorporated into Mexican
society. In fact, they had nothing to do with Mexico the nation, living
culturally and politically independent of the country in whose territory
they resided. These borderlands Indians had yet to be conquered.[15]

In the late nineteenth century, some of Mexico's indigenous
groups were so isolated from Mexican national discourse that they
were not even aware that Mexico existed as such. When Yucatecan
Justo Sierra O'Reilly attempted to expel the Mayan Indians from
the Yucatán peninsula for their failure to assimilate, "the Mayas
responded to this argument by defending their right to the land
being threatened by the 'King' and the 'Spaniards'. . . . This dated
concept of the country's political structure laid bare how completely
the absolute separation of the races had been maintained" in Yucatán
(González Navarro 147–48).

While Martí was justified in encouraging "los pueblos que no se
conocen" (peoples as yet unfamiliar with each other) to get over old
squabbles and join forces in the face of the threat of Yankee imperialism, he seems to imply two things regarding indigenous peoples in
Latin America. On the one hand, he wrote:

Los que, al amparo de una tradición criminal, cercenaron, con el sable
tinto en la sangre de sus mismas venas, la tierra del hermano vencido,

del hermano castigado más allá de sus culpas, si no quieren que les llame el pueblo ladrones, devuélvanle sus tierras al hermano.
(Martí, "Nuestra América" 121)

[If those who under the protection of a criminal tradition, would tear the land asunder and wrest it from the defeated brother—the brother still being punished for his faults—with a saber stained with the blood of their own veins, if they do not want to be called a criminal people, let them return these lands to their brother.]
(Martí, "Our America" 295)

The ruling criollos, then, should treat the conquered indigenous groups as brothers, give them back their land, and join forces with them for the common good. After all, the indigenous are an essential part of "nuestra América." He rebuked those who are ashamed of their mother's "delantal indio" ("apron of the *indio*") (Martí, "Nuestra América" 121, "Our America" 296).

On the other hand, Martí's treatment of "the problem" of indigenous Americans reflects a paternalism that prefigured the Latin American *indigenismo*[16] that would become a major component of liberal nationalism in several countries in the early twentieth century. Like Manuel González Prada in Perú, author of the seminal 1908 essay "Nuestros indios" (Our Indians), Martí's rhetoric can be condescending.[17] When he referred to the "hijos de nuestra América, que ha de salvarse con sus indios" (children of our American, who must be saved along with her Indians) (Martí, "Nuestra América" 122, "Our America" 296), he portrayed the Indians as children or even inert possessions, as helpless beings in need of protection. Again, they are the conquered race who belong in "nuestra América" but are not quite capable of making themselves part of it.

Their best option seems to be to submit, to get over the fact that they are a vanquished race, and join mainstream Latin American society. They should come to terms with any jealousies they may have of their neighbors *de casa mejor* (of a greater house) and befriend the Spanish speakers who rule over the territories in which they live. Martí's scheme of unification involved both an elimination of racial prejudices and hierarchies on the part of criollos and an assimilation into national culture on the part of indigenous groups. This latter move naturally did not question the linguistic hegemony of Spanish, nor did it open the door for a discussion of local indigenous autonomy. In short, it was a precursor of twentieth-century *indigenismo*'s project to incorporate indigenous groups into mainstream Latin America. What it took for granted is that indigenous peoples, resentful as they may be, do indeed recognize themselves as citizens, to some degree, of the nations in which they reside.

Such a premise made little sense in Mexico. Through most of central Mexico, indigenous, white, and mestizo Mexicans had learned to live in relative peace as neighbors for generations. But in more peripheral zones such as Yucatán and the Northwest, groups such as the Mayas, Yaquis, and Seris lived independently of Mexican national culture, laying claim to their own territories. The strongest independent tribe of the north, the Yaquis battled with the Mexicans on and off from 1825 to 1936 (see Hernández Silva). Regarding the less numerous but bellicose Seris, "para 1880 . . . los seris eran los únicos indios de Sonora que, aún contando entre ellos a los apaches, se habían mantenido independientes de cualquier forma de dominio; sus formas de vida nómada y el grueso de sus costumbres permanecían prácticamente inalteradas" (by 1880 . . . the Seris were the only Indians of Sonora who, even counting the Apaches, had maintained their independence of any form of authority; their nomadic lifestyles and the bulk of their customs remained practically unaltered) (Figueroa Valenzuela 146).

Late nineteenth-century newspapers in Ures, Hermosillo, and La Paz ran daily reports of incidents, often violent, with "indios bárbaros" (barbarous Indians), not because their editors were racists but because northwestern Mexico was at war with local indigenous peoples throughout the century.[18] The conquest of Mexico in 1521, it must be remembered, occurred in the area of Mexico City. It did not fully consolidate itself in the northwestern borderlands until the early twentieth century. Martí's assumption—that indigenous groups constituted a race, one that had been conquered but not yet fully assimilated into Latin American culture—was not true, and in this historical context, his call for racial unity makes little sense.

While it is clear that northwestern Mexico, poor and sparsely populated, hardly represented national culture, its importance to Martí's project should not be underestimated. Mexico's attempts to "colonize" the region by offering land grants and other deals to both Mexican nationals and foreigners tended to fail. For example, the population of Sonora in 1877 was only one hundred ten thousand (and falling) and that of Baja California a scant 23,000, together making up less than 1.5 percent of the national total (see Moyano Pahissa 86). Although the population increased by over 75 percent by the century's end, it still remained insubstantial (see Ortega Noriega 210).

One of the principal reasons for the failures of colonization projects was the Indian "problem," which Miguel Tinker Salas notes gave Sonora a reputation of being "practically uninhabitable" (62). Settlers did not feel safe with "outlaw" indigenous groups frequently ambush-ing white settlements. It did not help that Alta California had been seen, since the mid-century gold rush, as a land of opportunity for immigrants from all over the world, including Mexico. Murrieta was one of many emigrants from Sonora in this era. Baja California and Sonora were seen, for the most part, as difficult, mostly desert land, isolated from central Mexico; and, if the problems with local indige-nous groups were not enough, the United States's relocations of recal-citrant Apaches to border reservations led to frequent raids by these displaced Indians into Mexican territory, at times apparently with tacit encouragement from the U.S. government (see Zorrilla 275–92).

Mexico's northwestern borderlands, then, remained not only underpopulated but generally vulnerable to invasions from the north. And while skirmishes with Seris and all-out war with Yaquis may have troubled Mexicans in the late nineteenth century, such conflicts were minor in comparison with the potential and occasionally real battles in which northwestern Mexicans were forced to engage against U.S.-based invaders.

Ever since Anglo settlers from the United States in Texas began to demand independence from Mexico—which they would win, enabling them to later incorporate Texas into the United States—Mexicans had been wary of U.S. imperialist gestures toward Mexico. The U.S. inva-sion of a vulnerable Mexico in 1846, which forced Mexico to give up the vast territories of Alta California and Nuevo México, only amplified Mexicans' anxiety. The 1850s then saw a series of filibuster expeditions into Sonora and Baja California by private armies led by such figures as William Walker and Henry Crabb (see Zorrilla 293–314). Newspaper reports, widely translated in Mexican journals, from San Diego and San Francisco showed that plans to incorporate Sonora and Baja California into the United States were popular among U.S. citizens and often had the backing of politicians. While the numbers of such raids mostly dwindled to nothing by the end of the 1850s, rumors of new fili-buster armies forming and the messianic rhetoric of "Manifest Destiny" appeared regularly in the Mexican press for much of the century.

Martí himself was most conscious of U.S. imperialism toward Mexico and the pronounced border tensions of the era. In 1886, he reported: "Es inminente en estos momentos el peligro de una guerra mexicana" (The danger of war with Mexico is now imminent) (Martí, "México y Estados Unidos" 45). He gave extensive coverage to the libel case of the journalist A. K. Cutting in Mexico, which was stirring up tensions on both sides of the border. Martí recalled the invasion of the 1840s and cited the "miedo justo de una invasión ansiedada

por la mayoría de los habitantes del otro lado de la frontera" (justified fear of an invasion felt by the majority of inhabitants on the other
side of the border) (Martí, "México y Estados Unidos" 46). Ten
months later, he reported on the American Annexation League and
its vigilance for internal unrest in Mexico, Honduras, and Cuba. Its
ten thousand members would lobby for a takeover at such a moment
of weakness. Cutting, then president of the Occupation and Development Company of Northern Mexico, sought to "desposeer a México
de los Estados del Norte" (dispossess Mexico of its northern states)
(Martí, "México en los Estados Unidos" 53). Martí, then, was fully
conscious of border conflicts between Mexico and the United States
but utterly oblivious to the conflicts within Mexico's national boundaries with unconquered, unincorporated indigenous groups.

*　*　*

RAMONA IN NUESTRA AMÉRICA

Martí's error was in assuming that Latin America's treatment of "the
Indian problem" was essentially different from that of the United
States. Whereas intermarriage, religious conversion, cultural syncre-
tism, and even a certain ease of cultural assimilation were characteristic of central Mexican society, particularly when compared with
U.S. society's fundamental principal of racial segregation, attitudes
in Mexico's northwestern borderlands—especially among its urban
oligarchy—were, in fact, not much different from those in the U.S.
Southwest concerning these issues. Just as mestizaje existed on both
sides of the border, belief in white supremacy ruled in certain social
strata throughout the borderlands region (see Tinker Salas 26). And
while some Indians did manage to assimilate to one degree or another
into the Mexican mainstream, many retained ethnic identities that
kept them segregated or even excluded them from national cultures.
Violent conflict with some groups led to public policy more akin to
racial extermination than assimilation or even segregation. Ramona
was raised in a well-to-do Mexican criollo family. Her decision to identify as an Indian, to abandon her criollo culture, and to marry into an
indigenous community would hardly have been looked upon favorably
by urban elites in late nineteenth-century Sonora or Baja California.

An interesting parallel can be seen in the case of Lola Casanova,
a young woman who was kidnapped by Seri Indians while traveling
from Guaymas in 1850.[19] Her decision to abandon her well-positioned
criollo family, marry a Seri chief, bear his children, and essentially live

the rest of her life as a Seri caused a huge scandal in late nineteenth-century Sonora and has lived on into the twentieth century as a legend, both among Mexicans and Seris in Sonora.

While Ramona might have been embraced in central Mexico as a new romanticized twist on the Malinche personage (though there was no character who was anything like her in the literature of the age), in the northwestern borderlands it would have been difficult to see her as anything but a traitor who, like the scandalous Lola Casanova, rejected her Mexican heritage to join forces with *indios bárbaros*. While Martí's reading of *Ramona* was not invalid for his project of continental unity, and may have been an appropriate vehicle for promoting his vision of racial integration through most of Latin America, its utter incompatibility with the reality of borderlands life on the Mexican side points to a weakness in the "nuestra América" project. Martí's mission takes for granted the conquest of indigenous America and the colonization of their lands. Without conquest and colonization, the borderlands and therefore Mexico and "nuestra América" remain vulnerable to Yankee imperialism. While Martí was more conscious than anyone of the U.S.-based annexation movement and the sentiment of Manifest Destiny behind it, he—like too many U.S.-based border studies scholars today—remained unconscious of the particular cultural conflicts and anxieties of the Mexican borderlands that must be considered in order to fully understand the complexities of racial conflicts in the Americas in the late nineteenth century. For Mexicans of the northwestern borderlands, then, *Ramona* was not "nuestra novela."

By the 1940s, things had changed in Mexico. The Yaquis were vanquished and subjugated and the Seris nearly entirely wiped out. Sonora and Baja California's populations had increased enormously. There was no longer any talk of filibuster raids or annexation movements or Manifest Destiny. There were certainly (and still are) tensions in the borderlands, but no fear of impending war. War, after all, was tearing up Europe and Asia, and the United States and Mexico were allies. The United States, in the era of "Good Neighbor Policy," recognized the importance of economic ties with Latin America and was in no position to promote a crudely imperialistic agenda in the hemisphere. In 1940s Mexico, indigenous culture received new attention in the arts. Postrevolutionary *indigenismo* promoted Mexico as a *mestizo* culture of which an indigenous history was an important part. Mexico appeared to be ready to move beyond the Malinche myth and the foundational fictions of assimilation. While muralism was its most internationally prominent manifestation, *indigenismo* was not limited to painting. Francisco Rojas González, for example, was one of three authors who incorporated the legend of Lola Casanova into Mexican literature in the 1940s. In addition, the cinematic *indigenismo* popularized in the work of director Emilio "*el Indio*" Fernández in classic films such as *María Candelaria*, a Palme d'Or winner at Cannes, encouraged the filming of other indigenous themed stories, including that of Lola Casanova by Matilde Landeta in 1948.

By the 1940s, *Ramona* had been made into no less than four movies in the United States, including a 1910 D. W. Griffith short film starring Mary Pickford, Edwin Carewe's Dolores del Río vehicle in 1928 for which the classic Mabel Wayne / L. Wolfe Gilbert song was composed, and Henry King's 1936 Loretta Young hit. But it was not until cinematic *indigenismo* became a major trend in Mexican cultural production that *Ramona* became a Mexican story for the first time with the 1946 Víctor Urruchúa production starring Esther Fernández. Now, of course, with Televisa's 2000 production of *Ramona* as a *telenovela* starring Kate del Castillo, *Ramona* has attracted a renewed interest in Latin America. And perhaps now it can be said that *Ramona* is "nuestra novela."

*   *   *

CONCLUSION

Martí may have been blinded by the urgency to generate united support in Latin America for the cause of Cuban independence. For this reason, he might be forgiven for overlooking the serious problems facing the northwestern Mexican borderlands in the late nineteenth century. American border studies scholars' ignorance of the Mexican borderlands is another story. It is based on a tradition of monolingual study and closed national dialogue that only recognizes those Mexicans who have crossed into U.S. territory and who communicate in English. My reading of *Ramona* is meant to draw attention to this blind spot in American, including Western American, studies scholarship in hopes that (Western) American scholars might begin to make the effort to make their field truly postnational.

NOTES

1. This and all other translations from the Spanish, unless otherwise noted, are my own. English quotes from *Ramona* are from Helen Hunt Jackson's *Ramona* (New York: Signet, 1998). Martí's translations are from *Obras completas* 24.

2. See my "*Ramona* and Postnationalist American Studies: On 'Our America' and the Mexican Borderlands," on which the present article is based.

3. Gillman's article is of particular interest because of its focus on *Ramona,* but the volume as a whole can be taken to represent this particular style of American studies that commits itself to productive dialogue with Latin American (and Latin Americanist) scholars and texts.

4. With names, I am using Martí's Spanish spellings (Orteña and Alejandro) in place of Jackson's approximations (Ortegna and Alessandro).

5. In Mexico, *criollo* was a common designation from colonial times through the nineteenth century that referred to native-born Americans of pure European descent.

6. On *Ramona*'s reception, see Mathes.

7. I choose this example because it is a typical one in terms of gender and race allegory. See Sommer 169–71.

8. Estrade notes that Marti invoked Juárez more than thirty times and with ever-greater frequency and weight in his later writings.

9. See Martí, *Obras completas* 8 (1963), 327–41.

10. For Sommer's analysis of *El Zarco,* see 220–32. Note that the novel was published posthumously and was actually written in the mid- to late 1880s, simultaneous to Martí's translation of *Ramona.*

11. See Bolton, *The Spanish Borderlands;* while Bolton's early work focused only on the U.S. side of the border, later studies such as *The Padre on Horseback* did treat the Mexican Northwest.

12. In addition to critical texts already discussed, see also Luis Leal's introduction to Ireneo Paz, Powell, and Streeby. I critique this work in detail in *Bandits.*

13. A similar critique of Anzaldúa appears in Tabuenca 89–90.

14. My point is not that no one is doing borderlands cultural history from a Mexican point of view, but that such work gets little attention, even among Latin Americanists. Several excellent recently published books are absent from Johnson's review essay, which includes texts published as early as 1996. Among them are Salas and Radding. The issue in Mexico is a different one: the tendency to present borderlands historiography as state or regional history, thereby limiting its apparent interdisciplinary value and doing little to attract readership outside of Mexico. A case in point is the essay collection coordinated by López Soto. For a more detailed critique of scholarship on the borderlands in multiple disciplines and locations, see my *Bandits* 1–37.

15. Although Yaquis often worked as laborers in Sonora, this did not necessarily imply their cultural assimilation. Indeed, during the 1880s, the Yaquis were at war with Mexico over control of the fertile Yaqui river valley. See Figueroa Valenzuela.

16. *Indigenismo* refers to a liberal state policy launched in Mexico, Peru, and several other Latin American countries with significant indigenous

populations in the second quarter of the twentieth century to better incorporate these populations into national culture. It has since been criticized for its underlying principals of assimilation, its tendency to view once glorious indigenous cultures as decadent, and its failure to take into account the perspectives of contemporary indigenous communities. For an astute critique of indigenismo, see Tarica.

17. Estrade notes that Leopoldo Zea identifies Martí as a precursor of the "*indigenismo* liberal" of González Prada and José Mariátegui 245.

18. For example, Guadalupe Beatriz Aldaco Encinas notes that reports of conflicts with indigenous groups were a major component of Sonoran newspaper reporting from 1856 to 1870 (363). Several typical reports under the routine headline "Indios Bárbaros" from *La Estrella de Occidente* of Ures in 1875 appear in Cuevas Aramburu 408.

19. I analyze the discursive battles over the signification of this legend in *Bandits* 91–143.

WORKS CITED

Aldaco Encinas, Guadalupe Beatriz. "La prensa decimonónica sonorense: El caso de *La Voz de Sonora y La Estrella de Occidente* (1856–1870)." *Memoria: XIV simposio de historia y antropología de Sonora* 2, 361–73 Hermosillo: Universidad de Sonora, 1990.

Altamirano, Ignacio. *El Zarco*. 1901. Mexico City: Porrúa, 1995.

Anzaldúa, Gloria. *Borderlands / La Frontera: The New Mestiza*. San Francisco: Aunt Lute, 1987.

Belnap, Jeffrey. "Headbands, Hemp Sandals, and Headdresses: The Dialectics of Dress and Self-Conception in Martí's 'Our America.'" In *José Martí's "Our America": From National to Hemispheric Cultural Studies,* edited by Jeffrey Belnap and Raúl Fernández, 191–209. Durham, NC: Duke University Press, 1998.

Bolton, Herbert Eugene. *The Padre on Horseback: A Sketch of Eusebio Francisco Kino, S.J. Apostle to the Pimas*. San Francisco: Sonora, 1932.

———. *The Spanish Borderlands: A Chronicle of Old Florida and the Southwest*. New Haven, CT: Yale University Press, 1921.

Cuevas Aramburu, Mario, comp. *Sonora: textos de su historia* 2. Hermosillo/ Mexico City: Gobierno del Estado de Sonora/Instituto de Investigaciones Dr. José María Luis Mora, 1989.

Cypess, Sandra Messinger. *La Malinche in Mexican Literature: From History to Myth*. Austin: University of Texas Press, 1991.

Estrade, Paul. *José Martí: Los fundamentos de la democracia en Latinoamérica*. Madrid: Doce Calles, 2000.

Figueroa Valenzuela, Alejandro. "Los indios de Sonora ante la modernización porfirista." In *Historia general de Sonora*, 4 vols. Edited by Cynthia Radding de Murrieta, 139–63. Hermosillo: Gobierno del Estado de Sonora, 1997.

Fountain, Anne. "Ralph Waldo Emerson and Helen Hunt Jackson in *La Edad de Oro*," *SECOLAS Annals* 22.3 (1991): 44–50.

Gillman, Susan. "*Ramona* in 'Our America'." In *José Martí's "Our America": From National to Hemispheric Cultural Studies,* edited by Jeffrey Belnap and Raúl Fernández, 91–111. Durham, NC: Duke University Press, 1998.

Goldman, Anne E. *Continental Divides: Revisioning American Literature.* New York: Palgrave Macmillan, 2000.

González Navarro, Moisés. "*Mestizaje* in Mexico During the National Period." In *Race and Class in Latin America*, edited by Magnus Mörner. New York: Columbia University Press, 1970.

González Prada, Manuel. "Nuestros indios." In *Fuentes de la cultura latinoamericana*. Vol. I. Edited by Leopoldo Zea, 429–38. Mexico City: Fondo de Cultura Económica, 1993.

Gutiérrez Jones, Carl. *Rethinking the Borderlands: Between Chicano Culture and Legal Discourse.* Berkeley: University of California Press, 1995.

Hernández Silva, Héctor Cuauhtémoc. *Insurgencia y autonomía: historia de los pueblos yaquis, 1821–1910.* Mexico City: CIESAS/Instituto Nacional Indigenista, 1996.

Irwin, Robert McKee. *Bandits, Captives, Heroines and Saints: Cultural Icons of Mexico's Northwest Frontier.* Minneapolis: University of Minnesota Press, 2007.

———. "*Ramona* and Postnationalist American Studies: On 'Our America' and the Mexican Borderlands." *American Quarterly* 55 (2003): 539–67.

———. "Toward a Border Gnosis of the Borderlands: Joaquín Murrieta and Nineteenth-Century US-Mexico Border Culture." *Nepantla* 2 (2001): 509–37.

Jackson, Helen Hunt. *Ramona.* 1884. New York: Signet, 1998.

Jacobs, Margaret. "Mixed-Bloods, Mestizas, and Pintos: Race, Gender, and Claims to Whiteness in Helen Hunt Jackson's *Ramona* and María Amparo Ruiz de Burton's *Who Would Have Thought It?*" *Western American Literature* 36 (2001): 212–31.

James, George Wharton. *Through Ramona's Country.* Boston: Little, Brown, 1913.

Johnson, Benjamin. "Engendering Nation and Race in the Borderlands." *Latin American Research Review* 37 (2002): 259–71.

Lape, Noreen Groover. *West of the Border: The Multicultural Literature of the Western American Frontiers.* Athens: Ohio University Press, 2000.

López Soto, Virgilio. *Sonora: historia de la vida cotidiana.* Hermosillo: Sociedad Sonorense de Historia, 1998.

Luis-Brown, David. "'White Slaves' and 'Arrogant *Mestiza*': Reconfiguring Whiteness in *The Squatter and the Don* and *Ramona*." *American Literature* 69 (1997): 814–39.

Martí, José. "Antigüedades mexicanas." 1883. *Obras completas* 8, 327–29. La Habana: Editorial Nacional de Cuba, 1963.

———. "Autores americanos aborígenes," 1884. *Obras completas* 8, 335–37. La Habana: Editorial Nacional de Cuba, 1963.

———. "Los indios en los Estados Unidos." 1885. Martí. *Obras completas* 10, 319–27. La Habana: Editorial Nacional de Cuba, 1963.

———. "Mexico en los Estados Unidos: sucesos referentes a México." 1887. *Obras completas* 7, 50–58. La Habana: Editorial Nacional de Cuba, 1963.

———. "México y Estados Unidos." 1886. *Obras completas* 7, 45–50. La Habana: Editorial Nacional de Cuba, 1963.

———. "Nuestra América." 1891. *Fuentes de la cultura latinoamericana.* Vol. 1. Ed. Leopoldo Zea, 121–27. Mexico City: Fondo de Cultura Económica, 1993.

———. *Obras completas.* 28 Vol. La Habana: Editorial Nacional de Cuba, 1963.

———. "Our America." In *Divergent Modernities: Culture and Politics in Nineteenth-Century Latin America* by Julio Ramos, 295–303. Translated by John D. Blanco. Durham, NC: Duke University Press, 2001.

———. "'Ramona' de Helen Hunt Jackson." 1887. Marti. *Obras completas* 24, 199–502. La Habana: Editorial Nacional de Cuba, 1965.

Mathes, Valerie Sherer. *Helen Hunt Jackson and Her Indian Reform Legacy.* Austin: University of Texas Press, 1990.

Mignolo, Walter. "Capitalism and Geopolitics of Knowledge: Latin American Social Thought and Latino/a American Studies." In *Critical Latin American and Latino Studies,* edited by Juan Poblete, 32–75. Minneapolis: University of Minnesota Press, 2003.

———. *Local Histories/Global Designs.* Princeton, NJ: Princeton University Press, 2000.

Moyano Pahissa, Ángela, and David Piñera Ramírez. "El noroeste: Baja California 1850–1870." In *Visión histórica de la frontera norte de México* 4. Coordinated by David Piñera Ramírez, 79–91. Mexicali: Universidad Autónoma de Baja California/Editorial Kino/El Mexicano, 1994.

Ortega Noriega, Sergio. *Un ensayo de historia regional: el noroeste de México 1530-1880.* Mexico City: Universidad Nacional Autónoma de México, 1993.

Ortiz, Fernando. *Martí y las razas.* La Habana: Publicaciones de la Comisión Nacional Organizadora de los Actos y Ediciones del Centenario y del Monumento de Martí, 1953.

Paz, Ireneo. *Vida y aventuras del más célebre bandido sonorense Joaquín Murrieta: sus grandes proezas en California.* 1904. Houston: Arte Público, 1999.

Paz, Octavio. *El laberinto de la soledad.* 1950. Mexico City: Fondo de Cultura Económica, 1989.

Powell, Timothy. "Historical Multiculturalism: Cultural Complexity in the First Native American Novel." In *Beyond the Binary: Reconstructing Cultural Identity in a Multicultural Context,* edited by Timothy Powell, 185–204. New Brunswick, NJ: Rutgers University Press, 1999.

Radding, Cynthia. *Wandering Peoples: Colonialism, Ethnic Spaces, and Ecological Frontiers in Northwestern Mexico, 1700–1850.* Durham, NC: Duke University Press, 1997.

Sommer, Doris. *Foundational Fictions: The National Romances of Latin America.* Berkeley: University of California Press, 1993.

Starr, Kevin. *Inventing the Dream.* New York: Oxford University Press, 1985.

Streeby, Shelley. "Joaquín Murrieta and the American 1848." *Postnationalist American Studies,* edited by John Carlos Rowe, 166–99. Berkeley: University of California Press, 2000.

Tabuenca, María Socorro. "Aproximaciones críticas sobre las literaturas de las fronteras." *Frontera Norte* 9.18 (1997): 85–110.

Tarica, Estelle. *The Inner Life of Mestizo Nationalism.* Minneapolis: University of Minnesota Press, 2008.

Tinker Salas, Miguel. *In the Shadow of the Eagles: Sonora and the Transformation of the Border During the Porfiriato.* Berkeley: University of California Press, 1997.

Zorrilla, Luis G. *Historia de las relaciones entre México y los Estados Unidos de América 1800–1958.* Mexico City: Porrúa, 1965.

CHAPTER 9

POSSESSING LA SANTA DE CABORA: THE UNION OF SACRED, HUMAN, AND TRANSNATIONAL IDENTITIES

Desirée A. Martín

*We are defined by life itself and only in life can we see ourselves
reflected. And I? I have been a little bit of everything: a little saint,
a little virgin, a little married, a little in love, a little idealist, a
little revolutionary, a little visionary. Who am I, after all?*

—*Brianda Domecq*[1]

In the novel *La insólita historia de la Santa de Cabora* (*The
Astonishing Story of the Saint of Cabora* 1990), the Mexican writer
Brianda Domecq portrays Teresa Urrea, "La Santa de Cabora" of
Sonora, Mexico, demanding entrance at the heavenly gates shortly
after her death. The scene that ensues reflects the ambiguity and
contradiction that surrounded Urrea during her life and after her
death. The gatekeeper angel and God engage in a comical debate, for
they cannot find Cabora, her former home, on the registry of global
place names, nor can they find her name on the official list of saints:
"'She said she wanted to see you, that you would know who she was
if I told you she was Saint Teresa of Cabora.' 'Doesn't ring a bell.
Let's see, bring me the list of saints; maybe one slipped by without
my noticing. There are so many of them now!'"(1). Muttering that
there are so many saints nowadays that even he cannot keep track of
them, God then dismisses her as an "apocryphal saint" of the kind

that arises during popular rebellions on earth. He then sends the angel to turn Teresa away, instructing him not to fall prey to any feminine tricks, such as tears or the display of a false hymen to prove virginal martyrdom. His ultimatum is this: "If she makes a fuss, ask her for her genealogy. Women can never trace their genealogy back more than two generations. Tell her we don't admit saints without genealogies" (2). Yet Teresa defies God's contempt by boldly reciting her matrilineal genealogy to herself through more than twenty generations, flaunting her illegitimate origins while claiming her right to be called a saint.

While it might seem obvious for God to reject Teresa, for she is clearly not a saint in the orthodox Catholic tradition, his definition of sanctity implies that only male saints are able to articulate their genealogies. Thus, he dismisses her not merely because she is an apocryphal saint, but because of her humanity—specifically, her gender, as demonstrated through a stereotypical reading of her femininity. Domecq's representation of Teresa explicitly rejects the religious hierarchy and orthodox convention that God espouses, but even more importantly, it reveals that Teresa's claim on sanctity is frequently positioned against her human characteristics, especially in relation to gender. Thus, Domecq demonstrates that Teresa is criticized as much because of her humanity as because of her sanctity.

The conflict between Teresa Urrea's humanity and sanctity is only one of the contradictions she faces. This literary anecdote reveals the manner in which she has been misunderstood, underestimated, and dismissed throughout her history since she began to be considered a saint in 1889 in Sonora. In fact, she was all but forgotten in Mexico and the United States, at least in a national sense, until authors like Domecq began to intensively research her life in the 1980s and 1990s. However, as a popular *regional* saint, her memory lived on in the western U.S.-Mexico borderlands, especially in Arizona, New Mexico, Sonora, and Chihuahua. As the anecdote suggests, there has been plenty of doubt surrounding Teresa Urrea since the 1880s, for she has repeatedly been condemned for being too feminine, too childlike, too ignorant, or still worse, demented. At the same time, she has been celebrated for her intelligence, spirituality, strength, healing powers, and compassion, as well as for her resistance to authorities she considered to be corrupt, particularly the clergy, medical doctors, and the government of Porfirio Díaz. To this day, she is characterized as both visionary and hysterical, often in the same breath.

In the past twenty years there has been a resurgence of interest in Teresa Urrea. Artists, authors, and intellectuals on both sides of the border have begun to interrogate earlier representations of Teresa, particularly those like the Mexican author Heriberto Frías' novel *Tomochic* (1893) that characterize her as a lunatic or a victim. Contemporary representations of Teresa Urrea emphasize her connection to progressive gender politics, migration, transnational identities, and the affirmation of popular spirituality as a conscious revolutionary choice. Nevertheless, Teresa's sacred and human characteristics are still frequently characterized in conflict with each other, and it as such, are perpetually in question—even, at times, by Teresa herself. However, a critical reading of contemporary texts, particularly Domecq's *The Astonishing Story,* demonstrates that the sacred and the human are in fact deeply intertwined in Teresa Urrea's life. This link is established through a variety of ways, revealing new interpretations of the intersection between traditional forms of popular sanctity and secular or modern cultural production. Moreover, border and national spaces are essentially rearticulated through the union of sacred and human characteristics. In this essay, I argue that the two most important points of connection between sacred and human, as well as the primary modes of representing and understanding La Santa de Cabora, are "spirit possession," in which characters or authors and artists themselves desire to possess or be possessed by Teresa, literally or metaphorically becoming her through the texts, and the construction of transnational identities in the western United States and Mexico.

The focus on spirit possession in many recent texts about Teresa demonstrates the persistence of spirituality in modern life. Spirit possession imbues ostensibly secular or modern forms of cultural production with spirituality, demonstrating that spirituality functions as a part of modernity. In *The Magic of the State,* the anthropologist Michael Taussig describes the popular Latin American rituals of possession and reincarnation in which the dead—especially the sanctified figures of Indians and blacks—pass into the bodies of the living (3–5). This "magical harnessing" of dead political and historical bodies serves to construct the modern nation-state, as popular figures are merged with national heroes like Simón Bolívar as objects of worship and sources of possession (3). The nation is thus imagined through its transformative potential for others, demonstrating the link between the production of faithful worshippers and productive citizens. In the case of Teresa Urrea, however, spirit possession relates explicitly to the creation of transnational or borderlands identities, as critics, writers, and artists such as Domecq, the Chicano writer Luis Alberto Urrea, and the historian Paul Vanderwood emphasize the historical intersections across the U.S.-Mexico borderlands.

Following border studies theorists such as José David Saldívar, Guillermo Gómez-Peña, and Gloria Anzaldúa, the critics and authors who embrace spirit possession through Teresa demonstrate that border space has frequently been perceived as a separate "third space" by border residents and migrants, distinct from dominant national space both because of its distance (literal and figurative) from the national centers of Mexico City or Washington, D.C., and because of its historical fluidity, as demonstrated by border crossers and migrants who may feel equally at home on both sides. Of course, many border crossers are not free to choose which side of the border to live on, or whether or not to cross at all. It is precisely the dichotomy between agency and restriction regarding the borderlands that Teresa Urrea exemplifies through the integration of sacred and human characteristics.

In turn, her struggle between humanity and sanctity relates to the construction of transnational identities along the border. Though in her time Teresa was an icon on both sides of the western borderlands, she was always excluded from national belonging in either Mexico or the United States because of her status as popular saint, independent woman, revolutionary, and exile. While Teresa's sacred and human characteristics—especially in relation to her gender—exclude her from national belonging, her sanctity and humanity also establish the potential for border crossing and transnational allegiances among her followers. That is, Teresa Urrea demonstrates the manner in which the borderlands function as both a boundary, which reinforces the limits of national space, and a transgressive space, which opens up the possibility of transnational identities. Thus, through a reading of *The Astonishing Story* and other contemporary texts, I contend that the antagonism that is usually posed between sacred and human characteristics is deconstructed through an emphasis on spirit possession and transnationalism. Ultimately, I argue that the antinomy between sacred and human that Teresa Urrea struggles with is overturned to produce a transnational identity between Mexico and the United States.

* * *

The Life of Teresa Urrea, Santa de Cabora

Teresa Urrea's story is told from many perspectives by sources ranging from official to popular and historical to literary, with much conjecture over the details of her life and her personal intentions. While all representations of Teresa's life are necessarily fictionalized to some extent, the basic story is as follows: Born in 1872 or 1873, in Ocorini, Sinaloa, she was the illegitimate child of Don Tomás Urrea, a wealthy white landowner, and a poor indigenous woman named Cayetana Chávez, who lived on Urrea's property. Teresa spent her early years in extreme poverty, until moving to Cabora, Sonora, in 1888 with the support of her father, who recognized her and gave her his name. At Cabora, one of the household servants, a *curandera* (medicine woman) called Huila, taught her the art of healing through the use of herbs and potions. In 1889, Teresa suffered a "cataleptic fit" or seizure that caused her to go into a coma for thirteen days. The family, believing she had died, prepared a wake, during which Teresa awoke, sat up, and announced Huila's imminent death, which occurred three days later (Holden 54–56). Teresa then slipped into a trancelike state for another three months. During this trance, she began her healing ministry in earnest, claiming to be inspired by visions and voices of God and the Virgin Mary. She appeared to have acquired telepathic and telekinetic powers and utilized a combination of laying on of hands, herbal remedies, and mixtures of soil and her own saliva or blood to effect her cures (Vanderwood 169–71). Thousands of pilgrims, especially indigenous people, began to worship her as a saint and flocked to Cabora to see her.

Predictably, these pilgrimages did not sit well with President Porfirio Díaz. The Mexican government was extremely wary of any public celebration of indigenous difference and perceived an intrinsic link between millenarianism and popular rebellion, particularly in relation to the volatile border region. Teresa was especially revered by the Mayo and Yaqui Indians and became known as the "Queen of the Yaquis." While the Yaquis were particularly feared for their aggressiveness, it was the Mayos who, in May 1892, attacked Navojoa, Sonora, crying "¡Viva la Santa de Cabora!" (Vanderwood 196, 199). Of even greater significance, however, was the peasant rebellion that erupted in Tomóchic, Chihuahua, in late 1891. The rebels, who wished to challenge the state's totalitarian control over their region, fought for a year against the much larger and more powerful Mexican army (Osorio 121–24). Though the Porfirian government immediately attributed the rebellion to La Santa de Cabora's influence, in reality the rebels of Tomóchic sought Teresa's counsel and benediction only after the first full-fledged attack on their town by the army. Inspired by their faith in Teresa's divine powers, the rebels fought on, temporarily forcing the Mexican army to retreat. But eventually, the government crushed the rebellion, massacring almost all of the Tomochitecos and burning the entire town down to the ground in

December 1892. Prior to this, however, in May 1892, immediately following the Mayo rebellion, Teresa and her father, Don Tomás, were arrested and exiled to the United States as threats to national cohesion and stability.

Teresa and Tomás Urrea initially resided in Nogales, Arizona, where she continued her spiritual ministry while remaining a symbol of revolutionary potential for Mexicans on both sides of the border. Though it is unclear whether she participated in it directly, Teresa was associated with an unsuccessful raid on a customs office in Nogales, Mexico, by a group of mostly Yaqui Indians in August 1896 and served in a symbolic capacity for the production of revolutionary propaganda (Vanderwood 299–300). In 1897, under pressure from the U.S. and Mexican governments, Teresa and Don Tomás moved away from the border region to Clifton, Arizona. This period marked a turn to domestic life for Teresa and, according to both her followers and her critics, the beginning of the supposed decline of her saintly powers. Against her father's wishes, in 1900 she married Guadalupe Rodríguez, a laborer in the mines, who forcibly tried to take her back to Mexico and attempted to shoot her when she resisted. He was immediately imprisoned and later hanged himself in his cell (Domecq, "Teresa Urrea" 44–46). Shaken, Teresa returned to her family, but the rift with her father had been set. She soon embarked upon a national tour with an American medical company led by the San Francisco businessman J. H. Suits, which purported to discover the source of her healing powers, but which ended up displaying her as a curiosity (Vanderwood 304–5). During this time Teresa fell in love with one John Van Order, the much younger son of a family friend who had been serving as her interpreter on the national tour. They had two daughters, but by the time she returned to Clifton in 1904, the lovers had parted ways. There, she used her earnings from the medical company tour to help build a hospital and died in 1906 of tuberculosis at the age of thirty-three (Domecq, "Teresa Urrea" 46).

The fact that many believed that Teresa Urrea had lost her saintly attributes after marrying, divorcing, and having children with another man indicates the manner in which she embodies the tension between the extremes of the physically human and the mythically divine. However, the conflict between humanity and sanctity both limits and liberates her. Though Teresa's human characteristics—especially those associated with her gender—contribute to her development as a popular saint, these characteristics also potentially nullify her sanctity. This is evident through the stereotypical association of Teresa's supernatural powers with female hysteria. Meanwhile, though her sanctity grants her the freedom to be an independent woman at a time when women's options were limited, this sanctity also confines her by denying her human qualities. Her revolutionary activities, her female domesticity, and her independence are the very traits that provoke both critics and followers to declare her less than saintly. Yet at every point, Teresa's sanctity and humanity intersect through the blending of traditional forms of popular sanctity with more modern or secular cultural forms. These practices, both traditional and modern, include healing practices or mediation with the divine, the performance of sanctity as spectacle through public forums such as the media or photography, and an association with politics and revolutionary activities. Furthermore, spirit possession reflects the union of sanctity and humanity in Teresa Urrea's life by linking popular unorthodox spiritual practices, such as chanting, speaking in tongues, or channeling the spirits of the dead, to her function as a strong, independent woman.

*   *   *

POSSESSING TERESA URREA

Naturally, contemporary authors and critics modify the definition of spirit possession in their artistic and literary representations of Teresa even further. As well as reclaiming Teresa as a modern woman, authors and artists. such as Domecq, Vanderwood, and Luis Urrea, establish links across the western U.S.-Mexico borderlands, emphasizing the historical production of transnational identities through Teresa Urrea. While all of these authors and critics represent characters that attempt to possess or be possessed by Teresa, either by assuming her persona or literally "becoming" her, several of them also literally or metaphorically portray *themselves* as possessing or being possessed by Teresa. For example, the historian Paul Vanderwood engages in both representational and personal spirit possession even as he emphasizes historical veracity in his analysis of the Tomóchic rebellion, *The Power of God Against the Guns of Government*. While he argues for the importance of Teresa Urrea's spirituality, he also draws curious conclusions about the nature of her humanity.

Like others, Vanderwood links Teresa's human characteristics to her femininity. However, he seems to disparage her importance for contemporary feminists and Chicanas/os, declaring, "While ratifying her claims to special powers and buoyed by Teresa's own vacillations about their origin, both feminists and Mexican-Americans have chosen to cloak Teresa in a secular garb that more resembles their own . . . [they] seem to be reluctant to recall the spirituality that pervaded her life" (323). Here, Vanderwood assumes that "feminists and Mexican-Americans" are necessarily secular and that their work, perhaps because of its focus on marginalized communities, precludes spirituality. Moreover, he implies that there is a divide between "premodern" spirituality and "modern" secularism. Nevertheless, despite his claims on historical truth, and the divide between spiritual and secular he seems to promote, Vanderwood also expresses a desire to possess or be possessed by Teresa, particularly in his description of the celebration of the first annual Santa Teresa Day, held in Clifton, Arizona, in 1994. During the festival, local tourism promoter Luis Pérez reconstructed Teresa's life story to a mesmerized audience, describing the legendary cave in Cabora where Teresa was said to have collected soil to use in her healings and distributing some of this "holy soil" to the crowd. Citing people's "hunger for a personal experience with a higher being" (323) in the present day, Vanderwood writes,

> Twenty or thirty people—one in a wheelchair, another with fearsome physical hurts, several with unrestrained tears streaming down their cheeks—requested a few grains of that soil, myself included, all for our own private reasons. (328)

Vanderwood thus ends his history on a supernatural note, implicitly equating himself and his research with the pilgrims who seek spiritual and physical healing. By invoking the Santa de Cabora's mystical powers for the development of his research, in a sense he also pronounces himself a believer and thus a part of the multiple temporalities of the sacred and the secular that she represents.

However, by expressing Teresa's revival through nostalgia for a more perfect past, Vanderwood promotes a mystified version of Teresa. He interprets the recollection of the past as an effect of faith, further reflecting the union of spiritual and secular as he writes, "Faith is already working its miracles. People are recalling their history as needed to ponder, revalidate, and critique their present; they are reformulating their past to consider and serve their contemporary anxieties and demands" (329). At the same time, however, he suggests that only certain types of people can properly understand her, such as the devout pilgrims that he associates himself with. He privileges the historian's access to Teresa, suggested by his almost territorial claim on her spirituality, as opposed to the "feminists and

Mexican-Americans" he cites above. But Vanderwood also subsumes the pilgrims of Clifton under the intellectual privilege of the historian, implicitly comparing them, and Teresa, to relics that may exist within modernity, but do not form an integral part of it (Chakrabarty 48–49). By rendering Teresa as myth, Vanderwood underscores the antinomy between sacred and secular, or sacred and human, that he would seem to contest.

Indeed, such an idealized representation of Teresa produces just as inflexible a myth as her earlier characterization as a victim or a lunatic. This sort of mystification is further evident in the Chicano author Luis Alberto Urrea's representation of spirit possession and historical truth in relation to Teresa. Like Vanderwood, Luis Urrea's purpose in reclaiming Teresa involves the union of spirituality and historical truth (albeit with a different thrust), for he aims to "bring comfort to an ever-widening circle of pilgrims" throughout the borderlands, particularly Chicanos/as and Native Americans, as well as to retrieve his own lost family history, for he claims that Teresa Urrea was his great-aunt ("Saint Teresita de Cabora"). Yet his account of Teresa's life on his website is extremely idealized and often substantially different from that cited in most other sources ("Saint Teresita de Cabora"). For instance, on his website he implies that Cayetana, Teresa's mother, had a choice in rearing her away from the Urrea household and that Tomás Urrea took the initiative in seeking Teresa out at Cabora. Furthermore, while he ends his historical novel based on Teresa's life, *The Hummingbird's Daughter,* just as she and Don Tomás are exiled to the United States, on his website he states that on her deathbed Teresa joyfully reconciled with Cayetana, who had abandoned her so many years earlier—an account uncorroborated by any other historical source.

Although it is clear that all accounts of Teresa's life are at least partly fictionalized, Luis Urrea nevertheless calls his description "the truth—a truth more marvelous than the family legends," further idealizing and mystifying her ("Saint Teresita de Cabora"). Both Vanderwood and Luis Urrea engage in this type of mystification through their versions of spirit possession, even though they purport to provide historical or factual information about Teresa. In doing so, they reinforce the very dichotomies associated with Teresa, such as those between sacred and human, that they aim to challenge. As Domecq argues in her historical essays and in *The Astonishing Story,* such idealizations ignore the inconsistencies and contradictions in Teresa's persona. To this end, Domecq asserts that her own intentions are explicitly "literary, not historical," and that "history has had the luxury of overlooking" the contradictions in Teresa's life (Domecq, "Teresa Urrea" 12). By embracing the contradictions between Teresa's sacred and secular identities, Domecq contests the antinomies between sacred and human that shape Teresa Urrea's myth.

* * *

TERESA'S STRUGGLE BETWEEN SANCTITY AND HUMANITY

In *The Astonishing Story,* Domecq suggests that the consolidation of Teresa's myth prevents her from fully inhabiting either her sacred or human characteristics. The construction of this myth, by which people like Teresa Urrea are converted into icons, constrains her, for it not only reveals the collapse of her humanity into her sanctity, it reveals that she was never really allowed to be completely human or saint to begin with. Part of the appeal of saints is the accessibility of their imperfect bodies and the humanity they share with ordinary people. The humanity of popular saints actually links them to the divine. But for Teresa, physical imperfection is either denied or exaggerated, just as her divinity is denied and exaggerated, for reasons ranging from her gender to her association with indigenous rebellion. Thus, it is neither enough to recall her human attributes and imperfections, nor simply enough to return the emphasis to her spirituality. Instead, we must go to the root of the problem—the notion that the human and the sacred are incompatible—and embrace the contradictions between the human and the sacred in the representation of popular saints.

Domecq's representation of Teresa in *The Astonishing Story* reveals that she must accept her sanctity to embrace her humanity and vice versa. Like the other artists and authors I have mentioned, Domecq's representation of spirit possession demonstrates the intertwined construction of the sacred and the secular and puts her work into dialogue with the pilgrims who believe in Teresa's healing powers. Domecq's version of spirit possession deliberately links authorial identification with artistic representation, for she consciously identifies herself with Teresa and other characters as a trope in her work. Domecq also challenges earlier interpretations of Teresa as victim or lunatic and bases her fiction on copious historical research. But unlike Vanderwood and Luis Urrea, she makes no definitive claims upon the truth of her record. Instead, she establishes a parallel between herself and Teresa as women who have been chronically misread by others, and claims to have adopted her as "a sister in disgrace" in order to rescue her from oblivion (Domecq, "Teresa Urrea" 12). As well as chronicling Teresa's life, the novel focuses on a woman researcher who is obsessed with the Santa de Cabora, to the extent that her life begins to parallel Teresa's until she metaphorically and literally becomes her.

Around the time of the one-hundredth anniversary of Teresa's birth, the unnamed narrator of *The Astonishing Story* dreams repeatedly of a place called Cabora, eventually believing that Teresa has personally called her to her research (9–10). Teresa directs the narrator's actions, guiding her toward the discovery of Heriberto Frías' *Tomóchic,* where she describes her confusion at the contradiction between Teresa's representation as victim and threat. Domecq describes the researcher's identification with Teresa: "She so wanted to penetrate to the very soul of the forgotten woman . . . that she ended up losing almost all notion of her own reality and was living only to retrieve the other's existence" (5). As the narrator feels more and more alienated, the inability to distinguish between her own life and Teresa's compels her to visit Sonora in search of Cabora, where, in the midst of hallucinations relating various passages from her research and visions of Teresa, she finally arrives at the cave on the hill where Teresa supposedly collected soil for use in her healing ceremonies. After tasting the soil, as Teresa was said to have done, the woman experiences an overwhelming sensation of déjà vu; then, losing her footing, she slips and falls. In the novel this moment definitively unites the women, for it is also the moment that Teresa falls into a coma and metaphorically dies. During the fall, the two characters are fused into one body with a common history, a double moment of "death" that also represents Teresa's transformation into a saint and the researcher's transformation into Teresa (153).

The researcher, who suggests more than a passing resemblance to Domecq, is clearly meant to be a contemporary version of the saint. The similarities between the woman's research as a personal destiny determined by the Santa de Cabora herself—"She [Teresa] has brought me here" (68)—and Teresa's spiritual calling as healer and saint are obvious. While both characters struggle to find meaning in their lives through their respective callings—for the researcher, the study of Teresa's life; for Teresa, the path of sanctity—both of these missions are ultimately unsatisfactory or incomplete. In the novel, as the researcher dissolves into Teresa, Teresa must reconcile the opposing poles of sanctity and humanity. Yet while Domecq portrays her throughout the novel as a strong woman who rejects the societal dictates for women of her race and class, Teresa interprets her sanctity through an idealized view of masculinity as a marker of liberation. Prior to becoming a saint, Teresa insists upon learning to read, ride horses like a man, and play the guitar, while after her conversion she supports equal rights and autonomy for indigenous groups and the poor. She ministers as a saint against the wishes of her father, symbolically rejecting the patriarchal structure she is subject to. Indeed, from an early age, Teresa expresses the desire to be a man—specifically a powerful landowner like Don Tomás. She vows to refuse the constraints of femininity, which she understands through the vulnerability of the female body:

> She solemnly swore three things: first, that she would always keep her legs together; second, she would hide in the hills every time she bled so no man would ever smell her; and third, she would never, never get married or have children.   (62)

Although Teresa eventually breaks these vows, she decides at the time that the only way to challenge the limits of the feminine is to assume a masculine persona.

Before her transformation, Teresa rejects the humility and invisibility of her childhood relatives and the other indigenous women at Cabora, and she believes that she can achieve independence after entering her father's household by shifting social class levels. Once she realizes that wealthy women also face restrictions based on social mores, she understands that the only path away from the limits of women's bodies and toward independence is through sanctity. But while she is liberated from the constraints of her female body by becoming a saint, she also rejects family ties, personal relationships, and her role as feminine nurturer because of this sanctity. Whether coded as masculine or feminine, Teresa is unable to engage her own humanity throughout most of the novel. Although she initially perceives her humanity to be a prison, in a sense, her sanctity is no less of one.

Alongside the struggle between sanctity and humanity, Teresa is torn between longing for a normative life and rejecting the constraints of such a life. Throughout the novel she exists primarily through her spiritual works and her role as a revolutionary symbol. For the most part, Teresa realizes that she is only a saint because of the grace of God and the faith of others. Nevertheless, she is occasionally seduced by her own reputation. At one point, filled with hubris, she declares, "A lo mejor yo soy ese Cristo" (" . . . perhaps I am that Christ") (203),[2] but generally seems to fluctuate between self-doubt and narcissism. While treating a poor indigenous girl named Anastasia, Teresa realizes that the girl is beyond salvation because of her advanced tuberculosis. However, by absorbing the unwavering faith that Anastasia has in her as a saint, she calls on the girl to believe in the miracle as a condition of her salvation: "You have to believe in the miracle; only that way can I help you" (242). It seems as if Teresa is participating in the construction of her own myth. Later, as the government's persecution of Teresa increases and she faces imminent exile, she dreams that Anastasia has come to her, fully cured, bearing the gift of her diseased lungs. But the dream also reflects Teresa's instability, for the lungs pursue her and threaten to consume her. The example demonstrates that Teresa is ambivalent about her spiritual powers, for she is both emboldened and frightened by them. Ultimately, she is unable to reconcile her spiritual and political powers with their eventual failure, as she laments to a friend, "Do you know how it feels to want to do good and over and over again turn out to be an instrument of destruction?" (338).

* * *

TRANSNATIONAL IDENTITIES: THE BORDERLANDS AS BOUNDARY AND TRANSGRESSIVE SPACE

Meanwhile, Teresa's struggle between sanctity and humanity connects to the construction of transnational identities along the western borderlands. Particularly in relation to her exile to the United States, the conflict between sanctity and humanity reveals her permanent exclusion from national belonging and, by extension, exposes the illusion of national unity. After being exiled from Mexico, Teresa realizes that all of her identities are fluctuating and that she has never fully possessed them. These fluctuating identities extend, of course, to national identity and social class status. In Nogales, Arizona, she loses the class privilege that she had earned by moving to Cabora. More importantly, she loses the saintly myth of perfection she has come to rely on, for she intermittently loses the adulation of the masses that revere her as a saint. After giving birth to her daughter in 1901, her status as a mother, symbolic of a return to her humanity—especially the vulnerable femininity she has disparaged—marks the further deterioration of her spiritual powers in the eyes of many of her followers: "They say that I no longer attract much of an audience and it bothers them that I have a daughter. They think that's what took away my aura of 'saint'" (350).

However, it is not simply Teresa's embrace of her human characteristics that antagonizes the public, for her sanctity was a point of
contention between the Anglo and Mexican-American inhabitants of
Nogales from the moment she arrived there in 1892. She is immediately identified as "just another Mexican" by the powerful gringos
of Nogales:

> She was just another Mexican among all the refugees who crossed the
> border every day, an undesirable foreigner whose customs provoked
> first malicious laughter and then scorn, an outcast, a cultural hybrid,
> an abnormality within the context of Nogales. She didn't belong
> there. (279)

Teresa is lumped in with all the other "refugees," but it is her "customs"—her spiritual powers—that mark her as "abnormal." The fact
that these sacred "customs" have formed the basis of Teresa's myth
in northwestern Mexico is irrelevant, for to the Anglo residents of
Nogales, they are a hybrid practice presumably no different from
eating chiles or singing *rancheras* (traditional rural Mexican music).
More precisely, this example demonstrates that Teresa becomes
"Mexican," and thus undesirable, in the national context of the
United States as her sanctity is collapsed into her Mexican identity.
Yet even as she is equated with other border-crossing Mexicans and
indigenous peoples, it is clear that she has never been allowed to claim
Mexican national belonging in the first place. At the same time, while
she becomes a "culturally hybrid" Mexican only after she is banished
from Mexico, Teresa is an outsider in the United States, and she continues to be excluded from national identity. The double exclusion
that Teresa and other marginalized border crossers face reveals the
manner in which the border firmly serves as a boundary that reinforces national limits and national belonging, even as it might signal
the possibility of transgressive spaces and transnationalism.

Significantly, Teresa's exclusion from national identity in both
Mexico and the United States associates her with those marginalized peoples such as migrants, peasants, and indigenous peoples
who are her most fervent followers. Domecq particularly emphasizes
the connection between Teresa and her humble indigenous followers. Referring to the Yaquis and Mayos, she writes, "The majority
of them had arrived just as she [Teresa] had, fleeing from injustice,
fearful of being sent to the National Valley on the Yucatan Peninsula,
where they would die of hunger, malaria, and sorrow" (278). In the
United States, Teresa is not distanced from her indigenous followers

because of class, race, or her iconic status as a saint. Despite her earlier ambivalence about being associated with marginalized peoples, after her exile, she is now definitively united and allies herself with them. In fact, she embraces their connection, unlike most other Mexicans in Arizona whose main goal is to assimilate: "Other Mexican families stayed away, afraid of being identified with the motley groups of Indians. Their ambition was to conceal their mestizo traits, learn English, cover up their Latino background, and become accepted by the 'whiteys'" (279). While class and racial assimilation are still driving factors for many Mexicans living on the U.S. side of the border, Teresa finally understands that this path to dominant national belonging is impossible.

Unsurprisingly, Teresa's exile, which represents the moment of crisis both for her struggle between humanity and sanctity and her capacity for national belonging, coincides with her radicalization against the state in the novel. But while she attempts to find a place for herself and other marginalized peoples in the borderlands by openly supporting rebellion, as in the U.S. customs office raid, these revolutionary efforts are doomed to failure. Nevertheless, she knows that the Indians', and by extension, her own need for belonging, cannot correspond to national belonging:

> Teresa realized that the majority didn't need relief from physical ailments but from spiritual ones; they wanted the identity of a community . . . they wanted to reinvent lost traditions to feel that they belonged to some place, to some history . . . they wanted . . . what had been left behind in another world, in another moment of time. (278–79)

What has been "left behind" for Indians like the Yaquis and Mayos is not a Mexican national identity, since they have never truly pertained to one. Instead, the desire for lost traditions and history reflects a form of community that is specifically non-national, corresponding to fluid transnational identities that are predicated upon migration, border crossing, and awareness that national identity has always been illusory. The association of marginalized groups with non-national identities in Mexico and the United States also carries over to ideas of national citizenship in general. If migrants or Indians necessarily escape the bounds of national identity, any citizen might if they do not adhere to strictly held hierarchies of race or class or if they seek out past histories that pertain to "another moment in time" rather than relying upon official narratives of national identity. It is precisely this sort of past—and present—history that correlates to the transgressive space of the borderlands, a space that links the "lost traditions" of the past across history. This transnational space also connects current notions of borderless globalization, which often restricts marginalized groups to transborder communities that flout dominant national identities and convey agency for subjugated peoples.

Clearly, the conflict between sanctity and humanity prevents Teresa from belonging to either the United States or Mexico because of her status as holy saint and imperfect, independent woman. But while this conflict reveals the myth of universal national unity, it continues unabated until the end of *The Astonishing Story*. In exile, reporters and others still capriciously persist in classifying her as hero, martyr, or victim, and in positioning her saintly and human characteristics against each other (279–80). Meanwhile, Teresa continues to be plagued by self-doubt: "My life has been a lie. I don't even know if I exist or if I'm just a fabrication" (338). In an apparent contradiction, she remains trapped by the very antinomies that the novel so clearly contests. Nevertheless, from the opening of the novel, with its humorous depiction of Teresa at the Pearly Gates before the ultimate patriarch, ambiguity and contradiction between sanctity and gendered humanity are the order of the day—indeed, they are the means by which Teresa triumphs over God by reciting her matrilineal genealogy.

The Astonishing Story demonstrates, above all, the intrinsic relation between the sacred and the human in the life of Teresa Urrea. Along with other contemporary texts, Domecq's novel dismantles the antagonism between the sacred and the human through a focus on spirit possession, which demonstrates the blending of traditional forms of popular sanctity and secular cultural production, and by revealing the long history of transnational identities along the western borderlands. Although Teresa's exclusion from a national identity is quite specific, for it is predicated upon her threatening sanctity and gendered humanity, it nevertheless indicates the manner in which many marginalized groups are automatically excluded from national belonging. While this exclusion reveals the authoritarian function of the border as boundary or limit, it also opens up the transgressive possibility of transnational identities that reveal the illusion of universal national belonging promoted by the U.S. and Mexican states. In the end, *The Astonishing Story* asks us to interrogate antonimical identities, temporalities, and spaces, whether these are identified as premodern or modern, national or transnational, sacred or human. It is only by embracing the inherent contradictions between these shifting identities that we can truly understand Teresa Urrea as both human and saint.

Notes

1. *The Astonishing Story of the Saint of Cabora.* All translations are my own unless otherwise indicated.
2. Curiously, this line does not appear in the English translation of the novel.

Works Cited

Chakrabarty, Dipesh. "The Time of History and the Times of Gods." In *The Politics of Culture in the Shadow of Capital*, edited by Lisa Lowe and David Lloyd, 35–60. Durham, NC: Duke University Press, 1997.

Domecq, Brianda. "Teresa Urrea: La Santa de Cabora." In *Tomóchic: La revolución adelantada*, Vol. II. Edited by Jesús Vargas Valdez 11–47. Ciudad Juárez: Universidad Autónoma de Ciudad Juárez, 1994.

———. *La insólita historia de la Santa de Cabora.* México, DF: Planeta, 1990.

———. *The Astonishing Story of the Saint of Cabora.* Translated by Kay S. García. Tempe: Bilingual, 1998.

Frías, Heriberto. *Tomochic.* 1893. México, DF: Editorial Porrúa, 1999.

Holden, William Curry. *Teresita.* Owings Mills, MD: Stemmer House, 1978.

Osorio, Rubén. *Tomóchic en llamas.* México, DF: Consejo Nacional para la Cultura y las Artes, 1995.

Taussig, Michael. *The Magic of the State.* New York: Routledge, 1997.

Urrea, Luis Alberto. *The Hummingbird's Daughter.* New York: Little, Brown, 2005.

———. "Saint Teresita of Cabora." *Luisurrea.com.* April 30, 2008. http://www.luisurrea.com/teres/teresita.php.

Vanderwood, Paul. *The Power of God Against the Guns of Government.* Stanford, CA: Stanford University Press, 1998.

CHAPTER 10

MANIFOLD DESTINIES: ISABEL ALLENDE'S *DAUGHTER OF FORTUNE* AND TONI MORRISON'S *PARADISE**

Cheli Reutter

Toni Morrison's 1998 novel *Paradise* is unique among narratives of the American West. Conventional western narratives, including western dime novels, Louis L'Amour novels, and classic western films, inscribe an Anglo-Saxon, U.S. American, and masculine hegemony. Female-authored narratives of the West sometimes challenge the hierarchies of conventional westerns but are typically less ambitious in scope.[1] The extent of their challenge, moreover, is not often as great as might be hoped for. Willa Cather, the author most often cited by scholars of the American West, offers an immigrant female version of the pioneer prototype we have come to expect: that is, physically and emotionally strong Anglo women living through hardship and grief but ultimately emerging triumphant. In *My Ántonia,* Cather's heroine nearly achieves the status of a goddess, or at least earth mother.[2] Another women's strategy for writing the West is a dramatization of the violent effects of Western lifestyles on women. This strategy appears in Jean Stafford's post–World War II novel *Mountain Lion* and Annie Dillard's 1992 novel *The Living.* Yet a third strategy is to address the especial position of ethnic women in the West, as do (in strikingly different ways across a century) Helen Hunt Jackson and Leslie Silko in *Ramona* and *Ceremony,* respectively. Morrison and Isabel Allende employ all three strategies in *Paradise* and *Daughter of*

Fortune, respectively. Among these intriguing but muted challenges to Western hierarchies, Morrison's *Paradise* is most striking. Its subtle and sometimes ironic uses of these strategies yield a particularly comprehensive critique of conventions in narratives of the West.

The comparison between *Daughter of Fortune* and *Paradise* is useful in mapping turn-of-the-millennium responses to both conventional and feminine myths of the West. Both are set in the West and are written by women of color not generally associated with westerns. The novels, written a year apart in 1998 and 1999, respectively, demonstrate awareness of postnational or transnational discourse on the West. Beyond these comparisons, the two novels are a study in contrasts. Allende is a popular writer, whereas Morrison's considerable appeal to a popular audience is less notable than her value in the scholarly community. This difference in audience corresponds to a central difference in the manner in which the female protagonists are engaged with myths of the West. While Allende's novel is superficially transnational, it also employs conventional nationalist strategies. Morrison's novel, meanwhile, resists convention.

An author's primary challenge in writing literature of the West that is not also western lies in resisting the nationalist agendas inscribed in conventional narratives of the West. Alternatives to nationalist narratives include postnationalism and transnationalism. Nationalism offers a monolithic view of contested or ethnically amalgamated regions, ascribes cohesive and positive attributes to a nation or its peoples, and maintains conceptual borders congruent with political ones. Postnationalism resists the attribution of cohesive and generally positive characteristics to a nation-state (for current purposes, specifically the United States) but acknowledges that "the nation" does exist as a conceptual unit with actual political power.[3] As Robert Irwin suggests in "Helen Hunt Jackson's *Ramona,*" transnationalism can be understood conceptually as the consideration of the issues of a particular region, specifically a contested one, from both sides of a political border.

A litmus test for nationalism is Manifest Destiny. Allende's and Morrison's texts number among the manifold narratives involving the American West and Manifest Destiny. However, *Daughter of Fortune* conforms to the conventional treatment of the principle as it celebrates two Chilean women as paragons of Manifest Destiny. Morrison's *Paradise,* on the other hand, critiques the principle through its attention to the slaying of four female characters whose killers are motivated by a desire to be proponents of it.

Manifest Destiny locates the positive attributes of the United States within certain individuals or groups who, their proponents assert, are clearly destined to prosper in the land and have a sacred duty to plant their values or cultural legacy. Whereas *Paradise* belies this myth of Manifest Destiny as well as its applicability to African American settlers such as those in the fictionalized towns of Haven and Ruby, *Daughter of Fortune* merely issues a pluralist and feminist revision of it. In *Paradise,* the faith of the leaders of Ruby in Manifest Destiny is profoundly challenged. Meanwhile, in *Daughter of Fortune,* those presumed to be destined do in fact succeed.

The above notwithstanding, I guiltily confess my great pleasure in *Daughter of Fortune:* it is a lush, imaginative page-turner that, on a superficial reading, makes all the right moves as it presents strong and interestingly developed female characters and tropes. With its boatloads of Chilean harvests, or "delights of the Southern hemisphere" (355), it provides the trope of the West that Annette Kolodny identifies as the hallmark of feminine versions of the West. It also interestingly treats the issues of sexual passion, pregnancy, surrogation, and adoption, and it features a diverse and appealing cast of characters.

Moreover, *Daughter of Fortune* exemplifies the "pure pluralism" that Werner Sollors identifies. Allende's text, undeniably clever in its manipulations of western tropes, involves crossings of several boundaries, including geography and race (with national border crossings and the featuring of nonwhite characters as heroes). Gender is another boundary that is crossed, as for months Eliza dresses like her friend Tao Chi'en's little brother—until she decides that the time has come to present herself as a woman. Nor is Allende's narrative insensitive to the particular hardships some of these communities experienced.

Curiously, though, it is the Chinese community in San Francisco, particularly the "singsong" girls, not the Chilean or Mexican communities, upon whom Allende lavishes her sympathies. Narratives of the poverty and debasement of the young Chinese girls who have been sold into sexual slavery are heartbreaking. When readers are presented with the following description of the singsong girls, they cannot avoid recognizing the historical reality behind the fiction: "For the benefit of white visitors and sailors of all races they repeated in indecipherable English, 'two bittee lookie, four bittee feelee, six bittee doee,' as they exposed pitiful little breasts and tempted passersby with obscene gestures which, coming from those children, were tragic pantomime" (345). However, as Cathy Davidson explains in reference to the sentimental heroine Charlotte Temple, strategies of sentimentalization often ultimately result in dismissal of the demographic concern represented by the sentimental victim. It is moving that Tao Chi'en, inspired by his Eliza, comes to believe that these girls have souls, as Allende tells it, and devises a plan to rescue as many of them as he can. Yet the structure of the storyline thereby diverts attention from the fact that most of the historical counterparts for the singsong girls were not, in fact, rescued and that young girls in the contemporary world, including immigrants, often end up in similarly horrific circumstances. In this sense, a pluralist agenda merely reifies the hierarchy of the manifestly destined and the second-class minority. In *Daughter of Fortune*, Eliza Sommers and Paulina Rodríguez de Santa Cruz, who are, after all, American even if not U.S. American, are manifestly destined and the singsong girls from China are the second-class minorities.

Just as a pluralist gesture is not necessarily exemplary of transnational ideology, likewise the feminism of the text is not necessarily as far-reaching in its implications as might be hoped. *Daughter of Fortune* does replace hegemonic and masculine fantasies of the American West with romantic feminine ones. However, this angle is not new, nor, as a challenge to the conventions of the western genre, is it especially efficacious. Narratives of Belle Starr and Calamity Jane populate western literature as well as folklore. Allende's *Daughter of Fortune*, with its gender-bending female exceptions who prove the rule, still keeps the West safe for Anglo cowboys.

*   *   *

This proves to be the case because while *Daughter of Fortune* offers a strong and independent protagonist, the novel is masculine with respect to her identity construction. The novel details the life of a young Chilean woman who secretly follows to California a man named Joaquín, who provides the material around which Eliza's identity is shaped. Sophia McClennen mentions that "perhaps the strongest feature of the novel is the way that the protagonist recognizes that her identity does not depend entirely on the man she loves" (185). Indeed, Eliza eventually learns, at the end of the novel and after months of hard pursuit, that she is free of her unrequited love for her erstwhile partner Joaquín. She is free in this basic feminist sense that she understands she does not need him to love her in order to feel whole—though it must be noted that Eliza has this revelation only after walking out of a dark room holding another man's hand while contemplating the sight of Joaquín's head in a jar. Moreover,

Eliza is never really free of Joaquín because, even after her feelings for him have waned, he looms large. Several chapters before the end of the novel it becomes apparent that Eliza's quest to find Joaquín has become merely a pretext for the heroine's interesting adventures. Yet even though Eliza is no longer besotted with Joaquín in the same way as she was when she embarked on her voyage to San Francisco, she is shaped by him in the sense that she is narratologically indebted to him: he is the legend, she the interwoven story.

The Chilean Americans' stories in *Daughter of Fortune* are evidently the stuff of legend: Joaquín Murieta's legend, to be precise. Joaquín Murieta is a historical figure—or at least a character extant in the printed pages of mid-nineteenth-century yellow journalism. The stories circulating about him in the early 1850s are presumed to contain at least some kernel of truth, but also indulgent embellishments, as Allende hints through her journalist character, Jacob Freemont.[4] Robert McKee Irwin addresses in "The Many Heads and Tales of Joaquín Murrieta," the proliferation and variations of the Joaquín legend in narratives of the West:

> From the early newspaper reports and the first literary representations of Murrieta to the hundreds of reformulations of the legend in novels, plays, corridos, poems, histories, movies, etc. over the past century and a half in California and the United States, France, Spain, Chile and Mexico by gringo, Native American, Chicano, Sonoran, Latin American and even Russian writers, it seems that no one can agree on the many details of the case. Consensus occurs even less on the cultural meanings evoked by the many retellings of the Murrieta legend. (100)

Irwin also poses thought-provoking questions about the nature of the legendary outlaw and the nature of the embellishments of his legend:

> Is it Murrieta or Murieta or Muriata? Was there one Joaquín, were there five, or even more? Was Murrieta from Sonora or Chile? . . . Did he act out of revenge, desperation or a sadistic urge to kill? Did he exist or is he a mere literary invention? Was his head destroyed in the 1906 San Francisco earthquake or can it still be seen today? (100)

Though as Irwin suggests, consensus on "the cultural meanings evoked by the many tellings of the Murrieta legend" is hard to reach; it is somewhat easier to analyze the choices of a single author. It appears that Allende's treatment of this potentially transnational figure indicates a capitulation to nationalist ideals. The narrative is omniscient about Joaquín's origins—as Joaquín Andieta. He is from Chile, not Mexico, and is the illegitimate son of a destitute woman. He has fallen in love with his employer's niece, consummated his passion, and then grown weary of the girl. The rest of Joaquín's story is sifted through Eliza's experience as she struggles to locate him in California. While Allende never directly identifies his motives, she hints that he has acted out of some combination of the motives Irwin mentions, as well as pure desire for adventure. She hints throughout that the man Eliza tracks is indeed the same "Joaquín" she once passionately loved, but that he has changed his name and masked his origins.

In retaining his transnational first name and adopting the surname "Murieta," the Joaquín in Allende's account is becoming Pan-American. As Irwin explains, "Murrieta" (spelled with two "r"s) is specifically a Sonoran name; however, "Murieta" with one "r" is easier for Anglos to pronounce (104). Allende's choice to spell his name with the single "r" enables a transnational Latino—possibly even Chicano—identity.

This is why it is so ironic that Allende's final note includes the shrinking of Murieta's head. Eliza realizes, the moment after she sees her former lover's shrunken head and walks out with older Chinese widower Tao Ch'ien, that it is the latter whom she really loves. Tao Chi'en, has treated her with life-giving kindness on the ship and in California, and his wife, in ghost form and unbeknownst to Eliza, has sanctified this union. Kindness and respect have prevailed over Eliza's foolish romanticism. Such, at least, may be the instructional or moralistic conclusion. And yet, from a strictly transnational point of view, the text ultimately concludes that the best place for this potentially most challenging transnational character is in a jar as a western artifact. Nor is it challenging that Eliza's new lover is Chinese rather than Chilean. Eliza is free to accept Tao Ch'ien's love instead of Murieta's because Tao Chi'en, who has no real-life or legendary transnational equivalent, has been able to adapt and assimilate. He thus becomes an appropriate choice for Eliza, who has also adapted and become assimilated. After all, Eliza has discarded her alias of "Elías Andieta" to revert to the generic "Eliza Sommers."

Eliza, whose identity as an adopted daughter is ambiguous in the first place, will not return to Chile, at least not for good, but will remain in San Francisco, where she will become the daughter of fortune in the truest sense. She will belong to the United States, and she will prosper therein. Allegedly a foundling of uncertain origin, in fact the product of a clandestine affair between her adoptive mother's sailor-brother and a poor Chilean woman, this beautiful girl becomes the more-than daughter of the passionate but childless English aristocrat Miss Rose Sommers. Eliza, who can thus be described as "international," has chosen the Western United States from a variety of options, and it apparently has chosen her. She is destined for greatness—if not the stunning entrepreneurial success of her friend Paulina, at least the admirable role of the strong pioneer women familiar to us from Cather and Laura Ingalls Wilder, this time adapted to a Chilean American woman in San Francisco.

Paulina, meanwhile, is a Latina version of another familiar western female prototype. Paulina is as near as any of Allende's characters in *Daughter of Fortune* to being the admirable prostitute familiar from Anglo westerns from Bret Harte short stories to Larry McMurtry's *Lonesome Dove*. Like Cather's Ántonia, Paulina is once fallen, later redeemed. Like Cather's Alexandra, she looms high above the action of the plot as a legendary ideal of the entrepreneurial spirit of the West.

With the introduction of Paulina in the narrative, it becomes clear that even the most obviously feminine physical space—the fruit grove—is given over to conventionally masculine purposes. The groves, the gardens of the novel representing the feminine alternative located by Kolodny, are made little of in terms of horticultural beauty, but instead become the cattle, or even the gold, of conventional, masculine westerns. As Paulina writes, "Agriculture is the true gold of California. Farther than you can see are vast, sewn fields; everything grows luxuriantly in this blessed soil" (356). In this way a feminine alternative is turned into a conventional western gold mine, as Paulina becomes quite rich through the importing and exporting of this and other natural resources back and forth between California and Chile.

While the heroine, Eliza, offers the romantic intrigue of a voyage to San Francisco in pursuit of her wayward and gold-seeking lover, Paulina, the veritable empress of the agricultural trade, propels the myth of Manifest Destiny.[5] In order to fulfill her destiny, Paulina apparently acts on the principle that while some international narratives may be subsumed into the United States's national narrative, others must simply be replaced. Paulina replaces the Chilean imperative that a loose woman will bring shame to the family with a romanticized exotic legend of "Amazon women"—and subsumes the latter into the national narrative:

> Paulina was in her element in [San Francisco's] ambience; she liked the openness, the freedom, and the ostentation of that young society,

exactly the opposite of the hypocrisy of Chile. She glorified at the thought of how her father would rage if he had to sit down at the table with a corrupt upstart become a judge, or a Frenchwoman of dubious past decked out like an empress . . . it was possible to invent a new life and become a millionaire or a beggar in the wink of an eye. . . . Through the Golden Gate came masses of people escaping poverty or violence, hoping to find work and erase the past. It wasn't easy, but their descendants would be Americans. The marvel of this country was that everyone believed their children would have a better life than theirs. . . . No namby-pambies like her mother and sisters; here Amazons like herself reigned.   (356–57)

Just after spurning the "hypocrisy of Chile," the text extols U.S. culture: "It was possible to invent a new life." According to Paulina, the American West, even for those who approach it from the Pacific Ocean and not from across the Continental Divide, is "the land of opportunity" where immigrants' children may "be Americans"—that is, if they are destined to be there in the first place. Chilean society, the narrative implies, is outdated precisely because it cannot recognize the hierarchies of Manifest Destiny. In the youthful San Francisco, somehow the ancient, mythical "Amazon women," of whom Paulina is supposed to be one, prevail. Paulina may be from Chile, but she is the stuff of timeless legend imported to the United States. She, like Eliza, somehow transcends her original national identification. It is under these conditions, and not those of transnational agency, that her destiny becomes manifest.

*   *   *

Toni Morrison's *Paradise,* on the other hand, challenges the viability and sustainability of a pluralist West. Whereas Allende envisions California as a true "land of opportunity" for such Latinas as are destined to be there, Morrison challenges the notion of African American access to the fruits of the mythic harvests of the West. *Paradise* critiques an African American settler community's adaptations of the nation-building ideology of Manifest Destiny and, in so doing, challenges the principles of Manifest Destiny. The novel contemplates the strategies of an all-black community attempting to establish itself through the dominant ideology, despite the paradoxes of so doing. After all, the women who live in the former convent nearby, who are looking for something not even as ambitious as opportunity but only for Emma Lazarus's idealized refuge,[6] become the objects of a brutal attack by men striving with all their might to believe that the foundation myths, particularly Manifest Destiny, apply to them.

In its complex challenge, *Paradise* reveals that dangers to such Western communities, as represented by the town of Ruby, lurked not only outside but also within the belief systems of its members. Nor, the novel suggests, can the nearby convent—an unofficial shelter for women needing to escape the world—provide a lasting respite. Morrison's novel suggests that dominant ideologies and alternative communities are, ultimately, violently irreconcilable. Through such a focus, Morrison reveals the tensions between egalitarian and hierarchal ideals always at the heart of a faith in Manifest Destiny. In this way *Paradise* represents the true legacy of the American West.

At Fort Boonesborough State Park in Richmond, Kentucky, visitors are confronted with a four-sided plaque commemorating Kentucky's early heroes. One side honors "that gallant band of Axemen Pioneers and Indian fighters who at the risk and loss of life opened the doors of destiny to the white race in Kentucky and the West." On the face of the plaque, below the "testimony of gratitude" to the "gallant band" and before its attribution to the Daughters of the American Revolution in 1935, is a list of the "Indian fighters," including Daniel and Squire Boone at the top of the list and "a Negro man" and "a Negro woman" at the bottom. The paradox of including the "Negro man" and "Negro woman" in this plaque extolling "the white race" and affirming Manifest Destiny is multifaceted: they are at the bottom of the list; they are the only people on the list not mentioned by their given names, but only by their race and genders; and yet the fact that they are identified at all among those to be honored suggests that black men and women are complicit in the hierarchal logic of Manifest Destiny.

The challenges of African Americans' paradoxical conscription in the myths of the American West are marked in *Paradise*. The germs of paradox are most clearly evident in the "powerful memories" of the Morgan twins of Ruby, Oklahoma. Their ancestors founded the nearby town of Haven when Oklahoma was still a territory, and it is upon these ancestors and this original town that the twins reflect. Deacon and Steward Morgan—whose Christian names reflect their spiritual and ideological authority in the community—"remember the details of everything that happened—things they witnessed and things they have not" (13). As they "remember" it,

> Smart, strong, and eager to work their own land, they believed they were more than prepared—they were destined. It stung them into confusion to learn that they did not have enough money to satisfy the

restrictions the "self-supporting" Negroes required. . . . Then, remem-
bering their spectacular history, they cooled. What began as overheated
determination became cold-blooded obsession. (13–14)

The Morgan twins are born in 1924—a symbolic choice, as this
year marked the passage of the exclusionary Immigration Act.[7] This
act, not repealed until 1965, privileged and encouraged a Western
European population in the United States by allowing only very small
percentages of others besides Western Europeans to be accepted for
citizenship. The twins are born and come of age at exactly the historical moment when discrimination against all non-Western-European
minorities was supported explicitly by law, and yet they are doggedly
determined to assert that they and their community are destined
for success. The twins, not generally identical in their thinking, are
nevertheless symbiotic in their choice to "remember" that they, like
their postreconstruction ancestors who faced legal, interracial, and
intraracial challenges, have been destined for a "spectacular history."
The twins' "powerful memories" ensure that the heirs of their legacy
remember the community of Haven, Oklahoma, as being no less
exceptional than what Fort Boonesborough is to the Daughters of
the American Revolution who erected the plaque.

Morrison's *Paradise* considers the plight of a nationalist-minded
people. It may seem at first that Morrison's characters are not
nationalists in any sense, but rather, victims of nationalism. Benedict
Anderson's well-known conception of nationalism focuses on sentiment or beliefs held by a group of people conceiving of themselves
as members of a geographically specific and politically empowered
body or "nation-state." However, other scholars have focused on the
fact that political empowerment and geographic specificity are not
prerequisites for nationalism. Any people who understand themselves
as a discreet political force with a singularly agreed-upon purpose may
be nationalists. (Zionists, member of Haamas, and black nationalists
are just a few of many historical examples of nationalism without a
nation-state.) The people of Ruby and their forebears develop from
nationalists without a nation to nationalists with a nation-state of
their own (albeit a small one).

In cases where nationalism exists in the absence of a physical
nation-state or where the nation-state is a small geographic body
within a larger one (a town within a country, for instance), it can
also be said that this nationalism "challenges 'official' nationalism'"
(Rowe 2). However, Morrison's novel suggests that this "alternative" nationalism may be subject to the same cruel propensities as the

nationalism of the official nation-state. The distinction between these two nationalisms may be blurry at best, as, in the novel at least, the two are identical once the powerless nationalists gain geographic and political access. Nationalist pride is a pride easily threatened and readily aggressive in its own defense. So it comes to pass that Ruby's own young, progressive preacher Richard Misner reflects that "they think they have outfoxed the whiteman when in fact they imitate him" (302). The leaders of Ruby include the Morgan twins, who have not forgotten that prostitutes, Native Americans, and wealthier black communities used to "jeer" at their ancestors before Haven was established. Yet they nevertheless set out to destroy the women of the convent, whom they believe to blight the purity of their own community.

This is not the only paradox considered in *Paradise*. As Holly Flint explains, the settlers of Haven were modeled on a historical group called the Exodusters. The name, of course, draws on the biblical typology of the Exodus, a referent culturally or symbolically significant among African Americans as evidenced in nineteenth-century spirituals and turn-of-the-century literature by James Weldon Johnson and others. The Exodusters, like the Mormons discussed in Rüdiger Heinze's essay in this volume, are a chosen people: that is, if some Anglo-Americans understand the Eastern United States to be "the New Israel,"[8] the Exodusters were the Hebrews who had been enslaved and whose "Exodus" led them to a promised land in the Oklahoma Territory. Yet a paradox arises from the fact that it was the New Israelites—typologically allied with the once-enslaved Hebrews—who had enslaved them in the first place. Here is the case of a nation-state within a nation-state. Since the Western frontier was viewed as a promised land by the descendants of the (Anglo) New Israelites no less than the Exodusters and other African Americans, both groups must equally prove the manifest-ness of their own destiny.

So it is a complex critique that Morrison offers, one which examines on the one hand, the failure of the Emancipation Proclamation to guarantee a broad and true egalitarianism, and on the other, the fatal errors made by the leaders of Ruby (the fictional counterparts of the Exodusters) in their efforts to negotiate this failure. Katrine Dalsgård warns that Morrison's "deconstruction of Ruby's exceptionalism figures as a warning that the mechanisms of violence and marginalization are also at work in counter-discursive national historical narratives" (246). In their efforts to compete, the leaders of Ruby adopt the form of nationalism "aligned to the nation-state" (Rowe 2), including its mandate to purge perceived threats to this nation-state (namely, the women of the convent) through sacrificial violence.

The tragic failure of the community is in direct proportion to its insistence on its own exceptionalism, or, in other words, its Manifest Destiny. Manifest Destiny can further be defined as a belief in the virtue of a select group and a confidence concerning their mission and its success.[9] For the residents of Ruby this virtue is embodied in their "8-rock," or racially pure, heritage. Manifest Destiny is typically both a preemptive and a postoperative philosophy, which maintains a premise of superior virtue to justify disregard for the dispossessed. Preemptive in its "cold-blooded obsession" to establish itself as a town of superior merit, Ruby is postoperative in its destruction of the four women who represent a challenge to that superiority. That is to say that perhaps if Ruby were really so ideal, the refuge of the convent would not be necessary.

Susan Mizruchi suggests in *The Science of Sacrifice* that rites of sacrifice attempt to confirm the cohesiveness of a community when that cohesiveness is most in doubt. Certainly, the cohesiveness of Ruby in the novel's post–World War II present is in doubt. Death has entered the town, and unhappiness among some of the women and conflict among the elders have become evident. The final irony of the sacrifice ritual is that the same men who are said to keep Ruby's streets safe for Ruby's women are the same ones who kill the four women of the convent.

When Richard Misner begins to ponder the troubled nature of Ruby, he considers the stockpile of stories the residents tell about their predecessors: "Dangerous confrontations, clever maneuvers. Testimonies to endurance, wit, skill and strength. Tales of luck amid outrage" (161). Misner goes on to wonder, "But why were there no stories to tell of themselves? About their own lives they shut up. Had nothing to say, pass on. As though past heroism was enough of a future to live by" (161). It could hardly be true that the World War II veterans who lead the town of Ruby have "no stories to tell." Rather, the spinning of ancestral heroism into mythic tales simultaneous with the suppression of their own likely heroism suggests that they are clinging to artifice and ideology. Perhaps because their West has already been won both in point of fact and in exaggerated memory—perhaps because their Western town has been successfully modernized and even suburbanized—the present leaders of Ruby no longer respect themselves. In order to prove themselves exceptional and establish once and for all the manifest-ness of their destiny, these men must conquer a new frontier.

Stanley Corkin's *Cowboys as Cold Warriors* explains how during the Cold War, Americans, fueled by xenophobic projections, made of the Soviet Union a new frontier for conquest. In the case of the (fictional) all-black town of Ruby, the frontier was proportionally nearer and smaller but equally xenophobic. Moreover, this xenophobia is blatantly gendered. A shroud of fear and suspicion has been woven by Ruby's nostalgic patriarchs around the small community of women just outside its borders. Some of their women—Soane, for example—have contact with the women of the convent, and this lack of (in contemporary terms) "border security" is especially concerning. For a woman of Ruby to go to the convent—to seek, as the town leaders imagine, an abortion or to engage in "unnatural" sexual practices—represents to them the risk of defection from or even the annihilation of Ruby's way of life.

The leaders resort to what they perceive will be a fructifying violence, like that of the mythic Indian fighters. And yet the chilling opening scene—the calculated killing of the convent women by a posse of Ruby's town leaders—indicates that something has gone awry. The tenderly crafted ghostly reappearances of the dead women notwithstanding, the novel is not ultimately about the women but about the men and the poignant lessons they learn. The lessons that the men—and presumably the reader—learn involve understanding and acceptance. They begin to understand what it is that they did when they destroyed the convent women, and they begin to accept that Manifest Destiny is a myth, which provides, at best, an unstable foundation.

As townsfolk and readers learn, the convent does house women ungoverned by any men's rules. The women of the convent live together in a realm spun from their collective hopes about finding alternatives to their desperate lives. Of varying ages, experiences, geographic locations, and ethnicities (including one "white girl"),[10] the women have suffered abuses of various kinds, and leave behind painful pasts, including, in Mavis' case, the infanticide of her twins.[11] Yet Morrison illustrates the real innocence of these women, battered as they have been by life, eccentric as they may seem in their unsanctified (or at least unconventional) rituals. In a striking image toward the end of the novel, the women of the convent arise, mix dough, gather vegetables, and greet the morning:

> The women sleep, wake and sleep again with images of parrots, crystal seashells and singing women who never spoke. At four in the morning they wake to prepare for the day. One mixes dough while another lights the stove. Others gather vegetables for the noon meal, then set out the breakfast things. The bread, kneaded into mounds, is placed on baking tins to rise. (285)

This image equates the women of the convent with the natural world of air, earth, water and fire: the parrots, the shells, the mermaids or harpies, and the lighting of the fire. This is an earthy image to say the least, as the women dig their hands into soil and dough. Yet while the image is in part the stuff of idealized femininity, it also registers as historical commentary. What these women are doing is what pioneer women had to do, what the early women of Haven (Ruby's predecessor) must have done all their free lives. So it has come to pass that, in their desperate attempt to maintain the cohesion of the town and to honor the legacy of their nostalgic past, the posse of Ruby's patriarchs who gathered at the convent to destroy four women inside, end up destroying their own past—the feminine roots of their own past—and themselves.

* * *

How different this denouement is from that of *Daughter of Fortune!* As Sophia McClennen writes, "Allende blends history, politics, fantasy and passion into her work in a way that does not shock the reader and through tales that inevitably end happily" (184). Allende's *Daughter of Fortune* does indeed offer a happy ending. The happy ending is admittedly gratifying from a feminist perspective because the jilted heroine, seeing her heartless lover's head in a jar, has been vindicated (and the reader may derive pleasure from this vindication). And yet what McClennen suggests with her statement that Allende's texts invariably end happily is that, in the final analysis, no real challenge to the status quo is involved. Readers may be pleased that Chilean Americans may be included in the mythic narratives of the American West—and yet that is the extent of it.

If Allende leaves her readers with an ultimately disappointing happy ending, Morrison leaves hers with a challenge. The brilliance of Morrison's choices in *Paradise* lies in the fact that she neither attempts to co-opt traditional western myths nor to claim the possibility of alternative feminine spaces in the West. Isabel Allende does cleverly co-opt the traditional western, including the ideology of Manifest Destiny, for Pan-American and Latina purposes. However, as Morrison's *Paradise* relentlessly indicates, colonizing is colonizing, regardless of who is doing it. Because the leaders of Ruby have failed in their efforts to colonize their own women or those of the convent, readers have much to think about. If the deaths of the women were to mark the ending—or if, say, the men of the posse were all to proceed to kill themselves—the story could be a tragedy in the strictest Aristotelian sense. Bodies would litter the stage of the readers' imagination, and a cathartic purge would follow. The cathartic purge would be moving, but, like with all cathartic purges, would free the reader of further contemplative responsibility.

Yet the cathartic purge is denied to the reader of *Paradise*, for Ruby does move on. Its conscience, the Reverend Misner, gropes for understanding—pushing through his anger at the elders who killed the convent women and drawing some conclusions that may mark both the end of a quest for mythic circumscription and a beginning of a real community, however imperfect. The men from Ruby who shoot dead the four women of the convent evoke sympathy and understanding more than outrage. They are like young Ralph in Jean Stafford's *Mountain Lion* after his twin-bonded sister Molly's dead body is laid at his feet. Stafford's narrative concludes with the tragic revelation that it is Ralph's bullet that destroyed Molly. And yet when Morrison chooses not to end with the dramatic epiphany (in her case the death scene is at the beginning), but to push on through the rest of the novel and the rest of the men and women's lives before the shootings, she is truly postnational. For while nationalist ideology feeds on myth, true community survival is constituted from the continuity of life cut from the moorings of myths or even countermyths.

NOTES

*Special thanks to Stanley Corkin, Kwakiutl Dreher, Wolgang Hochbruck, and Reginald Dyck.

1. See Annette Kolodny's *The Land Before Her,* in which men chop down great forests and women plant small gardens.
2. The point of the scope of Willa Cather's challenge to pioneer prototype remains open for debate. See, for example, Reginald Dyck's "Willa Cather's Reluctant New Woman Pioneer," in which Cather's first Nebraska heroine, Alexandra Bergson, is read as a departure from the conventions of the woman pioneer.
3. See Barbara Curiel and John Carlos Rowe.
4. Allende writes, "Jacob Freemont took it upon himself to fan the flames of Murieta's celebrity: his sensationalist articles had created a hero for Hispanics and a devil for Americans. . . . Freemont suspected there were several 'Murietas,' not one, but he was careful not to write that because it would have diminished the legend" (338).
5. Allende writes that Paulina's business was so good that she "obtained a second steamship to expand her empire" (288).

6. Emma Lazarus is of course the poet whose words are inscribed on the Statue of Liberty.

7. Walter Benn Michaels notes the importance of these Immigrations Acts in history and literature in his article "The Vanishing American."

8. See John Winthrop's "Model of Christian Charity."

9. Though the term was coined in 1845, it became widely popularized in the 1890s during high nationalism and again in the twentieth century when America emerged as a world power.

10. For a full discussion of the role played by this ambiguous "white girl," see Linda Krumholz's "Reading and Insight in Toni Morrison's *Paradise.*"

11. Mavis' twins, though dead before the action of the narrative, haunt readers with foreclosed possibilities and painful realities. It is worth contemplating Morrison's choice to "twin" both Mavis' babies and the Morgan brothers.

WORKS CITED

Allende, Isabel. *Daughter of Fortune.* New York: Harper, 1999.

Anderson, Benedict. *Imagined Communities.* New York: Verso, 2006.

Cather, Willa. *My Ántonia.* Lincoln: University of Nebraska Press, 1994.

———. *O Pioneers!* Lincoln: University of Nebraska Press, 1992.

Corkin, Stanley. *Cowboys as Cold Warriors: The Western and US History.* Philadelphia: Temple University Press, 2004.

Curiel, Barbara Brinson, David Kazanjian, Katherine Kinney, Steven Mailloux, Jay Mechling, John Carlos Rowe, George Sánchez, Shelley Streeby, and Henry Yu. "Introduction." In *Post-nationalist American Studies,* edited by John Carlos Rowe. Los Angeles: University of California Press, 2000.

Dalsgård, Katrine. "The One All-Black Town Worth the Pain: (African) American Exceptionalism, Historical Narration, and the Critique of Nationhood in Toni Morrison's *Paradise.*" *African American Review* 35.2 (Summer 2001): 233–48.

Davidson, Cathy. "Introduction." *Charlotte Temple,* by Susanna Rowson. New York: Oxford Paperbacks, 1986.

Dillard, Annie. *The Living.* New York: Harper, 1992.

Dyck, Reginald. "Willa Cather's Reluctant New Woman Pioneer." *Great Plains Quarterly* 23.3 (Summer 2003): 161–73.

Flint, Holly. "Toni Morrison's *Paradise*: Black Cultural Citizenship in the American Empire." *American Literature* 78.3 (September 2006): 585–612.

Harte, Bret. *Bret Harte's Gold Rush: "The Outcasts of Poker Flat," "The Luck of Roaring Camp," and Other Favorites.* Berkeley, CA: Heyday, 1997.

Heinze, Rüdiger. American Outsiders at the Center: Mormons and the West." (Forthcoming).

Historical Markers and Tablets, The D. A. R. Fort Boonesborough Marker, Tablet #111.

Irwin, Robert McKee. "Helen Hunt Jackson's *Ramona:* A Transnational Reading of the Old West." (Forthcoming).

———. "The Many Heads and Tales of Joaquín Murrieta." *Bandits, Captives, Heroines and Saints: Cultural Icons of Mexico's Northwest Frontier.* (Forthcoming).

Jackson, Helen Hunt. *Ramona: A Story.* Boston: Little, Brown, 1884.

Johnson, James Weldon. *God's Trombones: Seven Negro Sermons in Verse.* New York: Penguin, 1976.

Kolodny, Annette. *The Land Before Her: Fantasy And Experience of the American Frontiers, 1630–1860.* Chapel Hill: University of North Carolina Press, 1984.

Krumholz, Linda. "Reading and Insight in Toni Morrison's *Paradise.*" *African American Review* 36.1 (Spring 2002): 21–34.

Larry McMurtry. *Lonesome Dove: A Novel.* New York: Simon and Schuster, 1985.

McClennen, Sophia A. "Isabel Allende: *Daughter of Fortune.*" *Comparative American Studies* 3.4 (December 2005): 184–85.

Michaels, Walter Benn. "The Vanishing American." *American Literary History* 2.2 (Summer 1990): 220–41. Reprinted in the *American Literary History Reader,* edited by Gordon Hutner. New York: Oxford University Press, 1995.

Mizruchi, Susan L. *The Science of Sacrifice: American Literature and Modern Social Theory.* Princeton, NJ: Princeton University Press, 1998.

Morrison, Toni. *Paradise.* New York: Knopf, 1998.

Rowe, John Carlos, ed. *Post-nationalist American Studies.* Los Angeles: University of California Press, 2000.

Silko, Leslie. *Ceremony.* New York: Viking, 1977.

Sollors, Werner. "A Critique of Pure Pluralism." In *Reconstructing American Literary History,* edited by Sacvan Bercovitch. Cambridge, MA: Harvard University Press, 1985.

Stafford, Jean. *Mountain Lion.* Austin: University of Texas Press, 1993.

Wilder, Laura Ingalls. *Little House on the Prairie.* New York: Harper, 1935.

Winthrop, John. "A Model of Christian Charity." In *The Puritans in America: A Narrative Anthology,* edited by Alan Heimert and Andrew Delbanco, 82–92. Cambridge, MA: Harvard University Press, 1985.

CHAPTER 11

THE LONESOME GERMAN COWBOY: NEGOTIATING GERMAN SKEPTICISM ABOUT AMERICA, 1893–2001

Hubertus Zander

With his parody *Der Schuh des Manitu* (*Manitou's Shoe* 2001) Michael "Bully" Herbig attacked two of Germany's most pervasive cultural icons: Karl May's "westman" Old Shatterhand and his noble Apache friend Winnetou. The enormous popularity of May's figures has been sustained for over a century, at first mainly on the strength of May's novels and since the 1960s increasingly also through their very popular movie adaptations. In wrestling with the clichéd aspects of these May variants, Herbig's parody also continues the theme of German skepticism about America present in the earlier May variants. Throughout their production and reception, May's adventure stories set in the American West have negotiated German uneasiness and skepticism of America's most pervasive myth: the West. Such a long negotiation of German skepticism was only possible because the two May modes of adaptation successfully culled the changing origins and currents of German uneasiness about this myth and the American ideology and policy that it helped sustain. While May's novels negotiated German uneasiness about America emerging as world power at the end of the nineteenth and beginning of the twentieth century, the movie adaptations negotiated German skepticism about American ideology and policy during the Cold War. Finally, *Der Schuh des Manitu* negotiates present-day German irritation about the way

America fills its new role as hegemon in world politics following the end of the Cold War.

This article will explore how Herbig's parody negotiates German irritation about American ideology by overtly satirizing May's iconic figures Old Shatterhand and Winnetou as well as their relationship. Before the parody can be analyzed in more detail, a brief clarification of two points is necessary. First, I will discuss how popular culture—and all three, May's novels, the 1960s films, and Herbig's parody, are part of popular culture—negotiates social and cultural values under strain and why popular fiction has to do so to be of significance. Second, I will outline the broad changes in the German attitude toward the United States from May's time to today. Both these aspects will necessarily be brief but should suffice as background for the discussion of Herbig's parody.

Referring to John Hall, Harry Ziegler has explained the century-long German fascination with May as follows:

> Only such social values were negotiated in popular fiction which were under strain within the society in which these texts were produced and consumed (Hall 96). . . . For May's stories to be attractive to audiences for more than a century, his readers have to be able to relate to his stories in one way or another, i.e., they have to negotiate such social values under strain which are of relevance to the audience.   (114)

Ziegler then points to some possible social values negotiated in May's stories, such as the symbolic power Claus Roxin attributes to May or the anticapitalist agenda Volker Klotz sees in the autonomy of May's heroes (115–16). At other times the autonomy and strength of May's heroes, along with their knowledge of and respect for nature, probably negotiated social issues related to German romanticism, which was frequently interpreted nationalistically in the first half of the twentieth century.[1] Indeed, Ziegler emphasizes that such stories "have to be polysemic, i.e., have to allow for different readings in different socio-historical circumstances, for every generation to be able to engage with [them]" (115). A further social value under strain that May's stories have negotiated, is German skepticism about the American western myth, and in this respect May's work has proven polysemic enough to negotiate this skepticism until today—at least in the form of the May film adaptations in the 1960s and in Herbig's parody.

The three versions of May's western myth can be related to major shifts in the German reception of the American western myth,

because they largely coincide with major shifts in the American interpretation of its own myth that sparked German reactions. May started
writing and publishing fiction in 1875, four years after the foundation of the first German nation-state. In Germany the foundation of
this nation-state was reflected in an increasingly nationalistic German
romanticism[2] that has a clearly discernible influence on May's writings as well. In the same time period, the American national western
myth was nearing its first nationwide, elaborate expression. As Stanley
Corkin explains,

> The lore of the West flourished in the period after the Civil War, at the
> point where the United States had taken domain over the lands from
> coast to coast as a result of imperial adventures justified by notions of
> manifest destiny in the 1830s and 1840s. Such adventures, buttressed
> and encouraged by jingoism, captured and helped shape the nationalist
> imagination, an aggregate that existed in relatively rudimentary form in
> the 1840s but that, as a result of technological changes in printing and
> transportation, was beginning to coalesce in the 1870s. (7)

This new ideology of American exceptionalism was transported back
by journalists and adventure novelists such as Charles Sealsfield,
Friedrich Gerstäcker, and Balduin Möllhausen to Germany where
it clashed with the romantic belief in German superiority. Unlike
Sealsfield, Gerstäcker, and Möllhausen, May had never set foot in
the Wild West[3] but had apparently extensively read both factual and
fictional reports from the American West. He found fault with the
American western myth and its results, especially with the treatment
of the Native Americans.[4] At the same time May was fascinated by the
adventurous and romantic possibilities the American West offered,
especially for German nationalists facing the dilemma that their sense
of mission clashed with the reality that other European nations had
already colonized the open spaces in the new worlds, leaving for the
romantic German only imaginary or megalomaniac imperial adventures.[5] May's popular fiction successfully negotiated this strain for a
large portion of the German public that shared his skepticism, mainly
by introducing the idea of the German *Edelmensch* (the noble human),
a term May takes from Berta von Suttner into the American West as
an alternative to the "uncivilized" American cowboys or, as May calls
them, "westmen." The concept of the *Edelmensch* is linked to a rather
typical expectation among May's contemporaries that humanity will
be saved by the emergence of a new human. A famous expression
of this is Nietzsche's idea of the "Übermensch." However, in May's

version the new human is far more benign, and still anchored in pre-revolutionary German romanticism with strong Christian influences (Scholdt 104–6). May's heroes Winnetou and Old Shatterhand are a literary expression of his concept of the *Edelmensch,* which May carefully crafted over the span of some years, as Otto Brucken shows for the case of Winnetou (293–96). Incidentally, Winnetou's transition from the most feared Indian between Sonora and Columbia to the Germanized American Indian version of the *Edelmensch* is completed with the publication of the first volume of May's *Winnetou* trilogy in 1893, the same year that Frederic Jackson Turner presented his seminal thesis about the American western myth, "The Significance of the Frontier in American History," to the American Historical Society.

May's critique of the allegedly uncivilized American westward movement, as embodied in his concept of the *Edelmensch,* retained its significance to many Germans throughout much of the first half of the twentieth century. However, after World War II, concepts of German superiority and of a German *Edelmensch,* even in May's benign version, had lost much of their allure. The Nazis had just demonstrated how an ideologically charged belief in the Übermensch, including racial hygiene experiments aimed at breeding the new human,[6] could lead to a worldwide catastrophe. At the same time America had been wavering between an isolationist interpretation of a closed geographic western frontier and an imperialist interpretation of a still open symbolic frontier that could "be transplanted conceptually to any number of locales" (Corkin 8). By the presidential election of 1952 the isolationist option no longer was "a viable political position" (Corkin 10). The American entry into World War II and into a Cold War with the Soviet Union after the defeat of Germany and Japan finalized America's rise to a world power. As Corkin shows, this cultural shift was negotiated to the American public by Hollywood western films during their heyday between 1946 and 1962:

> All of these films articulate the necessity of engaged heroes who morally ensure the rule of right. National interest is defined not simply by the goal of occupying contiguous land but also by the imperative of reordering them according to a distinctly U.S. vision of civil society.   (10)

Out of this distinctly U.S. vision, and the imperialism that served as the tool to fulfill it, grew a new point of contention over the American western myth in Germany. U.S. Cold War policies that were in part justified by recurring to this myth proved problematic in a divided Germany that found itself on the frontier of the cold confrontation between the United States and the Soviet Union, fearing to become the battleground should the confrontation turn hot. While Germany's first postwar chancellor, Konrad Adenauer, supported the U.S. policy of strength aimed at containing the USSR, the Social Democrats were decidedly more critical of America and the confrontational strategy based on the Hallstein Doctrine.[7] With the rise to power of Germany's first postwar social-democratic chancellor, Willy Brandt, the new German *Ostpolitik* (Eastern policy) took shape. This new policy called for a limited cooperation with the Eastern bloc, especially the German Democratic Republic (GDR), to facilitate a peaceful and stable coexistence (Hofmann 1–5). Its architect, Egon Bahr, describes the original motivation behind the development of the new Eastern policy as a presentiment to develop a *German* policy directed toward the *German* problem (Bahr 153). In other words, the new Ostpolitik was premised at least in part on (West) German skepticism of the American Eastern policy. This feeling was highlighted in the minds of most Germans by the construction of the Berlin Wall in 1961, which was a clear sign that Adenauer's policies of Western integration would not lead to a quick reunification (Bahr 125), and it stands at the beginning of the plans for the new Eastern policy realized during Brandt's turn as chancellor.

This change in the German attitude, and eventually policy, coincides with the production and release of the 1960s movie adaptations of May's western stories. The first film featuring Old Shatterhand and Winnetou, *Der Schatz im Silbersee* (*Treasure of Silver Lake* 1962) was released precisely when the American Cold War western had reached its pinnacle, and the successful string of May movie adaptations ran parallel to the decline of the western genre as main negotiator of Cold War tensions in America. Part of the success of the May films can be attributed to their successful negotiation of the new German skepticism about American containment policy at the time. This negotiation is achieved by the focus of the movies on the almost symbiotic relationship between the westman Old Shatterhand and his Apache blood brother Winnetou. Where American Cold War western films portray strong, individual western heroes civilizing the West according to "a distinctly U.S. vision," more often than not by driving out the Indian savages, the German May adaptations feature two heroes from supposedly different camps working together to civilize the Wild West, not by driving out the Indians, but by cooperating with them to form a new (utopian) West. This cooperative approach mirrors the conciliatory new German Eastern Policy and the German public's hope for a stable, peaceful future, which it saw threatened by America's Cold War imperialism.

However, the westman/cowboy is not yet discarded in the 1960s May adaptations; he is just transformed into a peace-loving Indian friend with a strong fist. This is in part a reflection of a protective need on the side of the Germans: without the strong military protection of the United States, the conciliatory policy may not have been possible, or at least would have been more risky. This need for protection from the USSR was removed with the end of the Cold War in the 1990s. The reunified Germany is no longer on the frontlines of present international conflicts, and Germans no longer feel that they need U.S. military protection against possible outside attacks. This change in geostrategic position along with the transition to full sovereignty after reunification has also caused a change in German foreign security policy. Since 1991 Germany has changed its position as an international military actor, and by 1999 the *Bundeswehr* (German Federal Defense Force) embarked on its first out-of-area combat mission in Kosovo. While this change was and still is controversial, a majority of Germans today accept this new role of the German military. However, the German public and German politicians have only been willing to support military intervention in clearly defined instances: in order to prevent a greater humanitarian crisis, when there is a UN mandate, or as a collective defense response to an attack on a NATO member.[8] This is in conflict with current U.S. policies of preemptive military action and of attempts to spread democracy by force. These have irritated the German public, which has largely blamed these policies on what it characterizes as the American cowboy attitude: the belief in the superiority of the American nation (Purdy). An indication of this is the frequent portrayal of today's most unpopular American in Germany—George W. Bush—as a cowboy who is trying to force the U.S. vision of a civil society onto the world.[9] Within this framework, the cowboy as individualistic trailblazer has outlived its purpose and become an anachronism in German eyes. This German irritation about U.S. policy and the western myth is negotiated by *Der Schuh des Manitu*, because by parodying and ridiculing the earlier German versions, it takes the final step not taken by May or the 1960s movie adaptations: it discards the cowboy figure as useless and outdated.

On the face of it, *Der Schuh des Manitu* is simply a spoof, mainly of the 1960s May movies, and not an elaborate renegotiation of German skepticism of America. It presents its variations in the visual guise of the original 1960s movies, most importantly by making the main characters Abahachi (Michael Herbig) and Ranger (Christian Tramitz) look like Winnetou and Old Shatterhand, respectively. The landscape is not quite the same as the original, since the movie was shot on location in Spain and not in Yugoslavia, which formed the iconographic backdrop to the 1960s movies. However, it serves the same function as in the original movies—it is mainly scenery for the protagonists to ride through. This visual similarity is immediately offset by a satirical aural defamiliarization caused by the protagonists' Bavarian accent. Having grown out of director and lead actor Michael "Bully" Herbig's TV comedy show, *Bullyparade* (1997–2002), the film appears to be mainly a commercial project. Its status as one of the most successful German movies of all time only adds to the impression of it being the movie equivalent of popular fiction. However, as John Hall points out, the argument "that mass culture is aesthetically poor because it is produced for profit [is a] vague anti-capitalist theory [which] combines uneasily with a love of high art in general, for it is obviously the case that, say, art galleries are as devoted to profit as perhaps is Harold Robbins" (81). Moreover, "the creators of popular fiction are very often motivated less by money than by a conviction of the importance of their moral vision and task" (Hall 81). That May's novels and the 1960s movies had political moral visions that negotiated German skepticism about Americans has been outlined above. By offering a new version of the May myth, Herbig's parody continues these negotiations and in part transposes them into a current discourse. In this way *Manitu* also points to those aspects in May that have led many Germans to abandon him as their negotiator of social values in general and of the American western myth in particular.

The parody is specifically aimed at three major aspects of both the May myth and the western myth: civilizing the West/Manifest Destiny, the superhero westman/cowboy, and the central role played by (homosocial) male bonding for sustaining and expanding western order. The central plotline in May's adventure novels set in the American West[10] is a slight variation to the American western myth of Manifest Destiny: the conquering of the West by strong men. In May's novels it is typically a young, adventurous German—most prominently May's alter –ego, Old Shatterhand[11]—going West, where he evolves into a strong westman, May's equivalent of the cowboy, and bonds with the noble Apache chief Winnetou. Together they fight the uncivilized American villains and the Indians corrupted by them, rescue the innocent settlers and thereby pave the way for a possible, but ultimately unattainable, utopian West in which these settlers live peacefully side by side with the Native Americans (Zahner 5). In *Manitu* the two protagonists also fight villainous westmen and corrupted Indians; however, the point is to rescue themselves. The movie begins with a failed adventure. Abahachi borrows money from the rival Indians of the Schoschonen to finance his retirement plan: an "Apache Pub." However, the real estate agent from Wyoming, from whom he buys the pub, turns out to be the villain Santa Maria (Sky DuMont), and the pub turns out to be no more than a stage backdrop. Unfortunately, the son of the Schoschonen chief is killed in the ensuing melee with Santa Maria and his men, and therefore Abahachi and Ranger have the Schoschonen on their heels for the rest of the movie. The bar-owner motive is continued later on, when Abahachi renews his friendship with Dimitri (Rick Kavanian), his Greek friend who has opened up a Greek tavern catering to local drunkards and those passing through, such as May. The significance of the introduction of this bar-owner motive is that it stands in contrast to the adventure spirit of the May novels and their movie adaptations, as well as the pioneer spirit encapsulated in the American western myth. Herbig's protagonists are not content with having adventures for the sake of adventures, and they do not seem to find their purpose in making the West a safer place for the settlers, except by providing them with drinks.

On a symbolic level, this turn away from western adventure reflects a turn away from adventurous dreams of saving the world and toward safer dreams of making a decent, easy living. Opening a bar is a rather clichéd but nevertheless typical dream of western male adolescents today. It stands for a longing for a job that allows you to do what you like best and get paid for it: hang around in a bar, drink beer, and watch sports on huge flat-screen TVs. Abahachi describes these pleasures as having barbeques, relaxing at night, and having Indian seminars in your own bar (*Schuh des Manitu*). Moreover, the fact that these western heroes even have the chance to open up a pub suggests that the West has already been won and that it is now time to enjoy the civilization that has been brought there (by hanging out in your own pub). On a political level the equivalent is to opt against military action unless your own status is threatened, as it is in the case of Abahachi and Ranger after Santa Maria has tricked them. Moreover, a refusal to participate in bringing (Western) civilization to the world by going out and fighting for it reflects an ambiguity about the justification for this fight. One possible justification can be found in the concept of American Manifest Destiny and the protection of the Western political system. This justification lay at the bottom of much of the American western output during the Cold War. Another justification could be found in a humanitarian interventionism that calls for military action to prevent humanitarian catastrophes. This concept is symbolically lived out by May's heroes. Old Shatterhand is particularly averse toward using violence, except when he has to, of course, and in May's fiction he often has to. Neither justification seems to convince Herbig's protagonists, who would prefer to spend their time running a bar, an attitude with which Herbig's German audience apparently could identify.

In *Manitu* the pointlessness of an adventurer's life on the frontier is further emphasized by Ranger, Herbig's version of Old Shatterhand, who is constantly bickering with Abahachi about it. When the two heroes are once again captured by the corrupted Indians, Ranger complains to Abahachi:

> I've had enough! I've been putting up with this for 16 years, man. Every other day we end up tied to a stake somewhere. . . . Did you ever think about how we spent our time? We stalk things that don't exist, hours and hours looking for tracks, and we ride around next to each other for no reason at all. (*Schuh des Manitu*)[12]

This is not just a pretty good description of the typical May plotline, for Ranger it also means that if he could choose freely he would prefer to stay home with his pregnant love interest Uschi (Marie Bäumer) instead of riding out with Abahachi through the Wild West. However, Uschi won't have that. Instead she insists that Ranger and Abahachi must seek their destiny since "the country depends upon [them]" (*Schuh des Manitu*). She then passionately argues for a fight for peace, freedom, and justice lying ahead of the two heroes, for them to create national parks, and free African Americans from the chains of slavery. At this point Herbig's parody of May's fiction directly confronts the American nation-building myth, thereby negotiating German skepticism today more convincingly than May's fiction does. May simply replaced the American adventurer with a German *Edelmensch,* whose goals and means were more benign, but this no longer convinces Germans today. If America today is looking to fulfill its Manifest Destiny by bringing democracy to the world, the concern of a majority of Germans is not that the Americans are too uncivilized to do so and that instead the Germans should step in. Neither do they really believe that a cooperative approach is feasible since, first of all, the U.S. government has been less than willing to cooperate, at least on an equal basis,[13] and secondly, they are rather skeptical of the motivation for the proactive American foreign policy. In a 2004 poll, 70 percent of Germans polled said that they now had less confidence that the United States wants to promote democracy in Iraq with the war there, and 60 percent stated that they believed that access to oil was a major motivation behind the intervention, while 47 percent even saw world domination as a motivating force ("Year after Iraq" 14 and 19). In this light, Herbig's potential bar owners seem a more convincing negotiation of German skepticism about America today than the German adventurers of May's novels and the film adaptations.

Indeed, the idea that the German westman and his Germanized Apache sidekick could step in and save the day is thoroughly ridiculed in *Manitu*. Herbig's two protagonists are far inferior to May's superhero westman and Apache chief as regards their heroic qualities. Whereas in May's novels Winnetou teaches Old Shatterhand the Indian ways, we see Abahachi being a relatively inapt student at the "Kiowa's Howgh School" when trying to learn how to be a good Indian warrior. Even more strikingly, Ranger is far removed from the extremely educated, extremely noble, and extremely strong Old Shatterhand. Neither Ranger nor Abahachi really understand the language of their Indian nemeses, while Old Shatterhand claims to be fluent in almost any language, including various Indian dialects (Cracroft 253).[14] And while Ranger easily beats up Santa Maria's men in a confrontation, he is nevertheless captured at the end of it. Indeed, whenever he and Abahachi escape from a tight spot, it is usually due to luck. This is in utter contrast to the qualities of Old Shatterhand, who in May's fiction is more reminiscent of a superhero than of a normal western hero. He knows almost everything, outwits everybody, and outfights even the strongest opponents. In other words, Ranger and Abahachi are far from May's romantic idea of the *Edelmensch*, of which Winnetou and Old Shatterhand are carefully crafted literary expressions. In a time when even comic superheroes are portrayed in motion pictures as struggling with their deficiencies (for example *Spider-Man* [2002] and *Batman Begins* [2005]), May's invincible superhero Old Shatterhand seems somewhat out of place, especially since he appears in a genre that has known broken and fallible heroes for quite a while.

Once again Herbig's variation on May reflects a broader change in German skepticism toward the American western myth. Whereas May seems to have believed in the possibility of a positive westward expansion, granted that it were led by German *Edelmenschen*, Herbig no longer grants the possibility that the German *Edelmensch* really exists. By extension, his skepticism about westward expansion runs deeper, as it challenges the concept of Manifest Destiny. It reflects today's Germans' irritation, as reflected in the opinion polls referred

to above, about the supposed American cowboy attitude: the belief
in the superiority of the American nation and in the divine mandate
for expansion of its beliefs.

Moreover, by transforming the almost symbiotic blood brotherhood of Old Shatterhand and Winnetou into an exemplary case of
failed male bonding dominated by constant bickering, *Manitu* challenges the romantic idealism the 1960s movies emphasize. As a team,
Abahachi and Ranger do not work smoothly. When they once again
find themselves in a shootout or tied to a stake, they do not start
making plans for their rescue but instead start arguing and blaming
each other for their misfortune. This character flaw is also part of
the larger issue of a troubled relationship between the two that goes
beyond the typical male-bonding issues facing western heroes. As
Ranger puts it in one of the best known quotes from the movie: "Ich
bin mit der Gesamtsituation unzufrieden" (*Schuh des Manitu*).[15] The
English-language version on the DVD translates this rather freely as:
"I am unhappy with our relationship." While not a very precise translation, this quite precisely captures the satirical male bonding theme
presented in *Manitu,* a relationship that is charged with homoerotic
undertones. This is not to say that either of the two protagonists is
homosexual or even that they are closet gays. In fact, they are decisively heterosexual, but this decisive heterosexuality is threatened
by the nature of their relationship. Eve Sedgwick has described this
problem of homosocial bonds between men as a mainly homophobic
rejection of the idea that there is a "continuum between homosocial and homosexual—a continuum whose visibility, for men, in our
society, is radically disputed" (1–2). The rejection of the connection
between male homosocial and male homosexual bonds is also a political one, since male homosocial bonds are essential in perpetuating the
"male-dominated kinship systems" (Sedgwick 3), such as the order
usually established by cowboys in the American western myth.

Herbig emphasizes this male bonding dilemma with the
introduction of a new character: Abahachi's decisively gay twin
brother, Winnetouch (also played by Herbig). The introduction of
Winnetouch and the resulting problematization of the homosocial
male bonding picks up a thread of revisionist western films that has
been clearly visible since John Schlesinger's *Midnight Cowboy* (1969),
and has recently been renegotiated in Ang Lee's *Brokeback Mountain*
(2005).[16] Lee Clark Mitchell traces cowboy eroticism all the way
back to Owen Wister's *The Virginian* (1902), in which the narrator's description of the Virginian among other things offers room
even for homoerotic interpretations (155–56). This eroticism and

its homoerotic undertones are carried into the western film genre, where the visual possibilities make the gazing at the male body both more varied and less obvious. An overt narration is no longer needed since the camera can more subtly direct the viewer's gaze. Mitchell even goes as far as saying that many western films are "covertly just about that: looking at men" (159). This can be variously interpreted as "deep-seated nervousness over homoeroticism" or as part of the process of "becoming a man" (Mitchell 159). According to the latter argument, the western (male) protagonist must be beaten up and ideally left-for-dead, so that he can make his triumphant, manly return.[17] In this respect, May's Wild West adventure novels for once are actually very close to the western tradition. The *Winnetou* novels are dominated by two strong, handsome males riding through the Wild West together. The periodically emerging female love interests are quickly gotten rid of, usually by being killed at the hand of a villain.[18] This has three important effects: (1) it creates a new plot line (the hunt for the villain); (2) it helps sustain the male-dominated kinship systems; (3) thus it frees the two protagonists to keep on doing what they have been doing ever since they met: riding side-by-side, looking for adventure.

Consequently, in picking up the homoerotic undercurrents of western movies and of May's novels, *Der Schuh des Manitu* points to potential identification problems with May's heroes—they are not the saviors of the innocent, but rather just two guys fighting out their relational problems while riding around the prairie.[19] Moreover, their supposedly heroic actions only help sustain the patriarchal order so reliant on similar homosocial bonds. Transferred to a symbolic, political level this means that the homoerotic potentials of the male homosocial bond, clearly emphasized by the emergence of Winnetouch, threaten the patriarchal order in part sustained by the American western myth, and criticize the current neoconservative American foreign policy associated in Germany with this western myth, and especially with the cowboy figure. After all, it is precisely the symbiotic aspects of his relationship with Abahachi that seem to bother Ranger after he meets Winnetouch. When Abahachi introduces the two, "Twin brother Winnetouch, blood brother Ranger. Blood brother, twin brother," Winnetouch answers by exclaiming, "Another brother!" (*Schuh des Manitu*). Ranger answers by fainting. He does not faint just because a homosexual Apache, dressed in pink, is too much for him to bear. He faints because this pink costumed Apache happens to be the twin brother of his blood brother, with whom he has been riding through the prairie for sixteen years. Thus he is now being included in a wholly new brotherhood. The homoerotic implications of this discovery seem to overwhelm the westman. They also threaten the basis of the male-dominated kinship system that sustains the Wild West the two protagonists have been riding through because they threaten the "'obligatory heterosexuality'" (Sedgwick 3) that is part of this system. By extension, Herbig's parody introduces the possibility of a continuum of male homosocial relations, including homosexual love, which reflects the German skepticism of the male homosocial bonds associated with the current American administration. This German skepticism is symbolized by the identification of President George W. Bush as a cowboy.

*   *   *

The cowboy, both the American Cold War variant and May's benign westman, has outlived his usefulness to many Germans today. In Germany today the cowboy is truly lonesome, if not poor, as he finds very few supporters. Politically and symbolically the Cold War cowboy stands for an American foreign policy that irritates Germans. American presidents who have supported a proactive, neoconservative foreign policy, from Ronald Reagan to George W. Bush, have frequently been identified as cowboys in the German media. Along with this irritation comes a turning away from the cowboy as a heroic figure to identify with. As a somewhat consternated journalist writing for the major German newspaper *Süddeutsche Zeitung* in 2004 notes, the cowboy is no longer a mainstay of young German boys' childhood fantasies (Rühle). The journalist recounts that during his childhood in the 1970s, the carnival costume of choice for any German boy but the individualist was the cowboy, and German TV programming featured a mass of western shows and films, including those based on May's novels. This author can attest that this was still the case in 1980s Germany. By the 1990s, however, the cowboys had been taken out of the main catalogue of Playmobil, one of Germany's most popular toy companies, where it had also been the perennial bestseller.[20] At today's carnival you are more likely to find a gay cowboy, Village-People-style, or a pink-costumed Indian, which is incidentally *Schuh –des –Manitu* style, than a John Wayne look-alike. A look at a weekly television guide in June 2007 reveals that there is currently not one single western series running on German television, even though there are now more than thirty channels as opposed to the three channels that were the norm until the mid-1980s. May's valiant westman does not fare much better as he falls into the same traps of trying to prove himself and forcing his will, albeit a benign one, on others. Moreover, it is hardly convincing that he could go out and bring peace to the world on the strength of his fist. There is no German *Edelmensch* or Übermensch who could achieve this.

In this context the petty and self-centered adventures of Herbig's protagonists, their less-than-superhuman qualities, and their own uneasiness about the nature of their relationship effectively negotiate contemporary German skepticism of the American western myth and of the ideology it helps sustain. In fact, in Herbig's version the westman and his Indian friend have become the objects of ridicule rather than of admiration to Germans. This is a risk the American government is also running with its current policies.

NOTES

1. While May is not as easily and frequently interpreted as nationalistic as, for example, Hermann Löns, May's fiction nevertheless offers some room for nationalistic readings largely related to his romanticism.

2. Romanticism as such is not necessarily nationalistic. However, as Lipowatz points out, it has been the vehicle for the myths of nationalism, such as the conspiracy (against the nation), the savior (a political incarnation of the national community), the Golden Age (the time when the nation was still pure), and unity (the community is fundamentally based on unity). Combined with the concept of *ius sanguis*, these romantic myths lead to a very strong German nationalism between 1871 and 1945 (64–68).

3. May took his first trip to America in 1908, years after the Wild West he wrote about in his novels had largely disappeared. Moreover, even on this trip the furthest west he got is Toronto. May also visited a few surviving Native Americans in reservations, who remained "alien" to him. However, this did not stop him from restating his belief that only a new "German-Indian" race, modeled on the prototype Winnetou, could fulfill the promise of the American West (Wollschläger 199 ff).

4. May began his *Winnetou* trilogy with an introduction that bemoans the annihilation of the "red men" at the hands of the "white men" (*Winnetou I* 5–9). For May's influence on the German image of Native Americans, see Seferns 86–87.

5. The new exhibition on Karl May's imaginary travels ("Karl May— Imaginäre Reisen"), which opened on 31 August 2007 at the German Historical Museum in Berlin, highlights May's importance for the German imagination during the late nineteenth century (Lewitscharoff 13).

6. The racial hygiene program in Germany during the Third Reich was the most radical attempt at "breeding" an *Übermensch* by eliminating those deemed inferior. The Nazis' means included "mass sterilization, the killing of handicapped persons, the murder of ethnic minorities, and the extermination of Jews" (Kühl xvi).

7. The Hallstein Doctrine is named after Walter Hallstein, a key advisor to Adenauer. The doctrine held that the Federal Republic was the only legitimate German state and consequently would not establish or maintain diplomatic relations with any state—except the Soviet Union—that recognized the GDR (Hofmann 132).

8. A recent poll indicates that 80 percent of Germans believe that a UN mandate is necessary to justify military action ("Year after Iraq" 4).

9. This impression is confirmed by German film director Wim Wenders in a 2004 interview for the German news weekly *Die Zeit*. Wenders, who has been fascinated with America and the American myth since childhood, and who has been living in the United States for longer periods on several occasions speaks about his irritation about the political culture among American citizens. Moreover, he explicitly speaks of the "Cowboy named George W." shoving his policies down America's and the world's throats. Moreover, poll numbers also support this view. In an opinion poll conducted by the Pew Institute in 2003, 85 percent of Germans indicated that they have an unfavorable opinion of George W. Bush ("Year after Iraq" 21).

10. May's novels are not really westerns in a narrow sense. As Cracroft points out they are rather closer to Cooper's adventure stories (256), albeit with a German twist. The combination of these two aspects has led Jeffrey Sammons to state that it is difficult to say "whether May's fiction is in any intelligible sense about America at all" (245). In this essay I claim that at least from a German perspective they are indeed about America in an intelligible way because they negotiate German skepticism about America.

11. In the early years of the twentieth century, May was equated by his fans with his first person narrator, named Karl, and eventually May himself claimed to have lived through all of the adventures he relates. This was soon discovered to be a fraud. May's history as a convicted impostor (overall he served eight years in prison) was publicized, and his plagiarism (for example, from Friedrich Gerstäcker) was uncovered. However, the discovery of this mendacity did not prevent May from becoming and remaining, by far, Germany's most successful author, in economic terms (Roxin 1974).

12. This quote is from the English language version on the DVD.

13. Opinion polls conducted in early 2004 clearly indicate that a majority of Germans are very skeptical of the American willingness to cooperate (47 percent said that the United States does not care "too much" about Germany's interests when making international policy decisions, and 22 percent said the United States does not care "much at

all") and therefore would prefer if Europe played a more independent role (63 percent) and if the EU were a counterweight to the United States (70 percent) ("Year After Iraq" 9 and 28).

14. For example, Abahachi does not complain about the outrageous credit conditions of the Schoschonen, a 35.8 percent monthly interest rate, because he supposedly cannot understand the strong dialect (*Schuh des Manitu*).

15. "I am unhappy with our general situation."

16. Both of these movies are not generally considered westerns since they lack many of its classical features. (E.g., they are not set in the Wild West because the Wild West no longer exists during their narrative present). However, they confront typical western themes, most notably the male bonding among cowboys (Le Coney and Trodd).

17. Clint Eastwood's character in Sergio Leone's *A Fistful of Dollars* (*Per un pugno di dollari* 1964) epitomizes this type of western hero. A man with no name is first beaten up, somehow nursed back to life, and finally makes his return as an avenging devil, killing all his former tormentors.

18. Winnetou's sister Nscho-Tschi is a victim of this necessity. She falls in love with Old Shatterhand while she nurses him back to strength, and subsequently is killed when she is on the way to get an education in the white man's ways so that she will be more acceptable to Old Shatterhand (*Winnetou I*).

19. *Der Schuh des Manitu* is certainly not a critique of homophobia. Actually, Herbig's portrayal of stereotypical homosexual males, which was a recurring joke in many of his TV skits, is rather homophobic or at least uses stereotypes to get cheap laughs.

20. "Western" is once again a category in Playmobil's catalogue. However, it is not listed on the company's homepage among its "products," where such categories as "Romans," "Pirates," and "Knights" dominate, and where even policemen and farmers are more easily found than cowboys. The latter have to be searched for under the "order catalogue," suggesting that it is mainly old-time fans or, as Rühle fears, nostalgic dads, who order such artifacts.

WORKS CITED

Bahr, Egon. *Zu Meiner Zeit.* Munich: Karl Blessing Verlag, 1996.

Brunken, Otto. "Der rote Edelmensch. Karl Mays '*Winnetou.*'" In *Klassiker der Kinder—und Jugendliteratur,* edited by Bettina Hurrelmann, 293–318. Frankfurt a. M.: Fischer, 1995.

Corkin, Stanley. *Cowboys as Cold Warriors. The Western and U.S. History.* Philadelphia: Temple University Press, 2004.

Cracroft, Richard H. "The American West of Karl May." *American Quarterly* 19 (1967): 249–58.

Hall, John. *The Sociology of Literature.* London: Longman, 1979.

Hofmann, Arne. *The Emergence of Détente in Europe. Brandt, Kennedy and the Formation of Ostpolitik.* London: Routledge, 2007.

Klotz, Volker. "Woher, woran und wodurch rührt 'Der verlorene Sohn'? Zur Konstruktion und Anziehngskraft von Karl Mays Elends-Roman." *Jahrbuch der Karl-May-Gesellschaft* 8 (1978): 87–110.

Kühl, Stefan. *The Nazi Connection. Eugenics, American Racism, and German National Socialism.* New York: Oxford University Press, 1994.

Le Coney, Christopher, and Zoe Trodd. "John Wayne and the Queer Frontier: Deconstructions of the Classic Cowboy Narrative during the Vietnam War." *Americana* 5.1 (2006). http://www.mericanpopularculture.com/ journal/articles/spring_2006/le_coney_trodd.htm (accessed 10 June 2007).

Lewitscharoff, Sibylle. "Auf den Flügeln des Größenwahns." *Süddeutsche Zeitung* 1 / 2 (September 2007): 13.

Lipowatz, Thanos. "Nationalistischer Diskurs und romantische Mythologie." In *Nationalismus und Romantik,* edited by Wolfgang Müller-Funk and Franz Schuh. Wien: Turia und Kant, 1999.

May, Karl. *Winnetou.* Vol. I. 1893. Bamberg: Karl May Verlag, 1951.

Mitchell, Lee Clark. *Westerns. Making the Man in Fiction and Film.* Chicago: University of Chicago Press, 1996.

Pew Research Center for the People. "A Year after Iraq War. Mistrust of America in Europe Ever Higher, Muslim Anger Persist." (16 March 2004). http://people-press.org/reports/pdf/206.pdf (accessed 5 June 2007).

Purdy, Jebediah. "Die Beiden Flügel der Freiheit." Translated by Tobias Dürr. *Die Zeit* (22 August 2002). http://zeus.zeit.de/text/ archiv/2002/34/200234_europa-amerika.xml (accessed 29 June 2007).

Roxin, Claus. "Dr. Karl May, *genannt* Old Shatterhand." *Jahrbuch der Karl-May-Gesellschaft* 4 (1974): 15–73.

———. "Ein *'geborener Verbrecher.'* Karl May vor dem Königlichen Landgericht Moabit." *Jahrbuch der Karl-May-Gesellschaft* 19 (1989): 9–36.

Rühle, Alex. "Western *von gestern.*" *Süddeutsche Zeitung* (15 October 2004). http://www.sueddeutsche.de/kultur/artikel/267/41226/ (accessed 5 June 2007).

Sammons, Jeffrey L. *Ideology, Mimesis, Fantasy: Charles Sealsfield, Friedrich Gerstäcker, Karl May, and Other German Novelists of America.* Chapel Hill: University of North Carolina Press, 1998.

Scholdt, Günter. "*Empor ins Reich der Edelmenschen.'* Eine Menschheitsidee im Kontext der Zeit." *Jahrbuch der Karl-May-Gesellschaft* 30 (2000): 94–111.

Schuh des Manitu. Directed by Michael Bully Herbig. Performers: Michael Bully Herbig, Christian Tramitz, and Sky Dumont. Constantin Film, 2001.

Sedgwick, Eve Kosofsky. *Between Men. English Literature and Male Homosocial Desire.* New York: Columbia University Press, 1985.

Seferens, Gregor. "'*Immer . . . wenn ich an den Indianer denke' eine Studie zur Entwicklung des Indianerbildes bei Karl May.*" *Jahrbuch der Karl-May-Gesellschaft* 24 (1994): 86–103.

Wenders, Wim. Interview with Katja Nicodemus. "*Der europäische Freund.*" *Die Zeit* 14 (October 20 2004). http://images.zeit.de/text/2004/42/Interview_Wenders (accessed 29 June 2007).

Wollschläger, Hans. *Karl May. Grundriß eines gebrochenen Lebens.* Göttingen: Wallstein Verlag, 2004.

Zahner, Silvia. "Karl May's 'Ich' in den Reiseerzählungen und im Spätwerk." PhD diss., University of Zürich, 2001. *Sonderheft der Karl-May-Gesellschaft* 123. Husum: Hansa Verlag, 2001.

Ziegler, Harry. "History and Popular Fiction: Two Worlds Collide. A Reply to Feilitzsch's Article on Karl May." *Journal of Popular Culture* 33 (1999): 111–21.

CONTRIBUTORS

Renny Christopher is associate vice president for Faculty Affairs at California State University, Channel Islands. Her book, *The Viet Nam War/The American War: Images and Representations in Euro-American and Vietnamese Exile Narratives* (University of Massachusetts Press, 1995) was named Outstanding Book on Human Rights by the Gustavas Myers Center for the Study of Human Rights in North America. She is working on an autobiography, *A Carpenter's Daughter: A Working-Class Woman in Higher Education,* which addresses her experiences as the first in her family to attend college.

Robert Crooks currently manages worldwide training and certification for Adobe Systems, Inc. Previously, he was a professor of English at Bentley College, specializing in literary and film theory. He has published theoretical and critical essays on a variety of topics including incestuous desire in *Mildred Pierce,* double suture (the political dimensions of film), and the role of voyeurism in Joyce's aesthetic.

Reginald Dyck, English professor at Capital University, is a teacher and community activist in Columbus, Ohio. He has published essays on the Western and Midwestern writers Willa Cather, Wright Morris, Louise Erdrich, and William Gass. His published essays have also focused on pedagogical topics as well as William Faulkner and Jean Toomer. He presently has a book in progress on work culture and class hierarchies in Native literature.

Rüdiger Heinze is currently junior professor for North American studies at Carolo-Wilhemina University, Braunschweig, Germany. Previously he served as assistant professor in American Studies at the Albert-Ludwigs-Universität, Freiburg. He has studied at Indiana University, Bloomington, and the Carolo-Wilhemina University. He has published on ethnic literature, superheroes and comics, ethical criticism, cultural theory, and popular culture.

Melissa J. Homestead, associate professor of English and women's and gender Studies at the University of Nebraska-Lincoln, is the author of *American Women Authors and Literary Property, 1822–1869* (Cambridge University Press, 2005). Her teaching and research encompass American literature from the Early Republic through the early twentieth century, with a particular focus on the History of the Book and women's authorship. She is currently working on antebellum novelist Catharine Sedgwick's engagements with the business of letters and, with Anne L. Kaufman, on a study of the nearly four-decade-long creative partnership between Willa Cather and Edith Lewis.

Robert McKee Irwin is professor and Chancellor's Fellow in the Department of Spanish and Portuguese at the University of California, Davis. He is author of *Bandits, Captives, Heroines and Saints: Cultural Icons of Mexico's Northwest Frontier* (2007) and *Mexican Masculinities* (2003). He is coeditor of *Hispanisms and Homosexualities* (1998), *The Famous 41: Sexuality and Social Control in Mexico, 1901* (2003), and *Diccionario de estudios culturales latinoamericanos* (forthcoming). He is currently principal investigator of a collaborative research project on the transnational reception of Mexican Golden Age cinema. His *Bandits, Captives, Heroines and Saints* received the Thomas J. Lyons award winner for Best Critical Book in Western Literary and Cultural Studies from the Western Literary Association.

Desirée A. Martín is assistant professor of English at the University of California, Davis. She is currently completing a book manuscript titled *Bordered Saints: Possessing Border and Nation in Chicana/o and Mexican Culture.* Her next project focuses on multilingualism, translation, and the limits of identity in Chicano/a and Latino/a studies.

Cheli Reutter is field service assistant professor of African American literature in the African and African American Studies Department at the University of Cincinnati. Reutter has also taught at Northern Kentucky University, the University of Louisville, and, as a Fulbright scholar, the Albert-Ludwigs-Universität, Freiburg. She has published on passing across the color line in Stowe's *Pearl of Orr's Island,* ethnicity and the American West, and cultural studies paradigms for medical humanities. Her next project examines the works and influence of nineteenth-century African American women writers.

Steven Rosendale is author of *City Wilderness: US Radical Fiction and the Forgotten Literary History of Social Justice Environmentalism* (University of Iowa Press, forthcoming), coeditor (with Laura Gray-Rosendale) of *Radical Relevance: Essays Toward a Scholarship of a*

"Whole Left" (SUNY Press, 2005), and editor of *Dictionary of Literary Biography 303: American Radical and Reform Writers* (Gale, 2004) and *The Greening of Literary Scholarship: Literature, Theory and the Environment* (University of Iowa Press, 2002). He teaches American modernism and ecocriticism at Northern Arizona University.

Jeffrey A. Sartain teaches literature and composition at Indiana University. He has written for journals such as *American Book Review, Ninth Letter,* and *Indiana Review.* Currently, he is editing an anthology of academic essays, *Sacred and Immoral: On the Writings of Chuck Palahniuk.*

Hubertus Zander is a lecturer at the IES EU Center in Freiburg, Germany. He is finishing work on a doctoral thesis on the "Public Cultural Memory of the Rosenberg Case." He holds a M.A. in political science, English philology, and economics from the Albert-Ludwigs-Universität, Freiburg, and has studied at the University of British Columbia. He has researched and lectured on Cold War America, the European Union, American popular music, and the postmodern North American novel.

INDEX